Va. Ordinances Norfolk Virginia.

The Ordinances of the City of Norfolk and Acts of Assembly of

Virginia

Relating to the City Government, with an Appendix. 1885

Va. Ordinances Norfolk Virginia.

The Ordinances of the City of Norfolk and Acts of Assembly of Virginia
Relating to the City Government, with an Appendix. 1885

ISBN/EAN: 9783744768443

Printed in Europe, USA, Canada, Australia, Japan

Cover: Foto ©Suzi / pixelio.de

More available books at **www.hansebooks.com**

THE ORDINANCES

OF THE

CITY OF NORFOLK

AND

ACTS OF ASSEMBLY

OF

VIRGINIA

RELATING TO THE CITY GOVERNMENT,

WITH AN APPENDIX.

1885.

NORFOLK, VA.:
LANDMARK STEAM PRINTING HOUSE.
1885.

THE CHARTER OF THE CITY.

CHAP. 33.—An ACT providing a charter for the city of Norfolk, and repealing the existing charter, approved April 21, 1882.

In force January 21, 1884.

1. Be it enacted by the general assembly of Virginia, That Boundaries the territory contained within the limits prescribed by the second section of an act passed in March, seventeen hundred and sixty-one, entitled an act for enlarging and ascertaining the limits of the borough of Norfolk, and for other purposes described therein as follows, to-wit: Beginning at the head of a creek called Newton's creek, and thence within a line to be run north fifty-nine degrees west, seventy-two poles to the head of Smith's creek; thence along the said Smith's creek, according to its various courses and meanders, to the mouth thereof, in Elizabeth river; thence bounding on the said river, the different courses thereof, to the mouth of the said Newton's creek; and thence up the said Newton's creek to the beginning; and by any act heretofore or hereafter passed by the general assembly of this State, shall be deemed and taken as the city of Norfolk, and the inhabitants of the city of Norfolk, for all purposes for which towns and cities are incorporated in this commonwealth, shall continue to be one body politic, in fact and in name, under the style and denomination of the city of Norfolk; and as such, shall have, exercise and enjoy all the rights, immunities, powers and privileges and be subject to all the duties and obligations now incumbent upon and appertaining to said city as a municipal corporation.

2. The administration and government of the said city Government; shall be invested in one principal officer, to be styled the mayor; how vested. a board to be called the councils of the city of Norfolk; and in such other boards and officers as are hereinafter provided for. The councils of the city of Norfolk shall consist of two bodies, namely: the common and select council, with such rights, duties, powers and privileges as are now vested in them by law, or as may be vested in them by this act or any act hereafter passed.

3. The said city shall be divided into four wards, which Division into number of wards the city councils may hereafter increase as wards. they may deem expedient. Until such revision be made, the boundary lines of wards shall remain as now established.

4. The election of the municipal officers hereafter men- Election of tioned, except those to be appointed by the councils, shall be officers; when held. held on the fourth Thursday in May, eighteen hundred and eighty four, and on the fourth Thursday in May in every second year thereafter, except the election of city treasurer and commissioner of the revenue, who shall be elected as hereinafter provided; and the said election shall be conducted under the provisions of the general election laws of the State.

5. Whenever any special election shall be ordered by the Special city councils for any object not provided for in the general elections.

election laws of the state, they shall communicate their order for the same to the judge of the court of the corporation, and the same proceedings shall be had as are provided by the laws of the state for special elections to fill vacancies in any municipal office.

Vacancies; how filled.

6. In case of vacancies arising in any municipal office provided for by this act, the councils shall appoint a qualified person to fill such office for the unexpired term, and in case of any vacancy arising in the office of councilman, the select or common council, as the case may be, shall elect a qualified person for the unexpired term.

Officers to be sworn.

7. The mayor and the members of the city councils, before entering upon the duties of their respective offices, shall be respectively sworn in accordance with the laws of this state. Such oaths may be administered to the mayor-elect, by any judge of a court of record commissioned to hold any such court within said city; and the members of the city councils by the mayor, being himself first sworn as aforesaid, or by a judge of a court of record, or a justice of the peace; and a certificate of such oaths having been respectively taken, shall be filed with the treasurer of the city, and entered upon the journals of the city councils. Every other person elected or appointed to any office under this act, or under any law or ordinance of the city councils, except laborers, teamsters, or temporary clerks, shall, before he enters upon the duties of such office, take and subscribe said oath and such other oaths as may be required by law or ordinance, before the mayor, or any justice of the peace of said city; and a certificate of the same shall be filed in the office of the treasurer of the city. The clerk of the corporation court of the said city shall notify all persons elected as aforesaid, and the treasurer of the city shall notify all persons appointed as aforesaid, of their election or appointment, as the case may be. If any person elected or appointed to any office in said city, shall neglect to take such oath for ten days after receiving notice of his election or appointment, or shall neglect within that time to give such securities as may be required of him by the city councils, as hereinafter provided, or as may be hereafter required by law or ordinance, he shall be considered as having declined such office, and the same shall be deemed vacant, and such vacancy shall be filled according to the provisions of this act.

CHAPTER II.

Mayor.

Election, term and salary of mayor.

8. The mayor shall be elected by the qualified voters of the city of Norfolk, for the term of two years, and until his successor shall be elected and qualify. His salary shall be fixed by the city councils, payable at stated periods, and he shall receive no other compensation or emolument whatsoever; and no regulations diminishing such compensation after it has once been fixed, shall be made to affect his compensation

until after the expiration of the term for which the mayor then in office shall have been elected.

9. He shall, by virtue of his office, possess all the jurisdiction, and may exercise all the powers and authority of a justice of the peace of the said city, in addition to the powers hereby given by virtue of this act, or that may hereafter be given him by virtue of any other act of assembly. *Jurisdiction and powers.*

10. It shall be his duty to communicate to the city councils annually, as soon as may be after the commencement of the fiscal year, and oftener if he shall deem it expedient, or if required by said councils, a general statement of the situation and condition of the city in relation to its government, finances, and improvement, with such recommendations as he may deem proper. *His communication to council.*

11. He shall exercise a constant supervision over the conduct of all subordinate officers, have power and authority to investigate their acts, have access to all books and documents in their offices, and may examine said officers and their subordinates on oath. He shall also have power to suspend or remove such officers for misconduct in office, or neglect of duty, to be specified in the order of suspension or removal; but no such removal shall be made without reasonable notice to the officer complained of, and an opportunity afforded him to be heard in his defence. On the removal or suspension of such officer or officers, the mayor shall report the same, with his reasons therefor, to the city councils, at their next stated meetings. *General duties of mayor.*

12. In case of the absence or inability of the mayor, any justice of the peace in the city, selected by the mayor, shall act as mayor, and shall discharge the municipal duties of the mayor during such absence or inability. *Absence of mayor.*

13. In case a vacancy shall occur in the office of mayor, the council shall appoint a qualified person to fill the vacancy for the unexpired term, except as provided in the next succeeding section. *Vacancies in mayoralty.*

14. The select and common councils, in joint session, two-thirds of the members elected to each council concurring, shall have power to remove from office the mayor of the city of Norfolk for malfeasance, misfeasance, corruption, neglect of duty or other misconduct in office, but he shall have at least ten days previous notice in writing of the motion to remove him, accompanied by a copy of the causes and charges alleged as the ground of his proposed removal, and shall have the right to be heard in person or by counsel in his defense, and in case of the removal of the mayor under the provisions of this section, the vacancy in the office of mayor shall be filled at a special election of the qualified voters of the city of Norfolk to be ordered by the councils, and to be held in twenty days after such removal. *Mayor; how removed.*

CHAPTER III.

Councils.

Councilmen; election and duties.   15.   There shall be elected on the fourth Thursday in May, eighteen hundred and eighty-four, and on the fourth Thursday in May biennially thereafter, thirty councilmen, who shall be apportioned to the several wards, as follows : To the First, Second and Third wards eight each, and to the Fourth ward six, and the same number of councilmen shall be so elected until a reapportionment shall be made according to law. The councilmen shall proceed at this first meeting after their election, or as soon thereafter as practicable, in such manner as they may deem proper, to elect eleven of their number to constitute a select council, which select council shall hold its meetings separate and apart from the remaining nineteen councilmen, who shall constitute the common council. The councils after their separate organization, shall in such manner and at such time as may be prescribed by ordinance, proceed to appoint all officers, clerks and assistants, whose election or appointment is not otherwise provided for by law.

Select council; duties and rights.   16.   The select council shall elect its officers, to consist of a president, vice president and clerk ; and the common council shall elect its officers, to consist of a president and vice president; the city treasurer shall be ex-officio clerk of the common council, and shall have an assistant. The select and common councils, respectively, may elect such other officers and clerks as they may deem necessary, which officers shall be liable to be removed by the councils respectively, each acting for itself in this regard, with power to the respective councils, each acting for itself, to supply any vacancy occuring. The president or the president pro tempore, who shall preside when the proceedings of a previous meeting are read, shall sign the same. The president shall have power, at any time, to call a meeting of his council, and in case of his absence from sickness, disability or refusal, the councils may be convened by the order in writing, of any five members of the common council, or three of the select council.

Ordinances of council.   17.   Ordinances and resolutions may originate in either the select or common council, to be approved or rejected by the other, and may be amended by either council with the consent of the other. But when the councils cannot agree upon any ordinance or resolution, the same shall be referred to a committee of conference, to be appointed by each council.

Quorum.   18.   The councils shall have authority to compel the attendance of absent members; to punish members for disorderly behavior, and by a vote of two-thirds of the council to expel a member for malfeasance of misfeasance in the office. They shall keep a journal of their proceedings; and their meetings shall be open. A majority of the members of the councils shall constitute a quorum for the transaction of business.

But on all ordinances or resolutions appropriating money, imposing taxes, or authorizing the borrowing of money, the yeas and nays shall be entered on the journal, and a majority of all the members elected to each council, shall be necessary to give them the force of law. No vote shall be reconsidered or rescinded at a special meeting, unless at such special meeting there be present as large a number of members as were present when such vote was taken.

19. The city council shall have, subject to the provisions herein contained, the control and management of the fiscal and municipal affairs of the city, and of all property, real and personal, belonging to the said city; and may make such ordinances, orders and by-laws relating to the same as they shall deem proper and necessary. They shall likewise have power to make such ordinances, by-laws, orders and regulations as they may deem desirable to carry out the following powers, which are hereby vested in them : *Powers of council.*

First. To establish markets in and for said city; prescribe the times and places for holding the same; provide suitable buildings therefor, and to enforce such regulations as shall be necessary or proper to prevent huckstering, forestalling, and regrating. *To establish markets.*

Second. To erect or provide, in or near the city, suitable workhouses, houses of correction or reformation, and houses for the reception and maintenance of the poor and destitute. They shall possess and exercise exclusive authority over all persons within the limits of the city, receiving or entitled to the benefits of the poor laws, and regulate pauperism within the limits of the city; and the councils, through the agencies they shall appoint for the direction and management of the poor of the city, shall exercise the powers and perform the duties vested by the law in overseers of the poor. *To erect work-houses.*

Third. To erect and keep in order all public buildings necessary or proper for said city. *To erect and care for public buildings.*

Fourth. To erect within said city a city prison, and said prison may contain such apartments as shall be necessary for the safe keeping and employment of all persons confined therein. *To erect, &c., public prison.*

Fifth. To establish and enlarge water works, gas works, and electric lights within or without the limits of said city, contract and agree with the owners of any land for the use or purchase thereof, or may have the same condemned for the location, extension or enlargement of their said works, the pipes connected therewith, or any fixtures or appurtenances thereof. They shall have power to protect from injury, by adequate penalties, the said works, pipes, fixtures and land, or anything connected therewith, within or without the limits of said city, and to prevent the pollution of the water, by prohibiting the throwing of filth or offensive matter therein, or in other places where the water may be affected thereby ; and such prohibition may be enforced by proper penalties. *To establish water and gas works.*

Sixth. To establish, construct, and keep in order, alter or remove landings, wharves and docks or land belonging to the *To establish landings and wharves.*

city; and to lay and collect a reasonable duty on vessels
coming to and using the same; and to regulate the manner
of using other wharves and landings within the corporate
limits, and prescribe the rates of wharfage to be paid by vessels using the same; to prevent or remove all obstructions in
and upon any landings, wharves or docks; to deepen and
clean the harbor and river. They may buy or build bridges
connecting the corporation with any suburb, town or village.

Powers and duties as to streets. Seventh. To close, extend, widen, narrow, lay out, graduate,
improve and otherwise alter streets and public alleys in the
said city, and have them properly lighted and kept in good
order, and they may make or construct sewers or ducts
through the streets or public grounds of the city, and through
any place or places whatsoever when it may be deemed by
the councils expedient. The councils may have over any
street or alley in the city, which has been or may be ceded to
the city, like authority as over other streets or alleys; they
may build bridges in, and culverts under said streets and
alleys; and may prevent or remove any structure, obstruction or encroachment over or under or in a street or alley, or
any sidewalk thereof, and may have shade trees planted along
the said streets. They may also regulate the size, materials,
and construction of buildings hereafter erected in such manner as the public safety and convenience may require.

To prevent incumbrances on streets. Eight. To prevent the cumbering of streets, avenues,
walks, public squares, lanes, alleys or bridges in any manner
whatever.

Railway tracks and horse cars. Ninth. To authorize the laying down of railway tracks, and
the running of horse cars thereon, in the streets of the city
under such regulations as they may prescribe.

Powers over railroads in the city. Tenth. To determine and designate the route and grade of
any railroad to be laid in the city, and to restrain and regu-
late the rate ef speed of locomotives, engines, and cars upon
the railroads within the said city, and may wholly exclude
the said engines and cars, if they please; provided no contract be thereby violated.

Wagons, carts, &c; tire to be regulated. Eleventh. To regulate and prescribe the breadth of tires
upon the wheels of wagons, carts and vehicles, of heavy
draught, used upon the streets of said city; provided however,
that this section shall not apply to vehicles coming into and
not owned in said city.

Inspection of liquors and measuring crops and other products Twelfth. To require spirituous liquors, wine, oil, molasses,
vinegar and spirits of turpentine in casks to be guaged and
inspected; and may make provision for the weighing of hay,
fodder, oats, shucks, or other long forage. They may also
provide for weighing and measuring grain, coal, stone, wood,
lumber, boards, potatoes, and other articles for sale or barter.

Sealed measures. Thirteenth. To require every merchant, retailer, trader, and
dealer in merchandise, or property of any description, which
is sold by measure or weight, to cause their weights and measures to be sealed by the city scaler, and to be subject to his inspection; and may impose penalties for violation of any such
ordinance.

Fourteenth. To provide or aid in support of public free schools, colleges and libraries. *Public schools*

Fifteenth. To secure the inhabitants from contagious, infectious, or other dangerous diseases; to establish, erect, and regulate hospitals; to provide for and force the removal of patients to said hospitals; for the appointment and organization of a board of health for said city, with the authority necessary for the prompt and efficient performance of its duties. *Hospitals.*

Sixteenth. To provide, in or near the city lands, to be appropriated, improved and kept in order, as places for the interment of the dead, and may charge for the use of grounds in said places of interment, and may regulate the same: provided that all moneys received for the use of such grounds shall be set apart and appropriated for the improvement of the cemeteries; may prevent the burial of dead in the city, except in the public burial ground; may regulate burials in said grounds, and may require the keeping and return of bills of mortality by the keepers or owners of all cemeteries. *Cemeteries.*

Seventeenth. To establish a quarantine ground for the city, to prescribe the quarantine to be performed by all vessels arriving within the harbor or vicinity of said city, and make regulations therefor, subject to the laws of the state and the United States; but if the place fixed on for the quarantine ground be without the limits of the city, the assent of the court of the county, wherein the quarantine ground is located must first be obtained. *Quarantine.*

Eighteenth. To require and compel the abatement and removal of all nuisances within said city at the expense of the person or persons causing the same, or the owner or owners of the ground whereon the same shall be; to prevent or regulate slaughter houses and soap and candle factories within said city, or the exercise of any dangerous, offensive or unhealthy business, trade or employment therein; and to regulate the transportation of coal and other articles through the streets of the city. *Nuisances.*

Nineteenth. If any ground in the said city shall be subject to be covered by stagnant water, or if the owner or owners, occupier or occupiers thereof, shall permit any offensive or unwholesome substances to remain or accumulate therein the councils may cause such ground to be filled up, raised or drained, or may cause such substances to be covered or to be removed therefrom, and may collect the expense of so doing from the said owner or owners, occupier or occupiers, or any of them, by distress of sale in the same manner in which taxes levied upon real estate, for the benefit of said city, are authorized to be collected: provided that reasonable notice shall be first given to the said owners or agents. In case of non-resident owners, who have no agent in said city, such notice may be given by publication, for not less than four weeks, in any newspaper printed in said city. *Stagnant water.*

Twentieth. To direct the location of all buildings for storing gunpowder or other combustible substances; and to regulate *Gunpowder and combustible matter.*

late the sale and use of gunpowder, fire-crackers or fire-works, manufactured or prepared therefrom, kerosene oil, nitroglycerine, camphene, burning fluid, or other combustible materials; to regulate the exhibition of fire-works, the discharge of fire-arms, the use of candles and lights in barns, stables and other buildings, and to restrain the making of bonfires in streets and yards, and to prohibit the carrying of concealed weapons.

Hogs, dogs,&c.   Twenty-first. To prevent hogs, dogs, and other animals, from running at large in the city, and may subject the same to such confiscation. levies, regulations and taxes, as they may deem proper; and the councils may prohibit the raising or keeping of hogs in the city.

Horses, &c., in streets.   Twenty-second. To prevent the riding or driving of horses or other animals at improper speed; to prevent the flying of kites, throwing stones, or the engaging in any employment or sports in the streets or public alleys, dangerous or annoying to passengers; and to prohibit and punish the abuse of animals.

To repress drunkeness and vagrancy in city.   Twenty-third. To restrain and punish drunkards, vagrants, medicants and street beggars.

Vice and immorality.   Twenty-fourth. To prevent vice and immorality; to preserve public peace and good order; to prevent and quell riots, disturbances and disorderly assemblages; to suppress houses of ill-fame and gaming houses; to prevent lewd and indecent and disorderly conduct or exhibitions in the city; and to expel therefrom persons guilty of such conduct who shall not have resided therein as much as one year.

Vending liquors with license and to minors.   Twenty-fifth. To forbid and prevent the vending or other disposition of liquors or intoxicating drinks to be drunk in any boat, store or other places not duly licensed; and to forbid the selling or giving to be drunk, any intoxicating liquors to any child or minor, without the consent of his or her parents or guardian; and for violation of any such ordinance, may impose fines in addition to those prescribed by the laws of the State.

Paupers and dangerous persons forbidden to come into the city.   Twenty-sixth. To prevent the coming into the city from beyond the limits of the state of persons having no ostensible means of support, or of persons who may be dangerous to the peace and safety of the city; and for this purpose may require any railroad company, or the captain or master of any vessel, bringing such passengers to Norfolk, to enter into bond, with satisfactory security, that such person shall not become chargeable to the city for one year, or may compel such company, captain or master to take them back from whence they came, and compel the person to leave the city if they have not been in the city more than ninety days before the order is given.

General authority of council as to penalties.   20. When, by the provisions of this act, the city councils have authority to pass ordinances on any subject, they may prescribe any penalty not exceeding five hundred dollars, except where a penalty is herein otherwise provided for, for a violation thereof; and may provide that the offender, on failing to

pay the penalty recovered, shall be imprisoned in the jail of
said city for any term not exceeding three calendar months;
which penalties may be prosecuted and recovered, with costs,
in the name of the city of Norfolk. And the city councils
may subject the parent or guardian of any minor or the master or mistress of any apprentice, to any such penalty for any
such offence committed by such minor or apprentice.

21. No ordinance hereafter passed by the city councils, for Publication of
the violation of which any penalty is imposed, shall take ordinances.
effect until the same shall have been published for five days
successively in two of the daily newspapers of said city, to be
designated by the said councils. A record or entry made by
the clerk of the common council, or a copy of such record or
entry, duly certified by him, shall be prima facie evidence of
the time of such first publication; and all laws, regulations,
and ordinances of the city council may be read in evidence in
all courts of justice, and in all proceedings before any officer,
body or board in which it shall be necessary to refer thereto,
either from a copy thereof, certified by the clerk of the common council, or from the volume of ordinances printed by the
authority of the city.

22. The councils shall not take or use any private property Private prop-
for streets or other public purposes without making to the erty; how tak-
owner or owners thereof just compensation for the same. But use.
in all cases where the said city cannot by agreement obtain
title to the ground necessary for such purposes, it shall be
lawful for the said city to apply to and obtain from the circuit or county courts of the county in which the land shall
be situated, or to the proper court of the city having jurisdiction of such matters, if the subject lies within the city for
authority to condemn the same, which shall be applied for and
proceeded with as provided by law.

23. In every case where a street in said city has been or Removal of
shall be encroached upon by any fence, building or otherwise, encroach-
the city councils may require the owner or owners, if known, ments.
and if unknown the occupant or occupants of the premises so
encroaching, to remove the same. If such removal shall not
be made within the time ordered by the councils, they may
impose a penalty of five dollars for each and every day that
it is allowed to continue thereafter, and may cause the encroachment to be removed, and collect from the owner all
reasonable charges therefor, with costs by the same processes
that they are hereinafter empowered to collect taxes. No
encroachment upon any street, however long continued, shall
constitue an adverse possession to, or confer any rights upon
the person claiming thereunder, as against said city.

24. Whenever any street, alley, or lane shall have been Streets, alleys
opened to and used as such by the public, for the period of and lanes
five years, the same shall thereby become a street, alley or lane
for all purposes, and the city shall have the same authority
and jurisdiction over and right and interest therein, as
they have by law, over the streets, alleys and lanes laid
out by it. And any street or alley reserved in the division

or sub-division, into lots of any portion of the territory, within
the corporate limits of the city, by a plat or plan of record,
shall be deemed and held to be dedicated to the public use;
and the councils shall have authority upon the petition of any
person interested therein, to open such street or alley or any
portion of the same. No agreement between, or release of
interest by the person owning the lands immediately con-
tiguous to any such alley or street, whether the same has been
opened and used by the public or not, shall avail or operate
to abolish said alley or street, so as to divert the interest of
the public therein, or the authority of the councils over the
same.

How same paid for. 25. Whenever any street shall be laid out, a street graded
or paved, a culvert built, or any other public improvement
whatsoever made, the city councils may determine what portion if any, of the expense thereof ought to be paid from the
public treasury, and what portion by the owners of real estate
benefitted, or may order and direct that the whole expense be
assessed upon the owners of real estate benefitted thereby.
But no such public improvement shall be made to be defrayed
in whole or in part, by a local assessment until first requested
by a petition signed by a majority of the owners of property
to be assessed for such improvement, or unless the councils
shall by a vote of a majority of all the members elected to each
council, declare the said improvement to be expedient; and
shall furthermore give public notice of such resolution in two
or more newspapers published in said city for twenty days, and
shall thereafter by a like majority vote, order and determine
that the said improvement shall be made.

CHAPTER IV.

Election of Officers.

Election of officers by the people. 26. There shall be elected by the qualified voters of the
city of Norfolk on the fourth Thursday in May, eighteen
hundred and eighty-four, and on the fourth Thursday in May
in every second year thereafter, the following officers: One
collector of city taxes and levies; one city attorney; one
inspector of streets; one clerk of the market; one physician as
health officer; one keeper of the alms house; one superintendent of the cemeteries; one weigher of hay; one wood measurer;
one sealer of weights and measures; one guager and inspector
of liquors, who shall hold their offices for the term of two
years from the first day of July ensuing their election, and
until their successors shall be elected and qualified, unless
sooner removed.

All other officers, clerks and assistants, whether required
by law or ordinance, shall be appointed by the councils at
their first regular meeting after their election, or as soon
thereafter as may be practicable, and the councils shall have
power to create such offices, clerks and assistants as they may
deem necessary, not inconsistent with the provisions of this

act, or the constitution and laws of the state or of the United States.

27. There shall be elected by the councils, at their first By the councils of justices meeting after their election, one justice of the peace for each ward, who shall reside in the ward for which he may be elected, during his term of office, and the councils shall designate one of said justices to hold the police court, and he shall collect a fee of fifty cents in each case, one half of the same to be paid by him to the treasurer for the use of the city.

28. There shall be elected by the councils at their first High constable; how meeting after their election, one high constable for the city of elected and Norfolk, who shall hold his office for two years, and until his duties. successor is elected and qualified. He shall give bond with sureties, to be approved by the corporation court of said city, in the penalty of five thousand dollars, payable to the commonwealth of Virginia, and conditioned for the faithful performance of his duties, said bond to be filed in the office of the clerk of said court. He shall perform such duties, have such powers, and be subject to such penalties as are now or may be hereafter prescribed by law in reference to constables. Said high constable may appoint, with the approval of the councils, one or more deputies to attend to and execute the duties of his office. But the surities on the bond of the said high constable shall be equally liable for the acts of the said deputy or deputies as for those of the principal. The councils shall have power to remove the high constable or any of his deputies, for cause, and appoint others in their place.

29. If any person having been an officer in said city, shall Vacation of office. not within ten days after he shall have vacated or been removed from office, and upon notification and request of the city treasurer, or within such time thereafter as the city councils shall allow, deliver over to the treasurer all the property, books and papers belonging to the city, or appertaining to such office, in his possession or under his control he shall forfeit and pay to the city the sum of five hundred dollars, to be sued for and recovered with costs. And all books, records and documents used in any such office, by virtue of any provision of this act, or of any ordinance or order of the city councils, or any superior officer of said city, shall be deemed the property of said city, and appertain to said office and the chief officer thereof shall be responsible therefor.

30. The city councils shall grant and pay to all city of- Compensation of city officers. ficers, clerks and assistants, elected or appointed under or in pursuance of this act, such salaries or compensation as the said city council may, from time to time deem proper, or shall be fixed by this act, or any other act of assembly hereinafter enacted.

31. The councils may, so far as is not inconsistent with How duties defined. the provisions of this act, or the constitutions and laws of the state and the United States, define the powers, prescribe the duties and compensation, and take from any of the officers

hereinbefore or hereinafter provided for, bonds, with sureties in such penalties as to the councils may seem fit, payable to the city in its corporate name, with the condition for the faithful performance of said duties. All officers appointed by the councils may be removed from office at their pleasure; but this power shall not be construed to interfere with the authority of the mayor to suspend or remove any city officer for cause.

32. The parties to bonds taken in pursuance of the preceding section, their heirs, devisees, executors, and administrators, shall be subject to the same proceedings on the said bonds, for enforcing the conditions and terms thereof, by motion or otherwise, before the corporation or circuit court of the city of Norfolk, that collectors of the county levy and their sureties are or shall be subject to, on their bonds for enforcing payment of the county levies.

City treasurer. 33. There shall be elected by the qualified voters of the city of Norfolk, on the fourth Thursday in May, in eighteen hundred and eighty-five, and every three years thereafter, one city treasurer, who shall hold his office for the term of three years, and until his successor be elected and qualified, unless sooner removed from office. He shall give bond with sureties, to the amount, of not less than fifty thousand dollars, said bonds to be approved by the city councils, entered on their records, and filed in the clerk's office for the court of the corporation. The said treasurer shall perform such duties, have such powers, and be liable to such penalties as may be prescribed by existing laws or ordinances, or as may be prescribed by laws or ordinances hereafter enacted or ordained, and he shall be ex-officio clerk of the common council.

Collector of taxes, 34. There shall be elected by the qualified voters of the city of Norfolk, on the fourth Thursday of May, eighteen hundred and eighty-four, and biennially thereafter, one collector of city taxes and levies, who shall hold his office for the period of two years, and until his successor shall be elected and qualified, unless sooner removed from office. He shall give bond with sureties, to the amount of not less than fifty thousand dollars, said bond to be approved by the city councils, entered on their records, and filed in the office of the city treasurer. The said collector shall perform such duties, have such powers, and be liable to such penalties as may be prescribed by existing laws or ordinances, or as may be prescribed by laws or ordinances hereafter enacted or ordained.

Duty of collector. 35. It shall be the duty of said collector to conduct all the proceedings, and render all service necessary to perfect the sale and transfer of real estate in said city where the same shall be sold or advertised for sale, for the non-payment of any tax or assessment imposed by the city councils as hereinafter provided.

Commissioner of the revenue 36. There shall be elected by the qualified voters of the city of Norfolk, on the fourth Thursday of May, eighteen hundred and eighty-four, and every four years thereafter, one commissioner of the revenue, who shall hold his office for the period of four years, and until his successor shall be elected and qualified, unless sooner removed from office. He shall give bond with sureties, to the amount of not less than ten thousand dollars, said bond to be approved by the city councils, entered on their records, and filed in the office of the city treasurer.

37. The said commissioner of the revenue shall perform His duties. such duties, have such powers, and be liable to such penalties as may be prescribed by existing laws or ordinances, or as may be prescribed by laws or ordinances hereafter enacted or ordained. In case of a vacancy in the office from any cause whatever, the councils shall appoint a qualified person to fill the said office for the unexpired term.

38. The board of water commissioners, the board of health, Boards of the board of fire commissioners and the board of street, sewer, water commissioners; of and drain commissioners shall continue as at present orga- health; of nized, until the first regular meeting of the council in July, streets, &c. eighteen hundred and eighty-four, at which time the said offices shall become vacant.

39. The mayor shall have power to appoint a clerk to serve Clerk to during his term of office, and perform such duties as he may mayor. require, who shall also act as the clerk of the police court, and of the board of police commissioners.

CHAPTER V.

Finances and Revenues.

40. The city council may, in the name and for the use of Issue of debt the city, contract loans, or cause to be issued certificates of certificates, &c. debt or bonds, but such loans, certificates or bonds shall not be irredeemable for a period greater than thirty-four years: provided, however, that they shall not contract such loans or issue such certificates of debt or bonds for the purpose of subscribing to the stock of any company incorporated for a work of internal improvement, or other purposes, nor indorse the bonds of any such company without first being authorized so to do by three-fourths of the legal voters of the city; and they shall not issue any such certificates of debt or bonds, or incur any indebtedness in the name of, or for or on account of the said city, or increase the said indebtedness, at any time, to an amount greater than twenty per centum of the assessed value of property. real and personal, set forth and contained in the rolls or books of assessment of the commissioner of the revenue of the city, for taxation by the city.

41. For the execution of their powers and duties, the city Taxes, how councils may raise annually, by taxes and assessments, in raised said city, such sums of money as they shall deem necessary to defray the expenses of the same, and in such manner as they shall deem expedient, in accordance with the constitution and laws of this state and the United States: provided, however, that they shall impose no taxes on the bonds of said city.

Powers of collectors

42. The councils may vest in the collector of the city taxes and of assessments for use of water, gas or other purposes, any or all of the powers which are now or may hereafter be vested in a sheriff or collector of the state taxes; may prescribe the mode of his proceeding, and the mode of proceeding against him for failure to perform his duties.

Powers of distress

43. All goods and chattels, wheresoever found may be distrained and sold for taxes assessed and due thereon; and no deed of trust or mortgage upon goods or chattels shall prevent the same from being distrained and sold for taxes assessed against the grantor in such deed, while such goods and chattels remain in the grantor's possession; nor shall any such deed prevent the goods and chattels from being distrained and sold for taxes assessed thereon, no matter in whose possession they may be found.

Payment

44. Any payment of taxes made by a tenant, unless under an express contract contained in his lease, shall be a credit against the person to whom he owes the rent; and where any tax is paid by a fiduciary on the interests or profits of moneys of an estate, invested under an order of court or otherwise, the tax shall be refunded out of such estate.

Lien for taxes

45. There shall be a lien on real estate for the city taxes, assessed thereon, from the commencement of the year for which they were assessed, and also for all local assessments made thereon. The city councils may require real estate in the city delinquent for non-payment of taxes or assesments, to be sold for said taxes or assessments, with interest thereon, at the rate of six per centum per annum, and such per centum as they may prescribe for charges, such real estate shall be sold, and may be redeemed under the provisions hereinafter made.

Notice by collector

46. The collector of city taxes snall, under the direction of the city councils, cause a notice of the time and place of such sales to be published in one or more of tne daily newspapers published in said city, at least ten days previous to said sale; and he shall also cause to be published in one or more of said daily papers, on some day not more than twenty days previous to such sale, a list of the several parcels of real estate to be sold describing therein each parcel of real estate in the same manner as the same is described in the assessment rolls, in which the said tax or assessment is imposed thereon, together with the name of the person to whom each parcel is assessed, and the amount of the tax or assessment thereon.

Sale by collector

47. If such tax or assessment, and the percentage, interest, and expense aforesaid, be not paid previous to the day for which said sale was advertised, or on some day immediately thereafter, to which said sale may be adjourned, the collector shall proceed to make sale accordingly of the said several parcels of real estate, or so much thereof as may be neccessary, to the highest bidder; and the sale may be adjourned from day to day until it shall be completed. On such sale the collector shall execute to the purchaser a cer-

tificate of sale, in which the property puchased shall be described, and the aggregate amount of tax or assessment, with charges and expenses specified; but the collector shall not for himself, cither directly or indirectly, purchase any real estate so sold.

48. If at any such sale no bid shall be made for any such parcel of land, or such bid shall not be equal to the tax or assessment, with the interest and charges, then the same shall be struck off to the city. On such sale the collector shall execute to the city a certificate of sale, in which the property purchased shall he described, and the aggregate amount of tax or assessment, with charges and expenses specified, and shall deposit such certificate with the treaurer. *bids at collector's sale*

49. The owner of any real estate so sold, his heirs, or assigns, or any person having a right to charge such real estate for debt, may redeem the same by paying to the purchaser, his heirs or assigns, within two years from the sale thereof, the amount for which the same was so sold, and such additional taxes thereon, as may have been paid by the purchaser, his heirs or assigns; or if purchased by the city, such additional sums as would have accrued for taxes thereon if the same had not been purchased by the city, with interest on the said purchase money and taxes, at the rate of six per centum per annum, from the time that the same may have been so paid; or the same may be paid within the said two years to the city treasurer, in any case in which the purchaser, his heirs or assigns, may refuse to receive the same, or may not reside, or cannot be found in the city of Norfolk. *Property so sold; how redeemed*

50. Any infant, married woman, insane person, or person imprisoned, whose real estate may have been so sold, or his heirs, may redeem the same by paying to the purchaser, his heirs or assigns, within five years after the removal of the disability, the amount for which the same was sold, with the necessary charges incurred by the purchaser, his heirs or assigns, in obtaining the title under the sale, and such additional taxes on the estate as may have oeen paid by the purchaser, his heirs or assigns, and the appraised value of any improvements that may have been made thereon, with interest on the said items, at the rate of six per centum per annum, from the time the same may have been paid. Upon such payment within two years after the removal of such disability, the purchaser, his heirs or assigns, shall, at the cost of the original owner, his heirs or assigns, convey .to him or them, by deed with special warranty, the real estate so sold. *Rights of persons under disability*

51. The purchaser of real estate sold for taxes and not redeemed, shall, after the expiration of two years from the sale, obtain from the city treasurer, a deed conveying the same, wherein shall be set forth what appears in his office, in relation to the sale. When the purchaser has assigned the benefit of his purchase, the deed may, with his assent. evinced by his joining .therein, or by a writing annexed thereto be executed to his assignee. If the purchaser shall have died, *Rights of purchasers*

his heirs or assigns may move the corporation court of said
city, to order the treasurer to execute a deed to such heirs or
assigns.

Title of pur- 52. When the purchaser of any real estate sold for taxes,
chaser; when
complete   his heirs or assigns, shall have obtained a deed therefor, and
within sixty days from the date of such deed shall have
caused the same to be recorded, such estate shall stand vested
in the grantee in such deed as was vested in the party assessed with the taxes, (on account whereof the sale was made)
at the commencement of the year for which the said taxes
were assessed, notwithstanding any irregularity in the proceedings under which the said grantee claims title, unless
such irregularity appear on the face of the proceedings. And
if it be alleged that the taxes for the non-payment of which
the sale was made, were not in arrear, the party making such
allegation must establish the truth thereof, by proving that
the taxes were paid.

Purchase by   53. In case that any real estate struck off to the city, as
city
hereinbefore provided, shall not be redeemed within the time
specified, the city treasurer shall, within sixty days after the
expiration of two years from the sale cause to be recorded
such certificate of sale, with his oath that the same has not
been redeemed ; and thereupon the said corporation or their
assigns shall acquire an absolute title to the same in fee. The
said certificate may be acknowledged or proved, and recorded in the same manner that deeds are recorded ; and the
said certificate, or the record thereof, or a copy of said record,
duly authenticated, shall, in all courts and places, be pre-
sumptive evidence of the fact therein stated, and of the regu-
larity and correctness of such sale, and all proceedings prior
thereto.

Board of sink- 54. The city councils, in joint session, at their first regular
ing fund com-
missioners   meeting in July, or as soon thereafter as practicalble, shall
elect three citizens, freeholders, a board of sinking fund commissioners, to hold their positions for four years, and until
their successors are appointed and qualify, and whenever a
vacancy shall occur in said board by death, resignation or
otherwise, shall elect some person to fill such vacancy, being
citizens and freeholders ; and said board shall have charge of
the sinking fund of the city, and the treasurer shall pay over
to them all moneys appropriated to said fund by any law or
ordinance; which board and their successors shall, by and
with the advice of the chairman of the committee of finance
of the councils of the city, for the time being, hold, manage
and invest the same in such manner as shall best conduce to
the extinguishing of the city debt; and the said commissioners may, at all times, either in their own names or the
name of the city of Norfolk, institute and prosecute all suits
in law or equity, which, in the opinion of such board, may be
necessary in the managing and conducting of said sinking
fund; and said commissioners shall, before entering upon
their duties, give bond to the satisfaction of the councils of
said city for the faithful discharge of the duties of their trust,

and all the property and rights of property of every description, belonging to said sinking fund, shall vest in and belong to said commissioners, as trustees for the time being, who shall have complete title thereto for all purposes of said trust, and it shall be the duty of the said board of sinking fund commissioners, together with the mayor and councils, to see that the city indebtedness is not increased beyond twenty per centum of the assessed value of real and personal property, as returned by the commissioner of the revenue of the city; and all issues of bonds shall, hereafter, bear upon their face a certificate to this effect from the board of sinking fund commissioners.

CHAPTER VI.

Police Department.

55. The police department of the city of Norfolk, shall be under the control and management of a board of police commissioners, which shall consist of the mayor and of two electors of said city, who shall be elected by the common council of said city, immediately after the passage of this act, and the mayor shall be the president of said board. The persons elected by the common council as aforesaid, shall continue in office until the first day of July eighteen hundred and eighty-six, and until their successors are elected and qualified. As soon as the commissioners elected by the common council as aforesaid, shall have taken the oath of office, the two police commissioners then acting as such under any law heretofore passed, shall immediately vacate their respective offices. *Police, board of*

56. The councils shall at their first meeting in July, eighteen hundred and eighty-six, or as soon thereafter as practicable, and biennially thereafter elect two police commissioners to serve for two years, and until their successors are elected and qualified. Any two of said commissioners shall form a quorum for the transaction of any business. Said board may adopt rules and by-laws for the government thereof, and also may establish, promulgate, and enforce proper rules, regulations and orders for the good government and discipline of said police force: provided that said rules, regulations and orders shall not in any way conflict with any ordinance of the city councils, or of the provisions of this act, or the constitution and laws of this State or of the United States. *Police commissioners*

57. The said police commissioners, after taking the oath of office as such commissioners, shall meet at the office of the mayor, or other suitable place, at such time as may be expedient, and as they shall from time to time designate, and on special occasions as the mayor in writing may appoint. They shall perform the duties of said office, without any compensation, reward or salary therefor from said city, except that nothing herein shall in any way conflict with the payment of the salary elsewhere provided to be paid to the said mayor. *Duties of police commissioners*

Appointment of policemen

58. It shall be the duty of said police commissioners to select from among the electors of said city, and appoint by warrant of appointment bearing the signatures of two of said commissioners, to be immediately filed with the city treasurer, so many permanent policemen, officers and patrolmen as may be authorized by city councils; and said board shall also appoint with the approval of the city councils, one chief of police, and such other assistants and officers as they may deem necessary, who shall hold office for the term of two years, through whom said board may promulgate all rules, regulations and orders to the whole force, and who shall have immediate direction and control of said force—subject, however, at all times to the rules, regulations and orders of said board, and to the orders of the mayor: provided that the orders of such single commissioner do not conflict with the rules, regulations or orders of said board then in force; and each policeman of said force appointed in manner as aforesaid, may hold his respective office during the term of good behavior, or until said board, by a majority vote, shall remove him. As soon as the appointments of policemen are made in the manner as herein provided, then all the policemen who shall be in service previous thereto, shall immediately vacate their offices respectively, unless re-appointed as herein provided.

Additional policemen

59. In times of exigency, said commissioners, or a majority of them, or any one of them, if the others should be absent from the city or unable to act, may appoint, temporarily, without authority from the city council, a suitable number of additional policemen for such time as shall appear necessary, not, however, to extend beyond the time of the next meeting of the city council.

Suspension of policemen

60. The mayor, at any time, upon charges being preferred, or upon finding said chief, or any other member of said police force guilty of misconduct, shall have power to suspend such member from service until the board of commissioners shall convene and take action in the matter: provided, however, that such member shall not remain so suspended for a longer period than thirty days without an opportunity of being heard in his defence; and upon hearing the proofs in the case, a majority of said commissioners may discharge or restore such member, in accordance with the decision of the majority of such board thereon; and the pay or salary of such member shall cease from the time of suspension to the time of restoration to service unless otherwise ordered by said board of commissioners in their written decision, which shall be filed with the clerk of the common council, and any violation of the rules, regulations or orders of the board, or orders of any superior, shall be good cause for dismissal.

Salary of policemen

61. The salary and pay of said chief and policemen shall be determined by the city councils, and all bills of expense on account of the police department shall be audited by at least two of said commissioners.

62. The said chief of police and every policeman duly appointed as aforesaid, shall have issued to him a warrant of appointment, signed by the president of the board and countersigned by the clerk of the common council, stating the date of his appointment, which shall be his commission; and he shall take such oath as the city councils may ordain, and subscribe the same in a book to be kept for that purpose by the said clerk of the common council. *Chief of police; warrant of appointment*

63. The said chief of police and policemen shall generally have power to do whatever may be necessary to preserve the good order and peace of said city, and to secure its inhabitants from personal violence and their property from loss and injury. Such number of the said police force, as the board of police commissioners may designate, shall, in criminal cases have the same powers and duties and be subject to the same penalties that are prescribed by law as to constables. *General duties of police*

64. The said board of commissioners may prescribe such uniforms and badges for the police force as they may deem proper, and direct in what manner they shall be armed. And if any person, other than a policeman, shall publicly wear such uniform and badges as may be prescribed as aforesaid, he may be subjected to such fine, not exceeding the sum of one hundred dollars, as the city councils may ordain. *Uniform of police*

CHAPTER VII.

Fire Department.

65. The city councils shall organize and maintain a fire department for said city, and appoint a chief engineer and fire wardens and assistants, with any or all of the powers which have been or may be vested by law in such officers. They may also make rules and regulations for the government of the officers and men of said fire department; may prescribe their respective duties in case of fire or alarms of fire; may direct the dresses or badges of authority to be worn by them; may prescribe and regulate the time and manner of their exercises; shall fix their pay, and may impose reasonable fines for the breach of any such regulations. They may also make such ordinances as they may deem proper, to extinguish and prevent fires, prevent property from being stolen, and to compel citizens to render assistance to the fire department in case of need. *Chief engineer and fire wardens*

66. For the purposes of guarding against the calamities of fire, the city councils may make such ordinances as they may deem proper to extinguish and prevent fires, prevent property from being stolen, and to compel citizens to render assistance to the fire department in case of need; and they may, from time to time, designate such portions and parts of said city as it shall think proper, within which no buildings of wood shall be erected, and may regulate the manner of construction of all buildings. They may prohibit the erection *Ordinances as to fires*

of wooden buildings in any portion of the city without
permission obtained from them, and shall, on the petition of
the owner or owners of not less than one-fourth of the ground
included in any square in the city, prohibit the erection in
such square of any building, or addition to any building,
unless the outer walls thereof be made of brick and mortar,
or stone and mortar, or some other fire-proof material; and
may provide for the removal of any such addition which shall
be erected contrary to such prohibition at the expense of the
owner or builder thereof. And if any building shall have
been commenced before said petitions can be acted on by the
councils, or if a building in progress appears clearly to be un-
safe, the councils may have such building taken down.

67. Whenever any building in said city shall be on fire, it
shall be the duty of, and lawful for the chief engineer to
order and direct such building, or any other building which
he may deem hazardous and likely to communicate fire to
other buildings, or any part of such buildings, to be pulled
down and destroyed; and no action shall be maintained
against any person or against the said city therefor. But any
person interested in any such building so destroyed or injured,
may, within three months thereafter, apply to the city councils to assess and pay the damages he has sustained. At the
expiration of three months, if any such application shall have
been made in writing, the city councils shall either pay the
said claimant such sum as shall be agreed upon by them and the
said claimant for such damages, or, if no such agreement shall
be effected, shall proceed to ascertain the amount of such
damages, and shall provide for the appraisal, assessment, collection and payment of the same, in the same manner as is
provided for the ascertainment, assessment, collection and payment of damages sustained by the taking of land for purposes of
public improvement.

Damages by
fire; how as-
sessed
68. The commissioners appointed to appraise and assess
the damages incurred by the said claimant, by the pulling
down or destruction of such building, or any part thereof, by
the direction of the said officers of the city as provided above,
shall take into account the probability of the same having
been destroyed or injured by fire, if it had not been so pulled
down or destroyed, and may report that no damages should
equitably be allowed to such claimant. Whenever a report
shall be made and finally confirmed in the said proceedings,
for appraising and assessing the damages, a compliance with
the terms thereof by the city councils, shall be deemed a full
satisfaction of all said damages of the said claimant. But
any party feeling aggrieved thereby, may appeal to the corporation or circuit court for the city of Norfolk; which court,
in taking jurisdiction thereof, shall be controlled by the laws
regulating assessments of damages to real estate in other
cases.

CHAPTER VIII.

Water Department.

69. The water department of the city of Norfolk, shall be Water commissioners under the general control and management of a board of water commissioners, which shall consist of three electors of said city, to be chosen by the councils for the term of two years, or until their successors are appointed and qualify. The commissioners shall elect from their body a president, a secretary and a treasurer. The treasurer shall give a bond in the sum of ten thousand dollars, and shall receive such compensation as the councils may authorize; the councils may also allow compensation for the services of the other commissioners. The water commissioners shall have such powers and perform such duties as may be prescribed by law or ordinance.

CHAPTER IX.

School Board.

70. The board of school trustees for the city of Norfolk, School trustees shall consist of two members from each ward of said city, together with the president of the common council, and the president of the select council, who shall be ex-officio members of said board.

71. There shall be elected by the qualified voters in each How elected ward of said city, on the fourth Thursday in May, eighteen hundred and eighty-four, and biennially thereafter, one elector as a member of the board of school trustees, who shall be a resident of the ward during his term of office, to serve for two years, and until his successor is appointed and qualified. The persons so elected in eighteen hundred and eighty-four, shall succeed the members of the present board, whose term will expire on the first day of July, eighteen hundred and eighty-four.

72. And the persons elected on the fourth Thursday in Vacancy in board May, eighteen hundred and eighty-six, shall succeed the members of the present board, whose terms will expire on the first day of July, eighteen hundred and eighty-six. In case of a vacancy in the board, the members thereof shall elect a qualified person to fill the same, from the ward in which such vacancy exists. for the unexpired term.

73. The said board of school trustees shall have and exer- Powers of school trustees cise all the powers and duties which have been heretofore, or may hereafter be vested in the school board of said city, by law or ordinance.

CHAPTER X.

74. The act entitled an act to amend and re-enact the Repeal or previous charter, &c. charter of the city of Norfolk, approved April twenty-first, eighteen hundred and eighty-two, and all acts and parts of

acts inconsistent with this act, are hereby repealed; and all acts and parts of acts in any way concerning said corporation and the rights of the people thereof, or any of them, not inconsistent with this act, shall be in as full force, to all intents and purposes, as if this act had never been passed.

Commencem't   75.   This act shall be in force from its passage.

TABLE OF CONTENTS

OF THE CHARTER.

REFERENCE TO FORMER CHARTERS.

The Original Charter of the BOROUGH OF NORFOLK was granted by Letters Patent of George II, on the 15th of September, 1736, and was confirmed by Act of the General Assembly in the same year. Acts were passed amending this Charter and enlarging the powers and jurisdiction of the Corporation in 1752, 1757, 1761, 1762, 1772, 1787, 1788, 1790, 1796, 1798, 1802, 1803, 1804, 1806, 1807, 1808, 1811, 1816, 1818, 1819, 1825, 1832, 1839, and on February 13, 1845, was passed the Charter of the CITY OF NORFOLK. This Charter was amended March 20, 1850, May 19, 1852, March 22, 1853, February 24, 1858.

After the Civil War, the Acts of Assembly relating to the City Charter are as follows:

The Charter of 1871. In force March 16, 1871. Acts of 1870-71, Chapter 139, amended as follows:

Act of March 4, 1872—Page 102,
Acts of 1872-73—Pages 175, 295.
"   1874   "   90.
"   1875-76   "   127.
"   1876-77   "   6.

THE CHARTER OF 1882,

was in force April 21, 1882, Acts of 1881-82, Chapter 70, Page 405, Sections 55 and 64 amended January 19, 1882, Acts of 1881-82, Page 22, Chapter 24—Police Department.

THE ORDINANCES

OF THE

CITY OF NORFOLK.

COMPILED BY

CHARLES G. ELLIOTT.

AND

PUBLISHED BY AUTHORITY

OF THE COUNCILS.

1885.

Date of Enactments including August, 1885.

TABLE OF CONTENTS.

ORDINANCES.

THE ORDINANCES OF THE CITY OF NORFOLK

CHAPTER I.

Alms House and Poor.

1. The keeper of the alms house shall, in all matters pertaining to the poor and the alms house, obey the orders and instructions of the joint committee of the councils who shall be appointed to superintend the affairs of the alms house, which committee are the overseers of the poor for the city. *Keeper to obey the alms house committee; who are overseers of the poor*

2. The joint committee shall inspect and superintend the alms house, and make all proper regulations for its government, for the reception and maintenance of its inmates, and for the admission and reformation of vagrants and others, and see that the keeper separates the inmates and arranges them in proper classes, keeping the vagrants, the poor and the sick, as far as practicable, separate and apart; the keeper shall provide employment for the vagrants and such of the poor as may be able to work; he may furnish junk or other material for this purpose, and may also employ them about the alms house and the grounds. The keeper shall receive into the alms house only such vagrants and others as the joint committee, (or a majority of them) shall direct; and the order for their admission shall be signed by the chairman of the respective committees of the select and common councils, or by any one of the joint committee that may be authorized by said committee for that purpose. *Duty of the committee and keeper; who shall be received*

3. The committee may employ nurses to attend upon the sick, and allow them such reasonable compensation as may be thought proper, and shall annually advertise for proposals and contract for the supply of rations and supplies, to be delivered at the alms house for the consumption of the inmates. *Committee may employ nurses*

4. Any person who shall bring any pauper or other person likely to become chargeable to the city within the same, or shall aid therein, shall pay twenty dollars for every such offence—one-half, when recovered, shall go to the informer, and the informer shall be a competent witness in the case. It shall be the duty of the inspector of streets and policemen to make inquiry after all persons likely to become chargeable to the city, not being residents, and report them to the committee, who shall take measures for their removal, and draw upon the treasurer for the necessary money for that purpose. *Penalty for bringing paupers to the city*

5. All accounts against the alms house shall be certified by the committee before being submitted for payment to the councils. The keeper shall render semi-monthly accounts of the receipts and disbursements of the alms house, and pay over to the treasurer any money on hand, and on failure to do so for five days, he shall pay a fine of twenty dollars. *Accounts to be submitted by keeper*

Duty of health officer

6. The health officer shall visit the alms house once every day at least, and more frequently when necessary, and there perform the duties of physician, surgeon and man mid-wife; and he shall also visit and administer to all patients or persons affected with infectious or contageous diseases who may be sent either to the alms house or pest house. The alms house committee may require the health officer to visit and attend such other of the sick poor people of the city as they may think proper.

Health officer to furnish certificate of death in certain cases

7. It shall be the duty of the health officer to view the body of any person who has died without having a medical attendant, and, after a satisfactory examination in each case, furnish a certificate stating sex, color, age and name of the deceased, and the disease known or supposed to have been the cause of his or her death; and in all cases of the inability to collect from the estate of the deceased the sum of one dollar, the same shall be paid by the city to the health officer.

Prescribing the system of accounts to be kept by the keeper of the alms house

8. The system of accounts for the regulation of the alms house shall be made to conform as nearly as possible to the rules regulating the receiving and accounting for stores, in the nature of quartermaster and subsistence stores, and for moneys and other property, that apply to the keepers of the military stores of the United States, and printed forms to this end shall be prepared by the alms house committee.

Reports

9. The keeper of the alms house shall present monthly reports to the alms house committee of the councils, according to the forms provided.

Articles to be furnished upon requisitions, countersigned by auditor approved by chairman of committee; duty of auditor

10. All subsistence stores and other articles for the use of the alms house shall be furnished upon the requisition of the keeper of the alms house, when approved by the chairman of the alms house committee of the councils, and borne upon the accounts of the keeper—all requisitions to be countersigned by the auditor of the city, whose duty it shall be to examine and approve the monthly accounts of the keeper of the alms house in all their details, and present consolidated quarterly statements therefrom to the councils. All requisitions from the keeper of the alms house shall specify the article, quantity and the time for which he has estimated; also the number of inmates—the number of inmates to be certified as correct by the physician upon all requisitions. The keeper of the alms house shall so prepare his estimates as to present requisitions for supplies and other stores on the first day of each month.

CHAPTER II.

City Advertising.

Printing and advertising only to be done by parties under contract with the city

1. Whenever any contract shall exist between the city and the owners of any newspapers for the publication of advertisements for the city, it shall not be lawful for any member of the councils or committee thereof or any officer or agent of the

city to publish in any newspaper not under contract with the city as aforesaid any notice or advertisement of any matter relating to the affairs of the city, unless special authority so to do shall be given by the councils.

2. Any officer or other person violating the provisions of the preceding section shall pay to the city the cost of advertising or publishing such notice. *Penalty*

CHAPTER III.

Public Buildings.

1. The committee of the councils on public buildings and grounds shall have the general supervision of the court house, and of all other public buildings, which are not specially placed under the control of some other standing committee, or the boards of commissioners. And no person or persons shall use or occupy any of said buildings for the purpose of holding any political or other meeting without the consent in writing of said committee on public buildings and grounds. *Who shall have control of public buildings; political or other meetings not to be held therein without authority*

2. If any person or persons shall use the court house or any public building, or shall forcibly enter therein, in violation of this chaper, he or they shall each pay a fine of not less than two nor more than twenty dollars. *Penalty for using or forcibly entering public buildings contrary to law*

CHAPTER IV.

Carts, Drays and Wagons.

1. Every person who shall have a cart, dray, truck or wagon in this city for hire or private use, shall first obtain a license for such a privilege. Before such license is issued there shall be paid to the collector, and his receipt therefor produced to the commissioner of the revenue, the annual tax of ten dollars, on the driver of a one-horse cart, dray, truck or wagon, and twenty dollars on the driver of a two-horse cart, dray, truck or wagon; and after that rate for any less period than a year. Country vehicles engaged in hauling produce to and from farms are excepted from the provisions herein contained, but dealers in produce, manufacturers and others engaged in business without the limits of the city, and who habitually use their vehicles upon the streets of the city, are not exempt from the requirements of this ordinance. *Who required to have license to use carts, drays and wagons; tax imposed*

But the collector will charge and collect for licenses issued to non-residents double the amount paid by the citizens of Norfolk city. *Double tax on non-residents*

Licenses shall be issued quarterly, say the first day of January, April, July and October; but in order to have them all expire at one date, the collector is authorized to issue to applicants a license for such a period as will enable him to carry out this provision, upon terms pro rata of the whole tax imposed. *When licenses expire*

Commissioner of revenue to keep register, mark and number; his fees

2. The commissioner of the revenue shall keep a register of the license and number of the same in every case, and shall furnish to every such person a tin plate painted black and marked white with the letter II, and the number corresponding to the number in the register, for which the commissioner of the revenue shall receive a fee of twenty-five cents in each case, to be paid by the driver, and the said plate shall be attached to the cart, dray or wagon in a conspicuous place. The commissioner of the revenue shall receive a fee of thirty cents for each license, and a like sum or fee for each transfer, to be paid by the party applying therefor.

Rates which may be charged; what constitutes a load; penalty for refusal to haul

3. In the absence of a special agreement there shall be paid for every cord of wood carried to either side of Cove street, or a line running parallel thereto, sixty cents; beyond Cove, to either side of Charlotte or Granby streets (above Stone Bridge), seventy-two cents; and to any other part of the city north of Charlotte and west of Granby streets, eighty cents; and after that rate for any greater or less quantity. For every dray or cart load, or part of a load of any other article carried to either side of Cove street, twenty-five cents; beyond Cove and to either side of Granby (above Stone Bridge) and Charlotte streets thirty cents; and for all west of Granby or north of Charlotte, thirty-five cents; and double these rates for wagon loads. Where wood or any other article is to be carted from the northern part of the city south, the reverse of these charges shall be paid, still making the above named streets the line. Three barrels of molasses, five other barrels, five sacks of salt, eight sacks of coffee, or one hogshead, shall be deemed a load. If any driver of a vehicle with the letter II., as aforesaid, being unemployed at the time, shall refuse the use of the same when called upon, he shall pay for every such offence a fine of two dollars.

Person under 18 not to drive

4. No person under eighteen years of age shall drive any public cart, dray or wagon in this city, and the owner of any such public cart, dray or wagon who shall permit the same to be so driven shall pay a fine of two dollars for every such offence, one-half of which shall go to the informer.

License may be transferred

5. A person obtaining a license under this ordinance may transfer the unexpired term thereof at the office of the commissioner of the revenue, and thereupon a new license shall be issued for the balance of the term.

Stand for public carts

6. All public carts, drays or wagons shall stand when not employed on Roanoke Square, or at the foot of the market house, on Water street; and for a violation hereof the driver of such cart, dray or wagon shall pay a fine of two dollars, one of which shall go to the informer.

Penalties

7. Any person who shall violate any provision of this ordinance, where no other penalty is imposed, shall pay a fine of not less than five or more than twenty dollars.

Collector to advertise expiration of licenses.

8. The collector shall advertise for three days in all the daily morning papers published in the city prior to the first days of January, April, July and October, the fact that licenses are required to be renewed on those dates as herein provided.

CHAPTER V.

Cemeteries—Cedar Grove and Elmwood.

1. The public burying grounds known as Cedar Grove and Elmwood Cemeteries are hereby set apart for the burying of the dead; and it shall not be lawful to bury the body of any person within the limits of the city except in the said cemeteries, or such other burying grounds as the councils may establish and set apart for that purpose Grounds set apart for burying the dead; unlawful to bury elsewhere

2. The said cemeteries shall be divided by the superintendent into lots of suitable and uniform size, with alleys and cross alleys and ornamented with trees. The superintendent shall keep a record of the lots so that the same may be known and easily found, should the boundaries become obliterated, and each lot shall have a separate number, and his record shall contain an account of all interments made in the cemeteries. Cemeteries to be divided into lots by superintendent and record of same kept

3. The treasurer of the city shall also keep in his office a copy of the plan of each cemetery and he shall sell the lots at forty dollars each, giving a receipt therefor to the purchaser specifying the number and location thereof and enter the same on his record. Record also to be kept by city treasurer; price of lots

Such receipt and entry shall give to the purchaser a title to the lot subject to such regulations as the councils may establish for the government of the said cemeteries. But no person shall be allowed to purchase a lot except for the use of his own family. Any lots that may be irregular in size shall be sold at prices in proportion to the regular lots. No lot sold except for use of family of purchaser

4. The superintendent of the cemeteries shall, under the orders and directions of the committee on cemeteries of the councils, take the care and oversight of the cemeteries, keep the walks and alleys in good order and have suitable trees and shrubs planted therein. Superintendent to take care of cemeteries and plant trees and shrubs

5. The superintendent shall enter in a book the name, age and calling of each person interred, and, as far as can be ascertained by him, the disease of which he died. From this book he shall make an abstract and report it on the first Monday in every month to the health officer, who shall publish the same in proper form on the Monday following, as provided in the ordinance concerning health. Record of name, age, &c. of deceased; monthly report to health officer; publication

6. The superintendent shall cause sunken graves to be kept filled up, the grass and weeds cut, the trees and shrubbery on and around each lot to be trimmed up twice a year. All assistance necessarily required by him for the proper maintenance of the cemeteries, and all workhorses, carts and implements required, shall be provided at the cost of the city, by the committee on cemeteries, and the superintendent shall be held accountable for the care and safe keeping of all such property. Superintendent's duties; assistance, how provided

7. No grave shall be dug or opened in any lot or other place in either of the said cemeteries, or in any other burying ground, except by the superintendent thereof. No person to dig a grave except superintendent

Public vaults   8. No person shall place, or cause to be placed, any dead body in the public vault in either of the cemeteries, or any other burying ground, between the first of April and the first of November in each year. Any person placing any dead body in said vault between the first of November and the first of April shall have the same removed and buried within sixty days after it shall have been placed there. Before the body of any person not a resident of the city, shall be deposited in said vault, there shall be placed in the hands of the superintendent of cemeteries a sum sufficient to defray the expenses of burial of such person, in case the body should not be taken out within the time required by this section.

Disinterments in summer prohibited   9. No grave shall be opened for the disinterment of any dead body in either of the cemeteries, or any burying ground of the city, from the first of May to the first of December in every year; nor shall any vault be opened for a like purpose; and if any person shall violate this section, such person shall pay a fine of twenty dollars for each and every offense.

Dimensions and prices of graves   10. The graves of adults shall be at least four feet deep, and of children four feet. The superintendent shall charge for the use of the city for graves opened in Cedar Grove and Elmwood Cemeteries the following rates: For single graves for children under five years of age, one dollar; for graves to be lined with brick or plank, for children under five years of age, two dollars; for single graves for children from five to twelve years of age two dollars; for graves to be lined with brick or plank, three dollars; for single graves for persons over twelve years of age, and for adults, two dollars; box graves, three dollars; for graves prepared so as to be lined with brick or plank, four dollars.

Work in cemeteries by superintendent for use of city; no other allowed to do work without a permit   11. All work appertaining to the cemeteries, including turfing, filling up lots, filling up graves, cutting of grass, cleaning of lots, cleaning of monuments, tombstones, &c., shall be done by the superintendent of cemeteries for the benefit of the city, and no person shall do or cause to be done, any work in Cedar Grove or Elmwood Cemeteries except that provided for in section 15, without the written consent of the committee on cemeteries, under a penalty of five dollars for every offence.

Disputes between lot owners; how settled   All grievances as to prices between lot owners and others with the superintendent, shall be referred to the committee on cemeteries for adjustment.

Scale of prices for work   12. The following are the prices established for doing work in the cemeteries Cedar Grove and Elmwood:

For filling up lots, 50 cents for every cart load of dirt used, and $2.00 per day for the laborer.

For turfing one lot, - - - - -	$8 00
For filling up and turfing one grave under 12 years old,	75
For filling up and turfing one grave over 12 years old,	1 25
For filling one grave under 12 years old, - -	50
For filling one grave over 12 years old - -	1 00
For cutting grass, trimming trees and shrubbery on lots twice a year, - - - - -	1 00
For disinterring bodies under 12 years old, - -	4 00

For disinterring bodies over 12 years old, - - $8 00
For depositing a body in the public vault, - - 50
For removing or taking out a body from the public
vault, - - - - - - - - 50
For depositing a body in a private vault, - - 1 00

13. The superintendent shall receive a salary of one thou- Superinten-
sand dollars per annum, and shall not be entitled to receive dent's salary, bond and
any other compensation for any services rendered by him by semi monthly settlements
order of the councils or committee thereof. But all moneys
received by him for opening graves, or other work, shall be for
the use of the city, and shall be accounted for by him, and paid
semi-monthly to the treasurer, who shall receipt for the same,
and a record thereof shall be kept in a book by the superintendent. The superintendent shall give bond with security
satisfactory to the councils, in the sum of one thousand dollars.

14. The committee on cemeteries shall set apart a portion Grounds set
of same for single graves. For each grave opened there shall apart for single graves;
be paid, for an adult five dollars, and for a child two dol- price of same
lars and fifty cents. Before any such grave shall be opened by
the superintendent the party applying therefor shall produce
the receipt and written order of the treasurer of the city.

15. The proprietors of lots shall have a right to enclose the Regulations
required of
same with a wall of stone not exceeding one foot in thickness, proprietors of
nor more than two feet in height above the surface, or with a lots
railing, (except of wood.) All such railings to be light, neat
and symmetrical. They shall have the right to erect any
proper stones, monuments, or sepulchral structure thereon;
and also to cultivate shrubs and plants in the same. If any
trees or shrubs situated in any lot shall by means of their
roots, branches or otherwise, become detrimental to the adjacent lots or avenues, or unsightly or inconvenient to passengers, it shall be the duty of the committee, and they shall
have the right, to enter the said lot and remove the said trees
and shrubs, or such parts thereof as are detrimental, unsightly
or inconvenient. Wooden enclosures and lettered boards designating graves will not be allowed.

Every owner of a lot, or trustee having a lot in his charge in Lot owners to
keep same in
either cemetery, is hereby required to place and keep his lot in proper condi-
a proper condition; and in case of failure so to do after due tion
notice from the superintendent, such person shall pay a fine
of five dollars for every seven days that his lot shall so
remain in an improper condition. And it shall be the duty of
the superintendent to issue such notice with the approval of
the committee on cemeteries.

16. The cemetery gates shall be kept closed day and night, Gates closed;
permits
and no persons admitted except officers of the city, without required for
permission from the superintendent, or the committee on cem- admission
eteries. The superintendent shall issue to the owner or part
owner of a lot a yearly ticket admitting him or his family to
the grounds at all times, but children must be under the
charge of some grown person.

Permits to visitors; improper characters excluded   Permits to visitors shall be given by the superintendent or committee, and lot owners may loan their tickets to their friends; but all lewd and improper characters shall be refused admittance with or without tickets as visitors.

Superintendent's duties   The superintendent or some person authorized by him shall be on the grounds to admit and aid visitors.

Duty of visitors   All visitors shall be required to observe strictly the decorum appropriate to the sacred grounds.

Superintendent and employees special policemen with power to arrest   17. The superintendent and all officers and employees connected with the cemeteries are hereby constituted special policemen, and they shall have power to compel any person disturbing the quiet or good order of the place to immediately leave the grounds; and they shall have power to arrest any person who shall violate any provision of this ordinance, or commit any trespass or depredation upon the premises.

Penalty for desecrating the cemeteries   18. If any one shall break or deface any part of the walls or gates of any of the cemeteries or burying-grounds of the city, or shall walk on the top of said walls, or shall climb over the same. or cut or deface any tree, post, monument, or tombstone, slab, shrub, flower or other thing in any of the cemeteries or burying-grounds, or hunt or shoot within the same, such person shall pay a fine of five dollars for every such offense, one-half of which shall go to the informer. No dogs, goats, or fowls of any kind, shall be allowed to enter the cemeteries, and owners of such dogs, goats or fowls shall pay a fine of five dollars for permitting them to go in the cemeteries.

CHAPTER VI.

Calvary Cemetery.

Grounds set apart for colored citizens under control of cemetery committee   1. All that piece or parcel of land belonging to the city of Norfolk, *lately purchased of T. R. Ballentine, lying on Tunner's Creek, north of Princess Anne road*, shall be set apart, and appointed as the burial ground of the colored citizens of the city. and shall be known as Calvary Cemetery. The joint committee of the councils on cemeteries shall have general control and management of interments in the said cemetery, of the preservation. improvement and embellishment of the grounds, and over the keeper and other persons employed about them, and the members of the said committe shall from time to time visit and inspect them.

Grounds to be laid off in lots to be sold by treasurer at price fixed by committee   2. The grounds of said cemetery shall be surveyed under the direction of the said joint committee, and divided into sections of convenient and suitable size, with alleys and cross alleys, and ornamented with trees; the sections or parts thereof to be sold by the treasurer of the city, at prices to be fixed by the said committee, with the approval of the councils; and the treasurer shall give a receipt for the purchase money, specifying the number and place of the lot sold, and enter in a book the names of the purchasers, which receipt and entry shall give title to the purchaser, subject to the regulations of the cemetery.

3. The provisions of the ordinance relating to Cedar Grove and Elmwood Cemeteries shall apply, as far as may be consistent, to Calvary Cemetery; provided, however, that the price demanded for opening graves shall be one dollar and twenty-five cents for single graves, and two dollars and fifty cents for double graves; and provided, further, that all money received by the keeper of Calvary Cemetery, under this ordinance, shall be accounted for and paid over to the treasurer of the city. For plank or brick graves, two dollars; for box graves, three dollars; for graves prepared so as to be lined with brick or plank, four dollars.

Same regulations as Elmwood and Cedar Grove; prices for opening graves

4. The committee on cemeteries shall set apart a portion of Calvary Cemetery for single graves for the interment of colored citizens and strangers, and for the ground and grave furnished for any person above the age of sixteen years, there shall be charged two dollars and fifty cents; and for any persons from twelve to sixteen years, one dollar and seventy-five cents; and for any persons from one day to twelve years old, one dollar.

Graves for strangers

5. All moneys received by the treasurer from the keeper of Calvary Cemetery as aforesaid, shall be held as a sacred fund, and devoted exclusively to defraying the cost of enclosing, improving and embellishing the grounds of the cemetery, under the direction of the said joint committee, and they shall not be used for any other purpose whatever, without the express authority of the councils.

Proceeds of sales to be kept as separate fund

6. The keeper of Calvary Cemetery (who, this ordinance contemplates, shall be a colored resident of the city) shall be elected by the councils at their first meeting in July to serve for two years and until his successor is appointed and qualified.

Keeper; when elected

The salary of the keeper shall be four hundred dollars, payable monthly, and he shall not be entitled to receive any other emolument from his said office. He shall enter into bond in the penalty of five hundred dollars with sufficient security for the faithful discharge of the duties of his office.

Salary and bond

CHAPTER VII.

West Point Cemetery.

1. All that parcel of land lying west of Elmwood Cemetery formerly known as "*Potter's Field*," shall hereafter be known and designated as "*West Point Cemetery*," and the committee on cemeteries is authorized to have the same laid off in suitable lots, alleys and cross alleys, and cause the plan thereof to be filed in the office of the treasurer of the city.

Name of Potter's field changed Cemetery committee to have same laid off into lots

2. All lots in said grounds owned by colored citizens shall be numbered and set apart to them, and the remaining lots may be sold by the committee on cemeteries, at a uniform price, to be fixed by said committee—on condition that the purchaser shall observe all the regulations governing the cemeteries, and keep his lot in good order free of expense to the city.

Lots belonging to colored citizens to be numbered and set apart; remainder to be sold

5

Money received dedicated to improvement of grounds

3. All moneys received by the treasurer for sale of lots and opening graves, etc. in said grounds, shall be held as a special fund, and devoted exclusively to the care and improvement of **West Point Cemetery.**

4. The superintendent of cemeteries shall also have the charge and over sight of West Point Cemetery, and shall charge for the use of the city, for single graves for children under twelve years, one dollar; for plank or brick graves, two dollars; box graves, three dollars; for graves prepared so as to be lined with brick or plank, four dollars.

Superintendent to open graves for deceased poor when ordered by committee

5. The superintendent of cemeteries shall open graves and furnish coffins for the interment of the remains of deceased poor persons in West Point Cemetery when directed so to do by the committee on cemeteries or any member thereof.

Same regulations as provided in Elmwood

6. All the provisions of the ordinance concerning the preservation of order in Cedar Grove and Elmwood cemeteries and prohibiting depredations therein shall apply also to the grounds designated as West Point Cemetery.

7. If any person shall violate any of the provisions of this chapter, where no other fine is imposed, he shall pay a fine of not less than five nor more than twenty dollars.

CHAPTER VIII.

Dogs.

Tax on dogs to be paid to collector; penalty for failure to pay tax

1. Upon every male dog kept within the limits of the city there shall be paid annually a tax of one dollar, and on every female dog two dollars, to be demanded and collected of the owner or keeper upon the first day of August of every year, or rateably after that time, provided that this ordinance shall not apply to dogs or puppies under the age of six months. The occupant or occupants of any house or lot to which any dog may belong, or which such dog may frequent, shall be deemed to be the owner of such dog or dogs, and be liable to the tax and fines herein imposed. If any such occupant or occupants of such house or lot, or the owner or keeper of any dog shall fail within ten days from the first day of August of every year to pay to the collector the tax upon such dog, such occupant or occupants shall pay a fine of five dollars, one-half of which shall go to the informer and the other half to the city.

Collector to furnish checks to parties paying tax, and to keep a register and make reports of the same

2. The collector shall also furnish to the owner or keeper of any dog, upon the payment of his license, a brass check, with the number of the license stamped thereon, to be attached to the collar. The collector shall keep a register showing the name of the owner of every dog upon which the tax has been paid, and the number of the license, and make monthly returns of a copy thereof to the treasurer and mayor, and post conspicuously in the mayor's office a list of all payments made up to the 15th of August.

3. It shall be the special duty of the police to report the name of any party owning or harboring a dog upon which the tax has been paid, and the mayor shall employ as many persons as he may deem necessary, whose business it shall be to take up and pen all dogs found outside the owner's enclosure without a collar, and the check on which is the number of the license. Every dog so taken up shall be penned for twenty-four hours from the time of his capture, during which time the owner may redeem said dog by the payment of two dollars to the officer in charge of the dog pen; and if not so redeemed, the dog shall be killed and buried outside the city limits. Every person so employed shall receive fifty cents for every dog he puts to death in accordance with this ordinance, after the same shall have been properly buried by him—the said amount to be paid by the treasurer of the city upon the certificate of the mayor—and the mayor shall order any dog to be killed whose owner has not paid any tax and will not pay the fine. *[Duty of police to report names of owners, &c., of dogs who fail to pay tax; provision for taking up, penning and killing dogs]*

4. Any female dog found going at large and creating a nuisance shall be penned, and the owner fined five dollars, one-half of which shall go to the informer and the other half to the city, and if the fine is not paid in twenty-four hours said dog shall be killed. *[Fine for permitting dogs to create nuisance]*

5. Any vicious dog may be killed by the order of the mayor or any magistrate. *[Vicious dogs; how killed]*

CHAPTER IX.

Fences and Party Walls.

1. Where party walls have been, or shall be hereafter erected, in a good and substantial manner, by any person within the city, any person who shall hereafter make use of or derive any advantage from such party wall, shall pay the proprietor one-half part of the value of such party wall at the time he shall make use thereof, or derive advantage therefrom; provided, that no person shall have power under this ordinance to demand more than one-half the expense of a nine inch brick wall, for any building not exceeding two stories high, nor more than one-half the expense of any fourteen inch brick wall for any building whatever, unless otherwise agreed upon in writing by the parties interested. *[How expense of party walls apportioned; proviso]*

2. All partition fences that have been, or hereafter shall be made within the said city, shall be made and maintained by such owners of the land on each side as may derive advantage therefrom, and each party shall keep or repair one-half part thereof, when it can be conveniently divided; and where any partition fence cannot be conveniently divided, the same shall be made and kept in repair at the joint and equal expense of such owners of the land on each side as aforesaid. *[How expense of maintaining partition fence apportioned]*

3. If any such person who ought to make and repair any part of any partition fence shall refuse to do so for six days after request made to such person, or in case of such person's absence, to the occupant of the premises, then it shall be law- *[What may be done in case of refusal to repair by one party, as provided; proviso]*

ful for the person who ought to make and repair the other part of such partition fence, as aforesaid, to make and repair the whole and to recover one-half of the expense thereof from such person or occupant, who ought to have made or repaired the half of such partition fence; provided, nevertheless, that the cost of any fence shall not exceed three dollars and fifty cents for every ten feet of running measure.

Power and authority of engineer and inspector to ascertain and fix lines and boundaries of streets, lots, &c

4. The engineer and inspector shall have full power and authority, when applied to by any person requiring the same, to ascertain and fix the lines of any streets, lanes and alleys, or any boundaries of any of the lots within the city and having fixed and established the same, to put up stones or land marks, to be provided by the person requiring the same to be done, and to make return thereof in writing, with the proper description thereof, under their hands, to the treasurer, who shall record the same in a book to be provided for that purpose.

How owners of lots must proceed in laying foundation of houses, or erecting walls or fences; duty of engineer and inspector; penalty for violation

5. No owner of any lot in the city shall dig or lay the foundation of any house in front of any street, or erect any wall or fence fronting thereon, before he shall have applied to the engineer or inspector to make out a true line of such street, unless the corners of the streets or square on which such improvements are to be made have been duly established; and the engineer and inspector are required to see that such foundation, building, house or wall does not encroach upon the line; and every person neglecting to apply as aforesaid shall pay a fine of five dollars for such neglect, and shall pay a further fine of five dollars for ever day he shall continue such neglect.

Authority of engineer and inspector when called upon to regulate party walls, &c., and report to treasurer; how engineer and inspector shall proceed

6. The engineer and inspector shall when called upon by any person requiring their attendance, regulate all party walls, partition fences, and the lines of any lot within the city, in such manner as they may deem most likely to promote justice between the parties concerned; and shall make and subscribe a written report of every such proceeding to the treasurer to be recorded. And when the engineer and inspector shall meet to establish any boundary of any lot, or regulate any party wall or partition fence, they shall give at least four days' notice, by advertisement, of the time and place of meeting.

How appeal may be taken from the determination of the engineer and surveyor

7. If any person shall think himself aggrieved by the determination of the engineer and inspector in fixing the lines of any street, or the boundary of any lots, every such person may, within five days after such determination, appeal from the same to the mayor, who shall appoint three disinterested persons (the determination of whom or a majority of them, shall be final) to settle all matters in dispute within ten days thereafter, and return their award to the treasurer to be recorded. And the said persons shall receive from the engineer and inspector all information which influenced them in said determination, from which the appeal was made; and each of the said persons shall receive from the person requiring their services the sum of two dollars for every day they shall attend.

CHAPTER X.

Fines and Penalties.

1. All fines and penalties not otherwise provided for shall be paid to the city of Norfolk, and shall be prosecuted in the name of the city of Norfolk. ^{Fines how prosecuted}

The mayor or justice imposing the fine shall collect the same, and, whenever any ordinance shall so provide, pay to the informer the moiety to which he may be entitled. ^{Justice to collect Moiety to informer}

2. In case of the failure on the part of any offender to pay the fine and cost imposed for the violation of any ordinance of the city, the mayor or justice, as the case may be, may cause the offender to be imprisoned in the jail of the city for any term not exceeding three calendar months, unless the said fine and costs be sooner paid. ^{Offender failing to pay fine may be imprisoned}

3. If a person liable to a fine or penalty be an infant or apprentice, the justice before whom the case is tried, may, in his discretion, impose a fine either on him, his father, or guardian; and if a married woman, on her husband. ^{Penalties on infants and married women; how recovered}

4. In all cases the informer, although entitled to part of the fine, shall be a competent witness on behalf of the city, and shall be entitled to one-half the fine, unless otherwise provided. ^{Moiety to informer who shall be a competent witness}

5. No application for the remission of a fine shall be considered unless accompanied with a statement of the circumstances and the evidence, certified by the mayor or justice of the peace who tried the case and imposed the fine. ^{See rules of order}

CHAPTER XI.

Fire Department.

1. There shall be a board of fire commissioners, to consist of three electors of the city, appointed every two years by the councils at their first meeting in the month of July, and at the same time the councils shall appoint a chief engineer, a first assistant engineer, and a second assistant engineer, of the fire department. ^{Fire commissioners to be appointed by the councils; also chief engineer and assistants}

The board of commissioners shall organize by electing one of their number president and the chief engineer shall act as secretary. ^{Organization of board}

The term of office of the present incumbents shall expire on the first day of July, 1886. ^{Term of office}

All vacancies in either of the offices named in this section shall be filled by the councils for the unexpired term. ^{How vacancies filled}

2. The board of fire commissioners shall appoint not more than one foreman, one engineman, one fireman, two hostlers and twelve extra men for each engine in active service, and the following officers and men for each hook and ladder truck: one foreman, one hostler and not more than twelve extra men. ^{Board of commission'rs to appoint employees}

Every steam engine in active service, may have one or more hose reels, one water tender, three horses and at least one thousand feet of hose and all minor accessories for efficient service. Each hook and ladder truck shall have one horse and all requisite harness and implements.

Board to adopt rules, prescribe uniforms, reduce number of employees when expedient; keep record

3. The board shall prescribe a suitable uniform to be worn by the officers and men ; and adopt such rules and regulations for their own government, and for the government of the fire department, as they shall deem expedient, provided such rules and regulations are not inconsistent with the laws of the State or ordinances of the city; they shall furnish each member of the fire department with a copy of such rules, and have a copy of the same and also a copy of this ordinance posted conspicuously in the office of the fire department, and in the several engine houses belonging to the department; they shall give notice when they are prepared to receive applications for membership in the fire department, and may reduce the number of extra men and other employees of the department when they think proper ; they shall keep a minute and correct record of their proceedings, subject to the inspection of the councils.

Board with chief engineer constitute a board of control

4. The fire commissioners, together with the chief engineer, shall form a board of control, and shall be responsible for the discipline, good order, proper conduct and economical administration of the department, and for the care of the horses, engines, hose reels and other furniture and apparatus thereto belonging ; they shall have the superintendence and control of all the engine and other houses used for the purposes of the fire department, and all the furniture and apparatus thereto belonging.

Board may suspend or receive any member of the department and also the chief or assistant engineers if councils approve

5. The board of fire commissioners shall have power to suspend and remove any member of the department appointed by the board and with the approval of the councils the board may also suspend the chief engineer, or either of the assistant engineers, for inattention or neglect of duty.

councils may remove any member of board or dep't

Nothing herein contained shall be construed to prevent the councils from removing from office any member of the board or fire department for malfeasance or misfeasance in office.

Pay of officers and men; how paid

6. The pay of the officers and men comprising the department shall be the following sums annually, which shall be paid monthly by the treasurer, upon a pay roll certified by the chief engineer, who shall deduct from the pay of any member the amount of any fines or assessments, levied by order of the commissioners, for any neglect of duty, that is to say:—

The chief engineer, $500; the assistant engineers, each $300 ; each foreman, $240 ; the enginemen, $720; the firemen, $600; the drivers of engines, $720; the driver of hose carts, $720; the driver of hook and ladder truck, $720; the extra men, each $120. The housemen shall give their undivided attention to their respective duties.

An extra compensation of $100 per annum shall be allowed

to the engineer who shall attend to the repairs or any other mechanical work required in the department.

7. It shall be the duty of the chief engineer and his assistants, whenever a fire shall break out in the city, to proceed at once to the place of such fire, and to take proper measures to see that the several engines and other apparatus be arranged in the most advantageous situation. The chief engineer shall have the sole command at fires over all other officers, all other members of the fire department, and all other persons who may be present at fires, and shall take all proper measures for the extinguishment of fires, and further protection of property, preservation of order and observance of laws of the State, ordinances of the city, and regulations of the fire commissioners respecting fires; and it shall be the duty of said engineer to examine into the condition of the engines and all other fire apparatus, and of the engine and other houses belonging to the city, used for the purposes of the fire department, as often as circumstance may render it expedient, or whenever directed to do so by the city councils or fire commissioners, and annually report the same to the city councils; and whenever the engines or other fire apparatus, engine or other houses used by the fire department require alterations, additions or repairs, the chief shall cause the same to be made, provided such alterations, additions or repairs shall not exceed in any instance the sum of twenty dollars; and if such alterations, additions or repairs exceed the sum of twenty dollars, the assent of a majority of the fire commissioners must be obtained for the same; and it shall be the duty of the chief engineer to receive and transmit to the fire commissioners, for the use of the councils, all the returns of the officers of the department and all other communications relating to the affairs of the fire department, and to keep fair and exact rolls of the number of officers and men of the department, specifying the time of admission and discharge, and age of each member, which he shall report to the fire commissioners, who shall safely file such reports. *Duty of chief engineer at fires and in case of apparatus; also keeping records and making returns*

8. In the absence of the chief engineer, the first assistant engineer shall perform the duties of the chief engineer, and have the powers of said officers, and in the absence of the chief and the first assistant, then the second assistant engineer shall perform the duties of the chief engineer and exercise his powers. *In absence of chief the assistants to discharge his duties in order of their rank*

9. If any person not a member of the fire department shall use the uniform determined upon by the fire commissioners, or any part thereof, such person shall be fined not less than ten dollars nor more than twenty dollars for each offense. *Uniform not to be worn by others*

10. If any person injure, deface or in any manner destroy any city fire apparatus, or if any person hinder or obstruct any member of the fire department from freely passing along the streets of the city to or from a fire, or in any manner hinder or prevent any member of the same from discharging his duty at any fire, each and every person so offending shall be fined not less than ten nor more than twenty dollars. *Penalty for injuring any property of department or obstructing members in discharge of duty*

Chief and assistants to have police powers during fires

11. The chief engineer and his assistants are authorized to exercise the powers of police officers in going to, while at, and returning from any fire or alarm of fire that may occur.

Duty of chief and assistants in precautionary measures against fires; preventing dangerous practices or structures

12. It shall be the duty of the chief engineer and assistant engineers to examine into all shops and other places where shavings or other combustible materials are collected and deposited, and report at the regular monthly meeting of the board the condition in this respect of the shops they have examined ; and whenever, in their opinion, the same may endanger the security of the city from fires, they shall direct the tenant or occupant of said shops or other places to remove such shavings or other combustible materials, and in case of such tenants or occupant's refusal so to do, they shall cause the same to be removed at the expense of such tenant or occupant, who shall in addition, be fined not less than ten nor more than fifty dollars for such neglect or refusal. The chief and assistant engineers shall also take cognizance of all buildings in the city in which any steam engine is used and all buildings in the city in process of erection or alteration, and make a record of such as in their judgment may for any cause be dangerous, and report the same to the fire commissioners. The chief and assistant engineers shall cause a prosecution to be instituted in all cases of infraction of the laws or ordinances in relation to the fire department or for the prevention of fire within the limits of the city.

Public cisterns controlled by board

13. The fire commissioners shall have full and sole control of all the public cisterns owned by and in the possession or control of the city of Norfolk ; and to the end that the same be at all times suitable for public use, the commissioners shall prevent the use of the same by any persons except for the purpose of preventing or extinguishing fires, and shall keep the same in good repair.

Fire marshal; when appointed

14. There shall be appointed annually, in the month of April, a fire marshal, in accordance with the provisions of chapter 55 of the Code of Virginia. The fire marshal shall have all the powers therein conferred and perform all the duties therein imposed.

Fire marshal's court; duties powers and fees; in absence of marshal chief engineer to act

15. As soon as convenient after the occurrence of a fire the fire marshal, with the chief engineer and one or more of the fire commissioners, shall convene a court of investigation, to be called the fire marshal's court, to investigate the origin of each fire, and, if in the opinion of such court, there be any ground to suspect incendiarism, such court shall certify the facts to the next corporation court of the city. The fire marshal shall for this purpose have the same power to summon witnesses and compel their attendance as coroners under the laws of the State ; and he shall be paid for such investigation five dollars in full for all services. In the fire marshal's absence the chief engineer shall perform his duties and receive his fees.

Fire marshal's oath

16. The fire marshal, before entering upon the duties of his office, shall take an oath before the mayor or some justice of the peace of the city, to discharge faithfully the duties of his

office. The certificate of which oath shall be returned and preserved by the clerk of the common council for the city.

17. No person shall keep in his house any stove for burning wood or coal unless the same be placed on a suitable foundation of brick, stone or metal and have its funnel or pipe leading directly through the shaft of a brick chimney or through a brick or stone wall or piece of metal. Any person violating this section shall pay a fine of not less than five nor more than twenty dollars. *Regulations as to stoves in houses*

18. All carpenters and others engaged in any trade by which shavings are made, shall at the close of each day, on leaving off work, cause the same to be securely stowed in some place remote from danger by means of fire, under the penalty of five dollars. If any person shall carelessly carry or kindle any fire in any street, such person shall pay a fine of five dollars for every such offense. *Shavings to be carefully stowed; kindling fires in streets*

19. If any owner or occupant of any stable, or any person in his employment, shall use therein any lighted candle, or lamp, except the same be securely kept within a lantern, every such person shall pay for every such offense a fine of five dollars. *Lights in stables*

20. If any person shall deposit any quicklime in casks, in any place in the city, without first having the same examined by the chief or assistant engineer, and obtaining his permission for such deposit, he shall pay a fine of ten dollars. *Quicklime; how deposited*

21. If any person having charge of any vessel, lying in any dock, or at any wharf of the city, shall keep fire, or suffer any fire to be kept on board any such vessel, otherwise than in proper chimneys, stoves or cabooses, he shall pay a fine of five dollars for every offense. *How fire kept on vessels*

22. If the chimney of any house shall take fire, so as to blaze out, unless it be actually raining, the tenant shall pay a fine of five dollars, Provided prosecution be commenced within one month thereafter. *Fine for allowing chimneys to take fire*

23. If any person shall set fire to any squibbs, crackers, or other fire works, or discharge any fire arms within the limits of this city, such person shall pay a fine of two dollars for every offense. But this shall not be construed to extend to a military exercise or review, or to Christmas, New Year, fourth day of July, or any other occasion when permission shall be obtained from the mayor. *Discharging fire works, &c* *See Gymnasium Association*

24. It shall be the duty of all owners or operators of foundries or other manufacturing establishments within the limits of the city, and of any railroad companies which shall employ their locomotive engines upon the streets of the city, to cause to be placed upon the tops of the chimneys of such foundries, manufacturing establishments or locomotive engines, respectively, proper spark catchers, and any one offending against the requirements hereof shall be subject to a fine of ten dollars and to an additional fine of five dollars for every day thereafter such foundry, manufacturing establishment or locomotive engine shall be used as aforesaid without such spark catcher. *Spark catchers to be used on chimneys of foundries, locomotives, engines, &c*

25. No person shall smoke any pipe, cigar or cigarette, on any lot or wharf or in any inclosure where cotton or other *Smoking pipes and cigars on wharves or lots prohibited*

6

inflammable material may be deposited or stored, if the owner
or occupant of the premises shall cause to be conspicuously
posted thereon a notice prohibiting smoking. Any person
violating this section shall pay a fine of not less than five nor
more than twenty dollars.

Duty of con-
stables in case
of fire
26. It shall be the duty of the constables of the city to proceed immediately, on the alarm of fire, to the place where such
fire may be, and obey such orders as may be given by the chief
or assistant engineers. For every failure so to do the constable
so failing shall pay a fine of five dollars.

CHAPTER XII.

Finance and Revenue.

Fiscal year;
year for
taxation
1. The fiscal year shall begin on the first day of July. The
year for which taxes shall be levied by the councils annually,
on real and personal property shall begin on the first day of
February.

Financial
estimates
2. The finance committee of the councils shall, annually
in the month of February, lay before the councils an estimate
of the amount required for the ensuing fiscal year, to provide
for the interest upon the city debt, and meet the necessary expenses of the municipal government; which estimate shall be
based upon information to be furnished said committee by
the officers of the city in charge of the several departments,
and also by the standing committees of the councils, and with
the advice of the treasurer.

Duty of com-
missioner of
revenue in
making
assessments;
laws of the
State to be
observed
3. All the property, persons and subjects upon which the
councils are by law authorized to levy taxes (except licenses)
shall be listed by the commissioner of the revenue upon rolls
or books of assessment for the city, and in making his assessments and in ascertaining and enumerating personal property,
the commissioner of the revenue shall be governed by the laws
of the State and the regulations prescribed for the assessment
of taxes by the State. The said rolls or books of assessment
shall be made out and completed by the commissioner of the
revenue for delivery to the collector of city taxes and levies by
the first day of July of each year.

Exemption of
Norfolk
College and
Leache-Wood
Seminary
from taxation
All property real and personal belonging respectively to the
Norfolk College for Young Ladies and to the Leache-Wood
Seminary is hereby exempt from city taxes for the term of five
years from January 1st, 1882.

Special assess-
ment of tran-
sient traders
4. All transient dealers who shall, after the roll of the
commissioner for the year has been closed, bring into the city
and expose for sale, any horses, mules, goods, wares, merchandise, or other subjects of taxation, shall cause the same to be
assessed specially by the commissioner of the revenue, and pay
the tax thereon to the collector; and the commissioner shall make
return of all such special assessments in the same manner as he
is required to do concerning licenses, provided that this section

shall not apply to agricultural productions, family marketing or live stock intended for food, brought to the city for sale.

5. In issuing licenses for the city, the commissioner of the revenue shall be governed by the laws of the commonwealth of Virginia in force, concerning the public revenue, in respect to the duration thereof, definition of subjects and all other matters pertaining thereto. *Laws of the State to be observed in issuing city licenses*

6. The lessee of any lease-hold property, when required to do so by his lease, shall have the right to pay the city taxes on any piece or pieces of real estate not assessed to the lessee, under a statute of the State of Virginia, approved March 20th, 1877, and the collector shall make out separate bills for each piece or such pieces of real estate, and settle the same with the lessee upon the same terms as prescribed in this ordinance for the settlement of other bills. *Lease-hold property; act of March 20, 1877*

7. If any person shall commence or engage in any business, trade, calling, profession or employment on which a specific license tax is imposed by ordinance passed by the councils, without first taking out the license, and paying the tax required, such person shall pay a penalty of twenty dollars, and the further penalty of five dollars for every day he shall so continue to do business without a license, one-half the fine to go to the informer. *Penalty for doing business without a license*

8. The mayor, justices of the peace, city engineer, inspector of streets, clerk of the market, keeper of the almshouse, keepers of cemeteries, and all other officers authorized to receive money for the city, except the collector of city taxes and levies, (who shall make his returns as provided in the ordinance defining his duties) shall each on the first and fifteenth day of each month, make a return of all money collected by them to the treasurer of the city, taking his receipt therefor. *Semi-monthly returns to be made of money received by certain officers*

A detailed statement of the sources from which, and the persons from whom, such sums were received shall be rendered by each of said officers to the auditor, together with a receipt from the treasurer for the amount paid to him by said officer; and the auditor after verifying the same, shall once in every month prepare an account naming the officer, the amount collected and amount paid over to the treasurer and present the same to the councils.

9. As soon as practicable after the passage of the annual tax bill or the amount to be raised by taxation has been estimated, the councils shall, by ordinance, appropriate the resources and funds of the city (not already by law specially appropriated) to the expenses of the several departments, or to the purposes to which said revenue should be applied, first providing invariably for the payment of interest upon the city debt; and it shall be the duty of the finance committee to prepare and report such ordinances at the proper time. *Councils to make annual appropriations*

10. A copy of the appropriation ordinance shall be delivered to the auditor immediately after its passage, and the auditor shall thereupon open an account on his books with each of the several departments, or subjects, in accordance therewith; and the warrants drawn by upon him the treasurer, shall not exceed *Duties of auditor*

the amounts appropriated in each case. And the auditor shall report monthly to the councils the warrants drawn against each appropriation, and the balance remaining to the credit of each department or subject.

Duties of treasurer in opening accounts and paying warrants.

11. The treasurer shall also open accounts upon his books corresponding with the annual appropriations, and he shall not make payment of any sums, which he is or may be authorized to expend, without the auditor's warrant, in excess of the amounts severally appropriated as aforesaid. And the treasurer shall make reports monthly to the councils showing the amount expended, and the balance to the credit of each appropriation.

Committees and police board authorized to expend $50 per month

12 Authority is hereby vested in the board of police commissioners and each standing committee of the councils, to order in writing such work or repairs, or the purchase of such materials, as they may deem necessary in cases requiring immediate attention, but not otherwise, not exceeding in cost the sum of fifty dollars in any month, and the bills therefor, when properly approved, shall be ordered by the councils to be paid by warrant upon the treasurer.

Special appropriations not to be used for other purposes

13. Whenever any special appropriation of money has been made by the councils for any purpose, the sum so appropriated shall not, without the consent of the councils, be used for or applied to any other purpose whatever.

No department to exceed in any month its proper allowance

14. It shall not be lawful for any department to incur any debt, or make any expenditures, in any one month, beyond one-twelfth of the annual appropriation to such department; provided, that any unexpended balance remaining from any such monthly allowance may used at any time during the year by the department entitled thereto; and provided further that this section shall not apply to the appropriations made to the board of health, to the police department or the interest on the city debt.

Board of health, police department and interest on city debt excepted

Duty of clerk of council in entering record of claims

15. When an account or claim against the city is allowed by the councils, the clerk of each council shall enter upon the same, in ink, over his signature, the order of payment and date thereof, and the clerk of the council last approving shall, within three days, deliver the same to the auditor. The

Auditor to issue warrants

auditor shall, on the twentieth day of the same moth, issue to the party in whose name the account is allowed a warrant upon the treasurer for the amount thereof, payable on the first day of the month next thereafter. The auditor shall number the said warrant, and keep a record of the same in a well bound book, showing the number, date, amount, to whom issued and on what account.

Form of warrant

The form of the warrant shall set forth on its face the date of approval of the proper committee, the date of allowance by the councils, and the department to be charged therewith, and the number, amount, date of issue, and department shall be endorsed thereon. The warrants so issued shall be

Transferable

transferable by endorsement, and when matured shall be receivable for dues to the city.

The auditor shall render to the councils monthly a detailed *Monthly reports by auditor* statement of all warrants by him issued, with his vouchers, which shall be cancelled and filed after examination by the finance committee.

16. The auditor shall issue his warrant upon the Treasurer *Auditor to issue warrants to the several departments* to the several boards of commissioners, on account of amounts appropriated by the councils to their respective departments, according to the provisions of the ordinance making annual appropriations, and to the board of health at such time as may be required by it with approval of the presidents of the councils

17. No bill or claim shall be allowed for stationery and *Stationery of clerk of court not to be paid for by city.* printing required for the use of the clerk of the corporation court, the same being included in the general allowance annually made to said clerk.

18. On the first day of each month the auditor shall issue *Warrants to be issued by auditor for salaries* his warrant to all officers whose salaries or allowances are paid by the city, for the amounts to which they shall be respectively entitled by law.

19. The members of the police force shall be paid semi-*Police force when paid* monthly, on the *ninth and twenty-fourth day of each month*, by the city treasurer, on a pay roll certified by two of the police commissioners, as required by the charter of the city.

20. The interest and principal of city bonds and all notes *Interest to be paid when due* in bank made by the city, shall be paid by the treasurer to the parties entitled to receive the same as they shall mature.

21. The treasurer shall not pay any bill or claim against *Duties of city treasurer as to payment of claims* the city except upon proper warrant of the auditor, other than those mentioned in the nineteenth and twentieth sections of this ordinance; and the treasurer shall state on his check book and in each check on the bank, the number of the warrant for the payment of which such check is drawn. He shall not pay any warrant before maturity of the same and the date of payment shall in every case be endorsed on the warrant by the treasurer.

22. Before issuing any warrant, it shall be the duty of the *Auditor's duty in issuing warrants* auditor to ascertain from the collector and the treasurer whether the party claiming the same be indebted to the city for any tax, assessment, or otherwise, and when said claimant is so indebted, the auditor shall issue the warrant for only so much as may be due to him, after deducting his indebtedness to the city; and he shall further draw a warrant for so much as may be applied to the claims of the city, making it payable to the city collector or treasurer as the case may be for account of the person indebted as aforesaid; and in rendering his monthly statement, the auditor shall set forth separately the warrants so issued.

23. Whenever a warrant shall be lost, the party entitled *Warrants lost, how renewed* thereto may apply to the auditor for a duplicate, after first having advertised for thirty days in one of the newspapers published in this city, the loss of his warrant, stating the number and amount thereof; and the auditor shall require the applicant to produce a certificate from the treasurer that the

same has not been paid, and thereupon he shall issue a duplicate warrant, numbered to correspond with the orginal, and bearing the words *"issued in lieu of original lost"* written across the face.

Lost city bonds, how recovered

24. When any bond or certificate of debt, payable by the city of Norfolk, shall be lost by the holder thereof, upon such person producing to the treasurer proof of having advertised the same once a week for three months in a newspaper published in said city, and filing in the treasurer's office an affidavit setting forth the time, place and circumstances of the loss, the councils may order the treasurer to issue a new bond or certificate in lieu of the one lost, upon condition that the holder shall first execute a bond to the city of Norfolk, with one or more securities approved by the presidents of the select and common councils, conditioned to idemnify the said city and all persons against any loss in consequence of the issue of such new bond or certificate.

Upon the face of any bond or certificate so issued the treasurer shall write, issued in lieu of lost bond, (or certificate.

CHAPTER XIII.

Sinking Fund.

1. Be it ordained by the common and select councils, that the treasurer of the city shall open an account on his books as treasurer, to be called and known as the sinking fund account.

2. That the assessments to be hereafter made for the payment of the interest on the bonds of the city shall not be less than that provided for by the tax bill passed by the councils of said city, on the 13th day of April, 1880, by the select council and the 1st day of June, 1880, by the common council, until the amount levied for this purpose shall equal one per centum of the total bonded indebtedness of the said city; but when such contingency shall happen it shall not be deemed to be in conflct with the objects of this ordinance for the said councils to so modify the assessments as to maintain an appropriation to the said sinking fund, of one per centum of the said indebtedness, yearly, and no more.

3. That the difference between the amount actually required for the payment of the accruing interest, on the bonds of the city, and the amount levied for that purpose, shall be credited by the treasurer to the sinking fund annually. That the amount so accummulating shall be applied by the treasurer under the direction of the commissioners of the sinking fund to the payment of the principal of such part of said new bonds issued at a less rate of interest, as may be redeemable, and the residue invested in the bonds of the city of Norfolk, or in the bonds of the United States Government, and the proceeds thereof shall be applied to the payment of the principal of said new bonds of the city of Norfolk, as they shall mature and become redeemable. Passed December 14, 1880.

CHAPTER XIV.

Appropriations, 1885.

The following amounts are appropriated for the use of the several departments of the city government hereinafter mentioned, during the fiscal year beginning July 1st, 1885, and terminating June 30th, 1886.

Appropriations for 1885.

INTEREST ON CITY DEBT. (*Not including Water Bonds.*)

July, '85 and Jan. '86 on $189,300 8 pr ct. C'p'n B'ds	15,144	00
July, '85 and Jan. '86 on 24,000 6 pr ct. "	1,440	00
July, '85 and Jan. '86 on 77,000 6 pr ct. "	4,620	00
July, '85 and Jan. '86 on 115,400 6 pr ct. "	6,924	00
July, '85 and Jan. '86 on 81,500 6 pr ct. "	4,890	00
July, '85 and Jan. '86 on 332,993 6 pr ct. Reg. St'k.	19,979	58
Sept. '85 and Mar. '86 on 202,700 6 pr ct. C'p'n B'ds	12,162	00
Oct. '85 and Apl. '86 on 101,500 8 pr ct. "	8,120	00
Oct. '85 and Apl. '86 on 320,000 5 pr ct. "	16,000	00
July, '85 and Jan. '86 on 91,000 5 pr ct. "	4,550	00
Dec. '85 and June '86 on 110,000 5 pr ct. "	5,500	00
July, '85 and Jan. '86 on 40,000 5 pr ct. "	2,000	00
Oct. '85 and Apl. '86 on 30,000 5 pr ct. "	1,500	00
	102,829	58

SINKING FUND.

2 per cent. on $202,700 8 per cent. Bonds, converted from 8 per cent. to 6 per cent. Bonds.............	4,054	00
1 per cent. on 320,000 6 per cent. Bonds, converted from 6 per cent. to 5 per cent. Bonds...	3,200	00
1 per cent. on $91,000 6 per cent. Bonds, converted from 6 per cent. to 5 per cent. Bonds.............	910	00
1 per cent. on $110,000 6 per cent. Bonds, converted from 6 per cent. to 5 per cent. Bonds..............	1,100	00
	9,264	00
	$112,093	58

Board of Health...	3,000	00
Markets...	300	00
Public Schools...............................	10,000	00
Almshouse..	14,000	00
Public Buildings.................................	2,100	00
Salaries..	21,490	00
Fire Department	13,770	00
Police Department...............................	35,040	00
Lights..	15,250	00

Amount forward.............................		$114,950 00
Contingent Expenses......	2,500 00	
Cemeteries [this appropriation is to include all revenues received from the Cemeteries on any account]...............	3,000 00	
Commissions for Collecting Taxes..................	3,500 00	
Public Printing. ....—......	1,500 00	
Court Allowances ... .—...	4,400 00	
Elections..........................	700 00	
Harbor Expenses...	500 00	
Juries...............	1,000 00	

Street Department—

For keeping Streets in repair.........	11,600 00			
For cleaning Streets...................	18,000 00			
For Maintenance of Sewers.........	6,197 00			
Incidental and General Expenses....	1,584 50	37,381 50	160,431 50	
Total for Interest and Sinking Fund brought forward......			112,093 58	
Total appropriations................... ....$281,525 08				

CHAPTER XV.

An Ordinance imposing License Taxes.

Sec. 1. Be it ordained, by the common and select councils of the city of Norfolk, that for the year beginning the first day of May, 1885, and for each year thereafter, the specific license taxes on persons and subjects herein named, shall be as follows: And the same license shall be required of a joint stock company, or corporation, as is required of persons or firms, for conducting any business.

SCHEDULE A.

Agents for selling books $12 per year. For a less time $2.50 per month, not transferable.

Agents, Land, $80.

Agents for sale of manufactured articles. or machines, $50 per year. For a less time, $5 per month, not transferable.

Agents for Labor, $25.

Agents: Each agent or firm for renting houses or collecting rents, $30, not transferable.

Agencies, Mercantile, reporting standing of merchants and others, $50.

Artists, Daguerrean and Photographers, $20 per year. For a less time, $5 per month, not transferable.

Architects, $20 per year or part of a year.

Attorneys at law, each, licensed five years and under, $25; licensed over five years and under ten years, $50; licensed ten years and over, $75; provided that no Attorney at Law shall be required to pay more than $25 whose receipts are less than $500 per annum.

Boarding Houses $10.

Barber shops, each, $12 per year.

Bill posters, $15.

Eating houses, stands and cook shops, $30 per year. For a less time, $3 per month, not transferable.

Livery stables, $50, and an additional tax of 50 cents for each stall in the stable.

Sales of Horses and Mules, $50.

Storage and Impounding, on every house or cart house, $50; on every yard, wagon yard or lot, $25, not transferable.

Street cars, $50 per car per year or any part of a year. *See R. Roads Tax on street cars amended*

Stallions and Jack keepers, for every animal let to mares, $10.

Physicians, Surgeons and Dentists, licensed five years and under, $1; licensed over five years and under ten years, $25; licensed ten years and over, $50; provided, no Physician, Surgeon or Dentist shall be required to pay more than $10 whose receipts are less than $500 per annum.

Physicians, Surgeons and Dentists, itinerant, $100.

Venders of medicines, salves, manufactured or patented articles, sold on the streets, $5 per week, not transferable.

7

Pawnbrokers, $200 per year or part of a year.

Peddlers, $6 per week; for a less time, $2 per day, not transferable.

Patent Rights, sellers, $10, not transferable.

Private Entertainment Houses, keepers, $25.

Waiter License, selling on streets, not peddlers, fruit, confections and victuals, $12 per year or part of a year.

SCHEDULE B.

Billiard, Pool and Bagatelle Saloons, $20 for each table, or any game pertaining thereto.

Bowling Saloons or Alleys, $10 for each alley.

Circuses, Shows and Menageries, for every twenty-four hours or part thereof, $60 each.

Musicians, itinerant, $1 per week, not transferable.

Public Rooms, on the proprietors or occupiers (such as the Norfolk Varieties), $200 per year, or part of a year, not transferable. This tax does not include bar license.

Skating Rinks, each rink, $20 per month, payable quarterly in advance.

Roller Coasters, $250 per year or part of a year.

Gymnastic, Baseball or other outdoor games where admission is charged, $1 per day for each day of performance.

Merry go-rounds or flying horses, whatever way propelled, $1 per day.

Theatres and Panoramas, or any public performance or exhibition of any kind, except for religious or charitable purposes, when the whole of net proceeds are applied to the said purposes, $3 for each performance, or $10 for each week of such performances.

SCHEDULE C.

Auctioneers, General, $100.

Auctioneers and Agents, Real Estate, $100.

Brokers and Private Bankers, $400 and 2 per cent on income over $600.

Commission Stock Brokers, $50 and 2 per cent. on income over $600.

Commercial and Merchandise Brokers, $40.

Brokers, Insurance, or Solicitors, $35, with privilege of negotiating insurance in companies licensed in the state.

Brokers, Ship, $30.

Commission Merchants, $40, and an additional tax on gross commissions over 1,000 of $1 and 50 cents for each $100. The tax hereby imposed shall be in lieu of all tax upon capital actually employed by said merchant or mercantile firm in said business.

Buyers and sellers of Corn, Cotton or other Produce, not required to be licensed under existing ordinances as Merchants, or Commission Merchants, and who do not account as such, shall, before they do any business, get a license from the city and pay for doing such business, $100 for a year or part of a year.

Seamens' Shipping Office, $25.

Common Criers, $80.

Express Companies, $250.

Insurance Agents, for each Marine Company, $50. Each agent or solicitor employed by any insurance agent, or who secures or places business with or through same for consideration, $35.

Insurance Agents, for each Life Company, $125. Each agent or solicitor employed by any insurance agent, or who secures or places business with or through same for consideration, $35.

Insurance Agents, for each Fire Company, $200. Each agent or solicitor employed by any insurance agent, or who secures or places business with or through the same for consideration, $35.

Junk Dealers, $100, and for each agent or canvasser, $10.

Merchants: On every license to a merchant or mercantile firm and persons engaged in the avocation of hucksters, both in and out of the market; butcher and butcher shops, oyster shippers, or dealers, fish mongers and shippers, green fruit, vegetable or produce dealers and shippers, undertakers, dealers in barrels, barrel covers, boxes and crates, there shall be paid a specific tax of $5—and an additional tax on purchases, graded as follows:

If $1,000 or under, $6.

If over $1,000 and under $2,000, $18.

If over $2,000 and under $3,000, $25.

If over $3,000 and under $5,000, $30.

From $5,000 to $20,000, 25 cents on the $100. From $20,000 to $50,000, 15 cents on the $100. From $50,000 to $100,000 10 cents on the $100. From $100,000 to $200,000, 8 cents on the $100; and on all purchases over $200,000, the tax shall be 5 cents on every $100, in excess of $200,000. The tax hereby imposed shall be in lieu of all tax upon capital actually employed by said merchant or mercantile firm.

Telegraph companies, each, $250.

Telephone companies, each, $250.

Fertilizing companies, dealers, their representatives or agents, who buy material to manipulate or to resell, same license as merchants.

Fertilizing Companies and Dealers, their representatives or agents, who buy no material to manipulate or resell, but sell on commission, same license as commission merchants.

Sewing Machine Agents, for each agent, $50 per year or any part thereof.

Undertakers' carriages, hearses and wagons, each $10.

Wholesale Liquor Dealers, $150—not to sell less than five gallons.

Wholesale and Retail Liquor Dealers, $200—not to sell less than one gallon.

Retail Liquor Dealers, $75—not to sell more than 5 gallons. When such dealers have a bar, or liquor is drunk on premises, then they shall pay $125.

Bar Rooms, $85.

Ordinaries, $80, and 5 per cent. on annual rent, or rental value of building occupied.

Wholesale Dealers in Malt Liquors, only, $100.

Retail Dealers in Malt Liquors, only, $50.

Sec. 2. In issuing licenses for the city, the Commissioner of the Revenue shall be governed by the laws of the Commonwealth of Virginia in force concerning the public revenue in respect to the duration thereof and definition of subjects.

Collector's commissions

Sec. 3. The Collector shall receive one and one-half per cent. for his compensation on all moneys collected by him under this ordinance.

Sec. 4. Nothing herein contained shall be construed to repeal the tax imposed by ordinances upon licensed hacks, and other vehicles or tax upon dogs, or upon persons, property or subjects not herein mentioned.

Sec. 5. All transient dealers who shall, after the roll of the Commissioner for the year has been closed, bring into the city and expose for sale any horses, mules, goods, wares, merchandise, or other subjects of taxation, shall cause the same to be assessed specially by the Commissioner of the Revenue, and pay tax thereon to the Collector; and the Commissioner shall make return of all such special assessments in the same manner as he is required to do concerning licenses; provided, that this section shall not apply to agricultural productions, family marketing, or live stock intended for food, brought to the city for sale.

Sec. 6. This ordinance shall be in force from its passage, and all ordinances or parts of ordinances in conflict therewith, are hereby repealed.

Adopted by the common council, April 7, 1885, by aye and nay vote, unanimously.

BARTON MYERS,
President Common Council.

Adopted by the select council, April 14, 1885, by aye and nay vote, unanimously.   W. H. HOLMES,

President Select Council.

       Teste: A. L. HILL,

Treasurer.

AN ORDINANCE

Imposing a License Tax on Banks.

License tax on banks

Sec. 1. Upon every Bank or Banking Association doing business in the city of Norfolk, there shall be paid a specific license tax, for conducting such business, of the sum of $300, for the year commencing the first day of May, and the further sum of 2 per cent. on the dividends derived from such business. And the tax herein imposed shall be in lieu of all tax upon the capital employed in such business; but nothing herein *Real estate not exempted* contained shall be construed to exempt from taxation any real estate belonging to such bank or banking association.

May 5, 1885.

Ordinances Authorizing the Issue of Bonds of the City. As the same were passed (without revision.)

------- .•.-------

AN ORDINANCE

Entitled an ordinance authorizing the issue of three hundred thousand dollars in eight per cent. Coupon Bonds.

Be it ordained by the select and common councils of the city of Norfolk, Va., that it shall be lawful for the said city to issue coupon bonds of one thousand dollars, five hundred dollars, and one hundred dollars, with coupons attached, to the amount of three hundred thousand dollars, payable in twenty years from date of issue, with the privilege of being redeemed in ten years, said coupons to be paid semi-annually, and receivable at par for all claims due the city, and to be so expressed.

$300,000 00
8 per cent.
due 1890

Passed common council August 5, 1870; select council, August 15, 1870.

BONDS SECURED BY DEED ON TOWN POINT LOTS, RAILROAD STOCK, ETC.

AN ORDINANCE -

To provide for the issuing of bonds in the name and for the use of the city of Norfolk.

Sec. 1. Be it ordained by the select and common councils of the said city of Norfolk, that coupon bonds of the said city, payable on the first day of April, A. D. eighteen hundred and ninety-two, to an amount not exceeding two hundred and fifty thousand dollars, bearing interest from the date thereof at the rate of eight per centum per annum, payable semi-annually, either at the Citizens' bank of Norfolk, Va., or the People's National bank of Norfolk, Va., or a part at the former and the residue at the latter bank, at the discretion of the committees hereinafter mentioned, be issued.

$250,000 00
8 per cent.
due 1892

Sec. 2. Full power and authority are hereby given to the finance committe of the said select and the finance committee of the said common council to prepare and issue the said bonds in such form, and each for such sum, as the said committees shall prescribe; and each of the said bonds shall be signed by the presidents respectively of the said councils, and countersigned by the treasurer of the said city, with the corporate seal of the said city affixed thereto; and each of the coupons shall have the name of the said treasurer affixed thereto.

Form

Sec. 3. Full power and authority are hereby given to the said committees, by one or more good and sufficient deed or

Power given finance committee to make deeds of R. & G. R.R. stock, N. & P. stock, A. M. & O. R.R. stock, tobacco warehouse, etc and Market rents, to secure bonds.

deeds, as they may deem expedient, to convey in whole or in part, that is to say, any part or parcel thereof by one deed, and other parts or parcels thereof by other deed or deeds, the following property of the said city—to wit, seven hundred and thirty-five shares of the stock of the Raleigh and Gaston Railroad Company, five hundred and fifty shares of guaranteed stock of the Norfolk and Petersburg Railroad Company, five thousand shares of the stock of the Atlantic, Mississippi and Ohio Railroad Company, the tobacco warehouse and wharf thereto attached, situated on Water street in the said city, the Town Point property of the said city, the wharf property at the end of Nebraska street in the said city (the said real estate to be conveyed subject to any existing leases thereof), together with the rents, issues, dividends and profits of all the said property, and all the revenues collected or to be collected from time to time from the markets of the said city, in trust, to secure the payment of the said bonds and coupons, the property embraced by each deed to be conveyed in trust to secure the payment only and exclusively of the bonds and coupons in such deed named and mentioned. And the said committees are authorized to convert, or to give authority to any person designated by them for the purpose, to convert the said five hundred and fifty shares of guaranteed stock of the Norfolk and Petersburg Railroad Company into stock of the Atlantic, Mis-

Power to convert N. & P. guaranteed stock.

sissippi and Ohio Railroad Company. And the rents, issues, dividends, revenues and profits of such of the said property as may be conveyed in trust by any deed as aforesaid shall be collected as in such deed may be directed, and deposited in such one of the said banks as may be therein named for that purpose, and applied by such bank to the payment of the coupons in such deed mentioned as they may fall due; and if in any year the said rents, issues, dividends, revenues and profits shall exceed the amount of such of the said coupons as may fall due and be payable that year, the excess shall be paid by such bank to the treasurer of the said city for the use of the said city, free from the trusts of such deed. And provision may be made in any one or more of the said deeds for the redemption by the said city of the bonds therein mentioned at any time after the expiration of five years from the date of the bonds mentioned in such deed or deeds, and the terms and conditions of such redemption shall be prescribed by the said committees and set forth in such deed or deeds; but the said committees may or may not, at their discretion, require such provision, or require it in one or more of the said deeds, and not in any other. And each of the said deeds shall be executed for and on behalf of the said city by the presidents respectively of the said councils, with the corporate seal of the said city thereto affixed.

Sec. 4. Full power and authority are hereby given to the said committees to exchange the said bonds, or any part or parcel thereof, for any matured bond or bonds of the said city, dollar for dollar, and to make sale of the same, or of any part or parcel thereof as they may deem expedient, provided that no such sale shall be made at a rate less than their par value; and farther, to do and perform all such other act and acts as may be necessary and proper to carry into effect this ordinance; and all monies realized by them under this ordinance shal be paid to the treasurer of the said city, and applied by him, under their directions, to the payment of the bonds and certificates of interest of the said city now due and payable. and to the payment of such other bonds and certificates of interest of the said city as may become due and payable on or before the first day of May next.

Sec. 5. The said bonds and coupons shall be exempt from any and all taxation by the said city, and the said coupons shall be received in payment of any and all dues to the said city, and of all taxes levied or assessed by the said city except the specific water tax. *Exempt from city taxes. Coupons receivable for taxes except water tax*

Sec. 6. The said committees, in the performance of the duties herein required of them, shall act jointly, and the concurrence of a majority of the members thereof shall be sufficient in every instance to determine their action.

Sec. 7. This ordinance shall be in force from and after its passage.

Passed common council March 18, 1872; select council March 7, 1872.

AN ORDINANCE

To amend and ordinance entitled an ordinance authorizing the issue of three hundred thousand dollars in eight per cent. Coupon Bonds, passed 5th August, 1870.

Whereas in the record of the ordinances passed on the 5th of August, 1870, authorizing the issue by the city of Norfolk of coupon bonds to the amount of three hundred thousand dollars, payable in twenty years from date of issue, with privilege of redemption in ten years, the rate of annual interest to be paid on said bonds was omitted to be stated in said ordinance; and whereas it was and is the intention of the select and common councils of the city of Norfolk that such rate of interest shall be eight per centum per annum: *Amending ordinance Aug. 5, 1870*

Now, therefore, be it ordained by the select and common councils of the city of Norfolk, Va., that to the holders of all bonds of said city heretofore issued, or which may be issued under and by authority of the aforesaid ordinance, passed on the 5th of August, 1870, there shall be paid interest on the face thereof at the rate of 8 per centum per annum, payable semi-annually. *Rate of interest*

Passed common council May 7, 1872; select council, May 10, 1872.

RESOLUTION

Concerning the issue of 8 per cent. Coupon Bonds.

The action of the select council, in amending the action of the common council in regard to issuing eight per cent. coupon bonds in exchange for old registered six per cent. bonds not *Resolution providing how bonds may be exchanged* mentioned, the said exchange to be made under direction of the finance committee, the amendment adding, "provided the amount of eight per cent. bonds be at least one-sixth less in amount than the sixth per cent. bonds for which they are exchanged," and as amended the action of the select council was concurred in.

Passed select council February 14, 1873; common council March 4, 1873.

AN ORDINANCE

To authorize the issue of Coupon Bonds in exchange for the Registered Stock of the city of Norfolk.

Six per cent. coupon bonds due 1894 in exchange for registered stock

Be it ordained by the select and common councils of the city of Norfolk, that the treasurer be, and he is hereby, authorized to issue the coupon bonds of the city of Norfolk, in sums of one hundred dollars and five hundred dollars, payable in twenty years from the first day of January, 1874, with interest at the rate of six per cent. per annum, in exchange for any of the six per cent. registered stock of the city of Norfolk, at the option of the holders thereof; that the coupons attached to said bonds shall be payable on the first day of January and first day of July of each year until maturity, at the office of the treasurer of the city, and shall be receivable for taxes and all dues of the city.

That any holder of the coupon bonds herein authorized may be allowed at any time to have the same registered by the treasurer.

That in issuing coupon bonds in exchange for registered stock, all past due coupons shall be detached and cancelled by the treasurer, and the interest accrued upon coupons not matured shall be accounted for by the holder of registered stock applying for such exchange.

That in addition to the publication required by law, this ordinance be published for one month in one newspaper in each of the cities of Richmond, Baltimore and New York, to be designated by the finance committee.

That this ordinance shall be in force from its passage.

January 21, 1874.

Repeal of foregoing Ordinance.

Ordinance of Jan. 21, 1874, repealed

That the ordinance to "issue coupon bonds in exchange for the registered stock of the city of Norfolk," in sums of one hundred dollars and five hundred dollars, payable in twenty years from the first day of January, 1874, with interest at the rate of 6 per cent. per annum, in exchange for any of the 6 per cent. registered stock of the said city, at the option of the holders thereof; that the coupons attached to said bonds shall be payable on the first day of January and July, in each year until maturity, at the office of the treasurer of the city, and shall be receivable for taxes and all dues of the city.

The above recited ordinance passed common council and select council, January 21, 1874, and is now repealed.
C. C., November 16, 1880.
S. C., December 14, 1880.

PAVING BONDS.

AN ORDINANCE

To authorize the issue of bonds for paving and repairing the streets of the city of Norfolk, and to provide for the payment of the same.

Sec. 1. Be it ordained by the common and select councils of the city of Norfolk, that the sum of one hundred and fifty thousand dollars be, and the same is hereby, appropriated to be expended by and under the direction of the councils, from time to time, for the special purpose of paving, curbing and grading the unpaved streets, and of repaving and repairing wherever necessary the paved streets of the city. *Paving bonds $150,000 8 per cent. 20 years*

Sec. 2. That to raise the amount appropriated in the first section, there shall be executed and issued by the proper officers, in the name of the city, coupon bonds, called street bonds, payable twenty years after date, bearing interest at the rate of eight per cent. per annum, payable on the first day of January and the first day of July of each year until maturity, at the office of the treasurer of the city.

* * * * * * * * * * * * * * * * * *

Sec. 5. That when any unpaved street is to be graded, curbed and paved, three fourths only of the cost shall be assessed upon the lands or lots lying thereon. Such assessment shall be collected by the city collector as other taxes. But the owner of any property so assessed may. if he prefer, execute his assessment bond for the amount by him due, payable to the city of Norfolk in five annual instalments, with interest at eight per cent. per annum, the said bond to be a charge against the said property as other taxes now are ; and all such bonds so taken shall be received by the treasurer, and recorded by him in a book kept for the purpose. But when an unpaved street is only ordered to be graded the whole cost shall be paid by the city. *Assessments for paving See amendment following*

Passed March 10th, 1872.

AN ORDINANCE

To amend the fifth section of an ordinance entitled an ordinance, to authorize the issue of bonds for paving and repairing the streets of the city of Norfolk, and to provide for the payment of the same.

Be it ordained, that the above recited section of the above mentioned ordinance be amended so as to read as follows :

Sec. 5. That where any unpaved street is to be graded, curbed and paved, three-fourths only of the cost shall be assessed upon the lands or lots lying thereon ; such assessment shall be collected by the city collector as other taxes, but the *Assessment bonds for paving to bear six per cent. interest*

owner of any property so assessed may, if he prefer, execute
his assessment bond for the amount by him due, payable to
the city of Norfolk in five annual instalments, with interest
at *six* per centum per annum from date, the said bonds to be
a charge against the said property as other taxes now are,
and all such bonds so taken, shall be received by the treasurer
and recorded by him in a book kept for the purpose. But
when an unpaved street is only ordered to be graded, the whole
cost shall be paid by the city.

Passed C. C., June 1st, 1875.

Passed S. C., June 8th, 1875.

* * * * * * * * * * * * * * * * *

Proceeds of
assessment
specially
applied

Sec. 9. That all moneys collected from property owners for
paving under this ordinance shall be kept by the treasurer
separate and apart from all other moneys belonging to the city,
and deposited specially with the bank keeping the account of
the city, in the interest department of said bank, as a sinking
or trust fund, and out of said fund the treasurer shall pay the
principal and interest, as the same shall mature, of the eight
per cent. coupon bonds authorized in section two of this ordinance; and the fund herein and hereby created shall not be
used or applied to any other purpose until the coupon bonds
before mentioned are fully satisfied and paid. But if the sinking fund herein provided should not be sufficient to pay the
coupons as they fall due, the same shall be paid out of any
funds in the hands of the treasurer.

* * * * * * * * * * * * * * * * *

The following amendment passed the common council
March 3, 1874, and the select council March 10, 1874:

Assessments
how settled

Sec. 12. That any person who shall be assessed with the
cost of paving in front of his property, under this ordinance,
may make payment of the assessment in the paving bonds of
the city authorized by the aforesaid ordinance at par. And
the collector shall receive the said bonds at par in payment of
assessments aforesaid, and turn them over to the treasurer,
and may retain his commission of one and one-quarter per
cent. thereon. And the treasurer shall cancel all such paving
bonds and coupons as may be paid in by virtue of this section.

AN ORDINANCE

Concerning the issue of coupon bonds in exchange for matured
Registered Stock.

Extending
provisions of
ordinance
March 18, 1872

Sec. 1. Be it ordained by the common and select councils,
that the provisions of section 4 of an ordinance, passed March
18th, 1872, which authorized the coupon bonds issued in pursuance thereto, to be exchanged at par for city bonds, due on
or before May 1st, 1872, be and the same are hereby extended,
and declared to apply to all bonds of the city of Norfolk
which are matured, and remain unpaid at the date of the passage hereof.

Sec. 3. This ordinance shall be in force from its passage, and all ordinances in conflict herewith are repealed.
Passed C. C. March 7th, 1876.
Passed S. C. March 14th, 1876.

Norfolk City Bonds, for retiring those that fall due in 1879.

AN ORDINANCE

Entitled an Ordinance authorizing the issue of ($77,000) seventy-seven thousand dollars registered or coupon bonds, under the Acts of Assembly, approved January 14th, 1878, (see Acts of Assembly 1877–78, page 11) for the purpose of retiring certain bonds of the City, as may become due and payable in the year 1879.

Be it ordained by the common and select councils of the city of Norfolk, that it shall be lawful for the said city to issue registered or coupon bonds of one thousand dollars, five hundred dollars, and one hundred dollars, bearing interest, to be paid semi-annually, at the rate of six per centum per annum, payable in twenty years from date of issue, with the privilege of being redeemed after the expiration of five years, to the amount of seventy-seven thousand dollars; provided, however, that the money arising from the sale of said bonds, shall be used and applied by the said councils for the payment and redemption of the registered and coupon bonds of the city of Norfolk, which shall fall due in the year 1879, and for no other purpose whatever. *$77,000, 6 per cent. 1896*

Sec. 2. Full power and authority are hereby given to the finance committee of said common and select councils, to prepare and issue the said bonds in such form, and each for such sum as the said committee shall prescribe; each of the said bonds shall be signed by the presidents respectively of the said councils, and countersigned by the treasurer of said city, with the corporate seal of the said city affixed thereto; and each of the coupons shall have the name of the treasurer affixed thereto. Full power and authority are hereby given to the said committee to exchange the said bonds, or any part or parcel therof, for any matured bond or bonds of the said city, dollar for dollar, and to make sale of the same or any part or parcel thereof, as they may deem expedient, provided, that no such sale shall be made at a rate less than their par value, and further to do and perform all act and acts as may be necessary and proper to carry into effect this ordinance. *Power to finance committee*

Sec. 3. The said registered and coupon bonds shall be exempt from any and all taxation by the said city, and the said coupons shall be received in payment of all dues to the said city, and of all taxes levied or assessed by the said city, except the specific water tax. *Exempt from tax, and coupons receivable for taxes*

Sec. 4. The fund to be derived from the sale of the said bonds, shall be deposited in bank as a separate and special fund, *Redemption fund*

which shall be known and styled as the bond redemption fund,
Sec. 5. This ordinance shall be in force from and after its
passage.
Passed common council November 7th, 1878.
Passed select council November 12th, 1878.

AN ORDINANCE

Entitled an ordinance, authorizing the issue of $150,000 (one hundred
and fifty thousand dollars) of registered coupon bonds, under an
Act of Assembly, approved January 11th, 1878, (see Acts of Assembly, 1877–78, page 11) for the purpose of retiring such bonds
of the city as may become due and payable in the year 1880.

$150,000
6 per cent.
March, 1879

2) years

Sec. 1. Be it ordained by the common and select councils of
the city of Norfolk, that it shall be lawful for the said city to
issue registered or coupon bonds of one hundred dollars, five
hundred dollars, and one thousand dollars, bearing interest to
be paid semi-annually, at the rate of six per cent. per annum,
payable in twenty years from date of issue, with the privilege
of being redeemed after the expiration of five years, to the
amount of one hundred and fifty thousand dollars; provided,
however, that the money arising from the sale of said bonds,
shall be used and applied by the said councils for the payment
and . redemption of the registered and coupon bonds of the
city of Norfolk, which shall fall due in the year 1880, and for
no other purpose whatever.

Sec. 2. Full power and authority is hereby given to the
finance committee of said common and select councils, to prepare and issue the said bonds in such form, and each for such
sum, as the said committee shall prescribe; each of the said
bonds shall be signed by the presidents respectively of the
said councils, and countersigned by the treasurer of the city,
with the corporate seal of the said city affixed thereto; and
each of the coupon or registered bonds shall have the name of
the treasurer affixed thereto.   Full power and authority is
hereby given to the said committee to exchange the said bonds,
or any part or parcel thereof, for any matured bond or bonds
of the city, dollar for dollar, and to make sale of the same, or
any part or parcel thereof, as they may deem expedient; provided, that no such sale shall be made at a less rate than their
par value, and further to perform all act or acts, as may be
necessary and proper to carry into effect this ordinance.

Sec. 3. The said registered and coupon bonds shall be
exempt from any and all taxation by the said city, and the
said coupons shall be received in payment of any and all dues
to the said city, and of all taxes levied or assessed by the said
city, except the specific water tax.

Sec. 4. The fund derived from the sale of said bonds shall
be deposited in bank, as a special and separate fund, and shall
be known and styled the bond redemption fund.

Sec. 5. This ordinance shall be in force from and after its
passage.
Passed select council March 11th, 1879.
Passed common council March 18th, 1879.

AN ORDINANCE

To amend and re-ordain Sec. 1, of the ordinance, entitled an ordinance, authorizing the issue of $150,000 (one hundred and fifty thousand dollars) of registered or coupon bonds, under an Act of Assembly, approved January 11th, 1878, (see Acts of Assembly, 1877-78, page 11,) for the purpose of retiring such bonds of the city as may become due and payable in the year 1880.

Be it ordained by the common and select councils of the city of Norfolk, that section 1 of the above recited ordinance be amended and re-ordained, so as to read as follows: *Amendment to ordinance of March 18, 1879*

Sec. 1. That it shall be lawful for the said city to issue registered or coupon bonds of twenty-five dollars, fifty, one hundred dollars, five hundred dollars, and one thousand dollars, bearing interest, to be paid semi-annually, at the rate of six per cent per annum, in twenty years from date of issue, with the privilege of being redeemed after the expiration of five years, to the amount of one hundred and fifty thousand dollars; provided, however, that the money arising from the sale of said bonds, shall be used and applied by the said councils for the payment and redemption of the registered and coupon bonds of the city of Norfolk, which shall fall due in the year 1880, and for no other purpose whatever.

Sec. 2. This ordinance shall be in force from its passage.

Passed common council June 3d, 1879.

Passed select council June 17th, 1879.

AN ORDINANCE

To amend and re-enact an ordinance passed select council March 11, 1879, and common council March 18, 1879, entitled an ordinance authorizing the issue of one hundred and fifty thousand dollars ($150,000) of registered or coupon bonds, under the act of assembly approved January 11, 1878, (see acts of assembly 1877-78, page 11), for the purpose of retiring such bonds of the city as may become due and payable in the year 1880.

Sec. 1. Be it ordained by the common and select councils of the city of Norfolk, that it shall be lawful for the said city to issue registered or coupon bonds of one hundred dollars, five hundred dollars, and one thousand dollars, bearing interest, to be paid semi-annually, at the rate of six per cent. per annum, payable in twenty years from date of issue, to the amount of one hundred and fifty thousand dollars: provided, however, that the money arising from the sale of said bonds, shall be used and applied by the said councils for the payment and redemption of the registered and coupon bonds of the city of Norfolk, which shall fall due in the year 1880, and for no other purpose whatever. *Amending ordinance of March, 1879*

Sec. 2. Full power and authority is hereby given to the finance committee of said common and select councils to prepare and issue the said bonds, in such form, and each for such sum, as the said committee shall prescribe; each of the said bonds shall be signed by the presidents respectively of the said councils, and countersigned by the treasurer of the city, with the corporate seal of the said city affixed thereto. 'Full power and authority is hereby given to the said committee to exchange the said bonds or any part or parcel thereof, as they may deem expedient: provided, that no such sale shall be made of such bonds at a rate less than their par value ; and further, to perform all act or acts as may be necessary and proper to carry into effect this ordinance.

Sec. 3. The said registered and coupon bonds shall be exempt from any and all taxation by the said city, and the said coupons shall be received in payment of any and all dues to the city, and of all taxes levied or assessed by the said city, except the specific water tax.

Sec. 4. The fund derived from the sale of said bonds shall be deposited in a bank as a special and separate fund, and shall be known and styled the bond redemption fund.

Sec. 5. This ordinance shall be in force from and after its passage.

Passed common council January 6, 1880.

Passed select council January 13, 1880.

AN ORDINANCE

To provide for the redemption of the bonds of the city of Norfolk issued under and by virtue of an ordinance passed by the common council of said city on the 5th day of August, 1870, and by the select council of said city on the 5th day of August, 1870, entitled an ordinance authorizing the issue of three hundred thousand dollars in eight per cent. coupon bonds.

Whereas by the provisions of the above entitled ordinance the privilege of redeeming the bonds issued under and by virtue thereof in ten years from the date of the issue was reserved by said city.

Providing for redemption of 8 per cents due in 1890

Sec. 1. Be it therefore ordained by the select and common councils of the said city of Norfolk, that coupon bonds of the said city, payable on the 1st day of September, in the year 1900, to an amount not exceeding two hundred and two thousand seven hundred dollars, bearing interest at the rate of six per centum per annum, payable semi-annually, be issued.

$202,700 6 per cents due Sep. 1, 1900

Sec. 2. Full power is hereby given to the finance committee of said councils to prepare and issue the said bonds in such form, and each for such sum as the said committee shall prescribe; and each of the said bonds shall be signed by the presidents respectively of the said councils, and countersigned by the treasurer, with the corporate seal affixed thereto, and each of the said coupons shall have the name of the treasurer affixed thereto.

Sec. 3. Full power and authority is hereby given to the said finance committee to make exchange or sale of the said bonds, or any part or parcel thereof as they may deem expedient, and all money realized by the said committee by the exchange or sale of the said bonds shall be paid to the treasurer of the said city and applied by him under the direction of the said committee to the redemption of the said bonds, and the coupons annexed or belonging thereto, and to no other purpose waatever.

Sec. 4. The said bonds and coupons shall be exempt from

any and all taxation by the said city, and the said coupons
shall be received in payment of any and all dues of the said
city, except the water tax.

Sec. 5. It shall be the duty of the treasurer to give notice
by publication in two or more newspapers printed in the city
of Norfolk and in other cities, if deemed by the said committee expedient to the holders of the bonds aforesaid, of the
election of the said city to redeem the same, according to the
privilege reserved as aforesaid.

Passed common council August 10, 1880.

Passed select council August 19, 1880.

Bonds issued to redeem bonds maturing in 1881.

Sec. 1. Be it ordained that coupon bonds of the city of
Norfolk, to the amount not exceeding $321,521, bearing interest
at the rate of not more than 5 per cent. per annum, payable
semi-annually, at the office of the treasurer of the city of Norfolk, or such banking institution as the finance committee may
determine upon, be issued. *321,521 5 per cents. issued Jan. 1, 1881, and July 1, 1881, due 30 years after date*

The said bonds to bear date on January 1st, 1881, and 1st
day of July, 1881, and be payable thirty years therefrom.

Sec. 2. Full power and authority are hereby given the joint
finance committee of the common and select councils, to prepare and issue said bonds in such form and each for such sum
as the said committee shall prescribe, and each of the said
bonds shall be signed by the presidents respectively of the
said councils, and shall be countersigned by the treasurer of
the said city with the corporate seal of the said city affixed
thereto ; and each of the coupons of the said bonds shall have
the name of the treasurer lithographed or engraved thereon. *Power to finance committee as to form*

Sec. 3. Full power and authority are hereby given to the
said joint finance committee to exchange said bonds or any part
or parcel thereof for any bond or bonds of the said city which
shall mature and become payable in the year 1881, at not less
than dollar for dollar; and to make sale of any part or parcel
of the said bonds as they may deem expedient. And all
moneys realized by them from such sale under this ordinance
shall be paid to the treasurer of said city, and applied by him,
under their direction, to the payment of the bonds of the said
city remaining unredeemed, which shall mature and become
payable in the year 1881, and to no other purpose whatsoever. *Power given finance committee to sell or exchange* *Proceeds how applied*

Sec. 4. That said bonds and coupons shall be exempt from
any and all taxation by the said city, and the said coupons
shall be received in payment of any and all dues to the said
city, and all taxes levied or assessed by the said city except
the specific water tax. *Exempt from taxation* *Coupons receivable for taxes*

Passed select council March 8, 1881.

Passed common council March 18, 1881.

Bonds in lieu of bonds maturing during the year 1882, and also for Sewerage and Drainage.

$155,000 5 per cent. Jan. 1, 1882 July 1, 1882 30 years after date Sec. 1. That coupon bonds of the said city of Norfolk be issued to an amount not to exceed $155,000, bearing interest at not more than the rate of 5 per cent. per annum, payable semi-annually, at the office of the treasurer of the city of Norfolk or such banking institution as the finance committee may determine upon   The said bonds to bear date of January 1, and July 1, 1882, and to be payable 30 years therefrom.

Form to be prepared by finance committee Sec. 2. Full power and authority is hereby given to the joint finance committee of the select and common councils. to prepare and issue the said bonds in such form and each for such sum as the said finance committee shall prescribe; and each of said bonds shall be signed by the presidents respectively of the said councils and countersigned by the treasurer of said city, with the corporate seal of said city thereto affixed. And each of the coupons of said bonds shall have the name of the treasurer of the city lithographed or engraved thereon.

finance committee to sell or exchange Sec. 3. Full power and authority is hereby given to the joint finance committee, to make sale of any part or parcel of said bonds as they may deem expedient, and all moneys realized by them from such sale under this ordinance, shall be paid to the **Proceeds how applied** treasurer of said city, and applied by him under the direction of the said finance committee, to the payment of the bonds of the city remaining unredeemed, which shall mature and become **Portion applicable to sewerage** payable in the year 1882, and to meet such appropriations as may be made by the councils from time to time for sewerage and drainage purposes.

Exempt from taxes Coupons receivable for taxes Sec. 4. That said bonds and coupons shall be exempt from taxation by the said city, and said coupons shall be received in payment of any and all dues to said city. and all taxes levied or assessed by the said city, except the specific water tax.

Passed common council February 7, 1882.

Passed select council February 14, 1882.

Bonds to meet certain Appropriations for 1884.

$40,000, April 1 1884 20 years Sec. 1. Be it ordained by the common and select councils of the city of Norfolk, that the finance committee of said councils, be and they are hereby fully authorized and empowered to sell the bonds of the city, payable thirty years after April 1, 1884, either registered or coupon, bearing interest not exceeding six per cent.   Said bonds if six per cent. not to be sold at less than par and accrued interest. or if five per cent. at not less than ninety-five per cent. of their par value with accrued interest. The said bonds to be issued, signed and attested, as other bonds of the city are required to be executed ; and the proceeds of the sale of said bonds are hereby ordered to be turned into the treasury of the city and applied to the payments of the several sums heretofore included in the appropriations made by the councils, or so much thereof as may be necessary, including the payments of any note or notes given in bank for temporary loans, and to meet the deficiency in the revenues as aforesaid. But the amount of bonds issued under authority hereof, shall not exceed forty thousand ($40,000) dollars.

This ordinance shall be in force from its passage, and the finance committee are authorized to advertise for proposals for sale of said bonds.

March 13th, 1884.

Bonds for Section B. Sewers and Drains 1884.

Sec. 1. Be it ordained by the common and select councils of the city of Norfolk, that in order to complete section B. of the Waring system of sewerage and drainage, coupon bonds of the city of Norfolk be issued to the amount of not exceeding $30,000, payable on the 1st day of January, 1912, with interest at the rate of five per centum per annum, payable semi-annually, on the 1st day of January and July. *($30,000 5 per cent. due Jan. 1, 1912, for sewers sec. B.)*

Sec. 2. Full power and authority are hereby given to the finance committee of the common and select councils to prepare said bonds to be executed in the same manner as other bonds of the city, and to make sale of said bonds at the best price that can be obtained therefor; provided that none of the said bonds shall be sold for less than ninety-five per cent. of their par value, and accrued interest.

Sec. 3. The proceeds of the sale of said bonds shall be placed by the treasurer to the credit of the street sewer and drain commissioners, and shall be used by them for the completion of section B., of the Waring system of sewerage and drainage and the expenses in connection therewith, and for no other purpose, except for said sewers and drains, to be expended in accordance with the contract authorized to be made by said board by the resolution of said councils, passed March 20th, 1884.

Sec. 4. The said coupons shall be exempt from all taxation by the city, and the coupons attached thereto shall be received for all dues to the city, except the special water tax.

Passed March 20th, 1884.

AN ORDINANCE

Authorizing the issue of bonds of the city of Norfolk, for the purpose of retiring and refunding certain bonds of said city which fall due in 1884–85.

Sec. 1. Be it ordained by the common and select councils of the city of Norfolk, by virtue of authority conferred by an act of the general assembly of Virginia, approved August, 1884, that the bonds of said city shall be issued to an amount not exceeding the sum of three hundred and thirty-three thousand dollars, ($333,000) for the sole purpose of redeeming or refunding bonds of said city which shall mature and become payable in the years 1884 and 1885. *(Amount of bonds authorized, $333,000)*

Sec. 2. The said bonds shall be dated on the first day of

Due Oct. 1, 1914 interest 6 per cent.

October, 1884, and be made payable on the first day of October, 1914, and shall bear interest at the rate of six per centum per annum, payable semi-annually.

Exemption from city taxes Coupons receivable for taxes

Sec. 3. The said bonds shall be exempt from all taxation by the city of Norfolk, and the coupons, issued as aforesaid, shall be receivable for all taxes, debts and demands due the said city, except for specific water tax.

How to be prepared and signed

Sec. 4. Full power and authority are hereby given to the joint committee on finance of the common and select councils to prepare said bonds in such form, either registered or coupon, and each in such sum as the said committee may prescribe. The said bonds shall be signed by the presidents of said councils, and countersigned by the treasurer of the city with the corporate seal of the city affixed thereto, and all coupons shall bear the name of said treasurer.

Finance committee authorized to sell or exchange

Sec. 5. The said committee on finance are further authorized and empowered to exchange the said bonds for any bonds of the city which shall mature and become payable in the years 1884 and 1885, if in their judgment they deem it best to do so, and to sell any part or parcel of said bonds as they may deem expedient; provided that no sale of said bonds shall be made, or shall be lawful at any price less than their par value thereof, with accrued interest.

Proceeds how received and deposited and applied

Sec. 6. All moneys received for the sale of said bonds shall be paid to the treasurer of the city, and by him specially deposited in bank upon the bond redemption account, and shall be applied to the payment and redemption of the bonds of said city which mature in 1884 and 1885, and said moneys shall not be used for or applied to any other purpose whatsoever.

Passed common council December 2, 1884.
Passed select council December 9, 1884.

CHAPTER XVI.

Norfolk Gymnasium and Athletic Association.

Target firing allowed on grounds of Gymnasium Association under certain restrictions

Sec. 1. That it shall be lawful for the members of the rifle team belonging to the Norfolk Gymnasium and Athletic Association to exercise at target practice within the bounds of the grounds of the said association now located upon Princess Anne avenue within and adjoining the city limits, under the restrictions and according to the rules and regulations provided by the managers of the said association, and provided that the target shall be of half inch boiler iron, affixed to a bulkhead 30 feet long by 16 feet high, constructed of two inch plank on the front and one inch plank on the back, joints to be battonned the space of one foot between the front, and planking to be filled in solidly with earth, the entire premises to be kept enclosed. And the members of the association when exercising within the said premises shall not be liable

to the penalty imposed by the ordinances of the city for discharging fire arms within the city limits.
June 10, 1884.

CHAPTER XVII.

Hacks, Carriages, &c., For Hire.

Sec. 1. Every person who shall use a public hack, carriage or other vehicle for the conveyance of passengers, for hire in the city of Norfolk, shall first obtain a license for the privilege of so doing. Before such license is issued, there shall be paid to the collector and his receipt therefor produced to the commissioner of the revenue, the annual tax of twenty dollars, and after that rate for any period less than a year. License tax required for using hacks, &c.

Licenses shall be issued quarterly, say first of January, April, July and October; but in order to have them all expire at one date, the collector is authorized to issue to applicants a license for such a period as will enable him to carry out this provision and at pro rata cost of the whole tax imposed. The collector will charge and collect for licenses issued to non-residents double the amount paid by the citizens of Norfolk. How issued and when expire
Double tax on non-residents

2. The commissioner of the revenue shall keep a register of the license, and the number of the same in every case, and shall furnish to every such person a tin plate painted black and maked white with the letter H, and number corresponding to the number on the register, for which the commissioner of the revenue shall receive a fee of twenty-five cents in each case, to be paid by the driver; and the said plate shall be attached to the vehicle in a conspicuous place, and the number shall be worn by the driver on his hat or on the lappel of his coat. The commissioner of the revenue shall receive a fee of thirty cents for each license, and a like sum for each renewal thereof, to be paid by the party applying therefor. Commissonr of Revenue to keep register of licenses and furnish tin plate with mark and number
His fee

3. No person under eighteen years of age shall drive any public hack in this city. Persons under 18 not to drive a hack

4. All public hacks licensed by the city shall stand to the west of the artesian well, on the middle of the Main street; and drivers of such hacks shall at no time be distant more than five feet from their vehicle. Stands for public hacks

5. The drivers of public hacks licensed by the city may charge twenty-five cents for carrying passengers from one part of the city to any other part of the same, and fifty cents for carrying passengers, with the usual amount of baggage, to or from any steamboat or railroad depot; and when hacks after night attend at any steamboat landing or depot they may charge one dollar each for passengers from eight o'clock P M., from the first day of October to the first day of April, and from nine o'clock P.M. from the first day of April to the first day of October inclusive. What drivers may charge for carrying passengers

6. Every driver of any hack or vehicle for hire shall have a copy of the fifth section of this ordinance placed inside of his hack or vehicle in some conspicuous place. Rate to be posted in vehicle

License may be transferred
7. Any person obtaining a license under this ordinance may transfer the unexpired term thereof at the office of the commissioner of the revenue, and thereupon a new license shall be issued for the balance of the term.

Penalty for violation
8. Any person who shall violate any provision of this chapter shall pay a fine of not less than five nor more than twenty dollars.

Collector to give notice of expiration of license
9. The collector shall give public notice in all the daily morning papers published in the city, for three days, prior to the first days of January, April, July and October, of the expiration of licenses and the necessity of prompt renewal thereof.

[NOTE.—See ordinance on health, prohibiting the conveying of any corpse of person dying of contagious disease.

CHAPTER XVIII.

Health.

Board to be appointed by councils biennially
1. The board of health shall consist of five members, electors, who shall be appointed by the councils biennially, at their first meeting in the month of July. The members of the board now in office shall serve until the first day of July, eighteen hundred and eighty-six, and until their successors are appointed and qualified.

Organization of board!
2. The members of the board shall organize by choosing a president and secretary from their own number, and divide the city into five districts, and assign one member to the particular care and oversight of each district.

Meetings of board
The board shall meet once in every week between the first day of March and the first day of November, and once in every two weeks between the first day of November and the first day of March, in every year, and at such other times as it may deem necessary, or as it may be called together by the president.

Quorum

Record
Three members shall constitute a quorum for the transaction of any business, and the board shall keep a record of all its proceedings.

Health officer and inspector to attend meetings of the board
3. It shall be the duty of the health officer, and also of the inspector of streets, to attend the meetings of the board, and to observe and carry into effect all orders within the sphere of their respective duties pertaining to the public health.

Duties of health officer
The health officer shall act as physician to the almshouse and quarantine officer in any case within the jurisdiction of the board of health of the city, which may not come under the jurisdiction of the board of quarantine commissioners.

Powers of board to adopt and enforce rules for preservation of health
4. The board of health shall have and exercise a general supervision of the sanitary condition of the city, and may adopt and enforce such rules and regulations for the preservation of the public health, as it may deem necessary.

Abatement of nuisances detrimental to health
5. It shall be the duty of the board, and it shall have full power and authority to determine what is a nuisance or detrimental to the health of any portion of the city, or the public, to abate and remove all nuisances to health, either through its

own officers and agents, or by contract, as it may deem best; to prescribe the manner, time and terms of removal of all night soil and excrementitious matter; and in case of contracting to have the service performed, it may confer the exclusive right of removal upon the person or persons contracting; provided, that all such contracts shall be ratified by the councils; and provided, that the occupant or owner of any lot may, within certain rules to be prescribed by the board, remove or cause to be removed the night soil from his own lot, if he shall so elect. *Removal of night soil by contract or otherwise* *Lot owners may remove night soil in certain cases*

6. The board may appoint an agent or assistant, to be known as sanitary inspector, to carry out its orders and regulations, and fix his compensation. *Sanitary inspector may be appointed by board*

7. It shall be the duty of the board to inspect, at least once in every two weeks, between the first day of March and the first day of November, in every year, and at such other times as it may think proper, all parts of the city; to enforce all ordinances relating to the sanitary condition of the city, and cause to be removed all nuisances. The board shall examine all lots, grounds, cellars, and all streets, lanes, and alleys; and whenever the board shall be of opinion that any lots, grounds or cellars are in a state of nuisance, or so situated that a nuisance may be created, it shall cause a written notice to be served upon the owner or occupant, or owners or occupants, directing the said nuisance or cause of nuisance to be removed; and if such owner or occupant shall fail to comply therewith he shall pay a fine of five dollars, and a further fine of five dollars for every day he shall so fail to comply with the said notice; and shall moreover pay the expenses incurred in case such nuisance shall be removed under the authority of the board, which the board is authorized to have done. *Duty of board to make frequent inspections and abate nuisances*

8. The expense of abatement of nuisances to health and the removal of night soil shall be paid by the person or persons causing the same, or occupying the ground where the same may be, to the persons performing the service, at the time of its performance; and in case of the failure or refusal to pay said expense within five days, the same may be collected and recovered from the owner of the property by the sanitary inspector by warrant or suit in the name of the city, and shall be a lien upon the property in like manner as taxes are now liens. *How cost of abating nuisances paid and collected.*

9. Whenever the board, or any member thereof, shall have cause to suspect that a nuisance exists in any house or enclosure, they, or any one of them, may demand entry therein; and if the owner or occupant refuse to open the same, and to admit a free examination of the premises, he shall pay a fine of five dollars. *Board may enter private premises*

10. Whenever the board shall be of opinion that any private docks are not sufficiently cleansed or deepened, or have any rotten or decayed wood about them, so as to be likely to become injurious to the public health, it shall cause a written notice to be served upon the owner or occupants of such docks to cleanse and deepen them, and remove such rotten and decayed wood, and otherwise correct the evil existing, or likely to *Board may require docks to be cleansed*

exist, in and about the premises, in such manner as shall be prescribed by the board; and if any such owner or occupant shall fail to obey any order in such notice, he shall pay a fine of five dollars for every day he shall so fail; and shall moreover pay the expenses incurred in deepening, cleansing, or otherwise repairing such dock, when the board shall see proper to have the work done, under its own direction, as it is hereby authorized to do, on such failure.

May order cellars and lots to be filled up 11. All cellars under warehouses, stores, dwellings and other houses shall, when deemed necessary by the board, be filled up with sound materials, and paved with hard bricks or stones; and all lots, when deemed necessary by the board shall be filled up above the level of the streets, so as to prevent the lodgement of water; and any person owning or occupying such place, and failing to comply with the requisitions of the board under this section, shall pay a fine of five dollars for every day he shall so continue to fail; and shall, moreover, pay the expense incurred in filling up such cellars and vacancies, and raising such lots, when the board shall see proper to have such work done under its direction, as it is hereby authorized to do.   The board may contract to have cellars, vacancies and sunken lots filled up.

The board with the approval of the presidents of the councils, may draw on the treasurer for all sums to be expended under this section.

Money expended by board in filling up lots, &c., to be a lien on property All sums of money paid by the city for filling up any lot or premises, as provided in this section, shall constitute a lien upon the property, to be enforced upon said property as liens for taxes are now enforced.

Who to be deemed owner of lots in certain cases 12. When any person shall be in possession of any property, or have charge thereof, within the city, as executor, administrator, trustee, guardian or agent, such person shall be deemed to be the owner of such property, and shall be bound to obey all orders of the board, as far as the same may affect such property, in the same manner and subject to the same penalties and fines as if such person were actually the owner of such property; and notice to such person shall be deemed to be sufficient.

When no owner can be found notice to be given in newspapers In case no owner or occupant, or other proper person, can be found on whom to serve the notice, the board is authorized after giving five days' notice in one of the newspapers of the city, to have the work done; and in all cases where the board shall cause any work to be done it shall return to the treasurer an account of the expense incurred, and he shall put the said account into the hands of the collector for the city for collection.

Board may order a general vaccination 13. Whenever, in the opinion of the board of health, there shall be danger of the introduction or increase of variola and kindred diseases, it shall have full power and authority to to cause a general vaccination of all persons residing or sojourning within the limits of its jurisdiction, and to that end may make such rules and regulations pertaining to the matter as it may deem necessary.

Penalties Any person refusing to comply with any of the rules or regulations of the board, made in pursuance of this section, shall pay a fine of not less than five nor more than twenty dollars; but nothing herein contained shall prevent any person ordered to be vaccinated from employing any physician he may deem proper, provided it be done within the time prescribed by the board.

14. When any physician knows that any person whom he is Physicians called to visit in the city is infected with smallpox, diptheria, required to scarlet fever or any other contagious disease dangerous to the of inspectors public health, or shall, in the practice of his profession, dis- diseases under cover that any section of the city is peculiarly the seat of pre- ment ventible disease, such physician shall immediately give notice thereof to the president of the board of health. Any person who shall violate the provisions of this section, shall pay a fine of not less than ten nor more than one hundred dollars.

15. No person shall bring or cause to be brought into the Second-hand city for sale any second hand wearing apparel or bed clothing. clothing not Any person who shall violate this section shall pay a fine into city for of twenty dollars, one half of which shall go to the informer. sale The mayor or any justice may require the party charged to show how, when and where the articles were bought.

16. When any householder knows that a person within his Householder family is taken sick with small pox, or any disease dangerous of any danger-to the public health, he shall immediately give notice thereof ous disease in to the president of the board of health, or to the mayor, or to president of any officer of the police. Any person who shall violate this board or section shall pay a fine of not less than ten nor more than policeman twenty dollars:

17. No dead body shall be brought into or be conveyed Dead body not through the city, nor be allowed to remain therein, without a in or conveyed written permission from the board of health, obtained through city without the health officer; and any person who shall bring into, permit convey or cause to be conveyed through the city, any dead body, or allow it to remain therein without the permission of the board of health, shall, on covniction thereof, pay a fine of twenty dollars.

18. It shall not be lawful for an undertaker or any other Undertaker person to remove, or cause to be removed, for the purpose of any dead body interment, the remains of any person dying within the limits for interment of the city, until he is furnished with a proper certificate of ficate of death death, signed by the medical attendant of the deceased; and should said medical attendant refuse to grant to said undertaker or other person a proper certificate of death, so as to enable him to comply with the law within a proper period, say twelve hours after death, he shall be subject to a fine of twenty dollars for every offence; and in case there is no such medical attendant, two respectable persons cognizant of the facts may give such certificate of death.

The certificate of death shall set forth the name in full of What death the deceased, date, place, and cause of death, both chief and shall state complicating, color, sex, age, place of birth, occupation, name of parents, whether married or single; and if married, the name of consort, and also the name of the informant, and his or her relation to the deceased, as now required by the State law.

Certificate to be returned to health officer who shall publish same
The said certificate of death, with date and place of burial of deceased appended, shall be returned within three days of its date to the health officer, who shall, on or before the second Wednesday of each month, return to the board of health a statement containing an enumeration of the causes of deaths of the previous month, as obtained from the before described certificates of death, in such form as may be prescribed by the board of health, and the health officer shall publish the same in the newspapers having the contract for advertising for the city.

Carrying dead bodies in carriages prohibited in certain cases
19. It shall be unlawful for any owner or driver of any public or private carriage to use the same as a hearse in carrying to either of the cemeteries the dead body of any infant or child, or other person, whose death was caused by any contagious or infectious disease, and the provisions hereof shall be kept posted in every public hack. Any person violating any of the provisions of this section shall pay a fine of not less than five nor more than twenty dollars.

Mayor to order police to report nuisances and make general sanitary inspection quarterly
20. It shall be the duty of the mayor to direct that the police shall report all nuisances of every description that may exist in any street, lane, alley, yard, vacant lot, marshes or docks, daily, to the chief of police, who shall make a daily report of the same to the mayor.

The mayor shall also order a general and thorough sanitary inspection of the city to be made by the police quarterly, on the fifteenth day of March, June, September and December of each year. They shall examine thoroughly all streets, lanes, alleys, docks, vacant lots, cellars, yards, &c., &c., and they shall report as to the actual condition of the same to the chief of police, who shall report the same to the mayor.

Mayor to order nuisances to be abated
The mayor shall order the immediate abatement of every nuisance so reported, by the person complained of, and in case of refusal or neglect to comply with his order, the mayor shall order the street inspector to cause the said nuisance to be abated and the expense thereof collected by the city collector from the party liable therefor.

Penalty for violating orders and rules concerning the public health
21. Any person violating any of the provisions of this chapter, or any lawful order of the councils, or of the mayor, or any of the orders, rules or regulations of the board of health, made under their authority, concerning the public health, shall, on conviction thereof, where no other penalty is imposed, pay a fine of not less than five nor more than twenty dollars, for each offense.

CHAPTER XIX.

Wooden Houses.

Wooden houses over certain dimensions not to be erected without permission of councils
1. No person shall, without special permission from the councils, build on any lot of land within the city limits, any house or building whatever of greater dimensions than twelve feet square and one story high, ten feet in the clear, un-

less the outer walls of such house or building be made of brick and mortar, or of stone and mortar, or of sheet iron, or some other fire-proof material and the roof covered with tin or slate. Nor shall any person, without permission from the councils, build upon the line of any street or fronting thereon, any wooden house of any size or dimensions whatever. *No wooden house of any size to be built on street line without permit*

All permits to erect wooden buildings shall be coupled with the condition that water shall be introduced upon the premises from the Norfolk city water works by the owner or builder, provided the house be situated along the line of the water pipe. It shall be the special duty of the inspector to see that this condition is complied with. Any person offending herein shall forfeit and pay a fine of twenty dollars, and a further fine of ten dollars for each week such building or buildings shall remain after due notice to remove the same shall have been given. *All wooden houses to be connected with water works.*

2. All petitions for permission to erect buildings in accordance with the provisions contained in section one of this ordinance shall be accompanied with a plat of said building or buildings and the written consent of the property holders adjoining the land where such building or buildings are to be erected, and such petition shall lay over for one month from the date of its presentation to the councils, and in no case shall the construction of said building or buildings be commenced until such petition shall have been granted by the councils. *Plat of building and consent of adjoining owners to accompany petition.*

Any person who shall violate this section shall incur the penalties prescribed in section one.

CHAPTER XX.

Instruments in Writing—Execution of.

1. All deeds, bonds, leases, contracts, conveyances and agreements of whatsoever nature or description, authorized to be made or entered into by the city, shall, unless otherwise specially provided by the councils, be signed and acknowledged by the presidents of the common and select councils respectively and sealed with the corporate seal of the city by the city treasurer, and all bonds shall also be countersigned by the said treasurer, and said deeds, bonds, leases, contracts, conveyances and agreements, when so signed and sealed, shall be taken as and for the true act and deed of the city of Norfolk; *provided* that nothing herein contained shall apply to the conveyance of lands sold for delinquent taxes, required to be made and executed by the mayor and treasurer under any resolution of the councils. *Deeds, bonds, etc. to be signed by the presidents of the councils* *Proviso as to deed for delinquent lands*

2. All negotiable notes of the city made by authority of the councils shall be signed by the presidents of the common and select councils respectively, and a record thereof shall be made by the treasurer of the city, showing the name of the payee, amount and the date of execution and maturity. *Negotiable notes: how executed*

3. Whenever the presidents of the councils, or either of

Vice president of council to act in absence of president

them, shall be absent from the city the duties in this chapter required to be performed by them shall be discharged by the vice-presidents of the councils respectively.

Record of bonds to be made by treasurer

4. Every bond or other evidence of debt issued in the name of the city shall be numbered by the city treasurer, and he shall keep a record showing said number, the name of the party to whom issued, and on what account and the date of issue and maturity thereof, and he shall also make a detailed record in like manner of all transfers of bonds made by him.

CHAPTER XXI.

Lights.

Council committee on light to have supervision of the subject and prepare contracts for the councils

1. The joint committee of the councils on light shall have the general supervision of the lighting of the streets of the city and public buildings, under the orders of the councils, and shall from time to time seek proposals and submit to the councils for their approval contracts for furnishing the lights required, either by the use of gas, electricity, or otherwise, as the councils may direct. If the contract be for gas, it shall

Gas to be furnished at rate of four feet per hour

provide for a good and constant light at the rate of four feet per hour; and in all cases the contractor shall be required to

Contractor to light and extinguish lamps

light and extinguish the lamps and keep the apparatus and fixtures clean and in good order at his own cost.

Contractor to be fined in case of negli- in lighting lamp

2. If from the negligence or fault of any contractor, his servants or agents, any lamp or lamps or apparatus employed for giving forth the light shall not be lighted when the same ought to be done, according to the terms of the contract, then the contractor shall be subject to a fine per lamp for the time the same may not be lighted, during the night, ratably with the compensation per lamp allowed him by the contract.

Policemen to re-light extinguished gas lamps and report same to chief

3. When gas is used for lighting, the several policemen, in going their rounds, shall relight any gas lamp that may have been extinguished from any cause, and make report of the same to the chief of police.

Penalty for breaking lamps or injuring same

4. If any person shall break, take down, deface or injure any pillar or lamp, or break the glass or any part of the same or in any wise injure or break the tubes or burners of any lamp belonging to the city or any contractor or extinguish the light therein, he shall for every such offense pay a fine of five dollars, one-half of which shall go to the informer; and it shall be the special duty of the police to prosecute for violations of this section.

CHAPTER XXII.

Markets.

Market days and limits of market

1. Every day in the week (Sunday excepted) shall be a public market day within the city, and the limits of the market shall be follows: Beginning at the lower end of Campbell's wharf and the lower end of Newton's wharf and running

from thence to the south end of the market-house; from thence, including both sides of the market-house and Union street, to Main street; thence along the south side of Main street to Bank street crossing, and thence westerly along the north side of Main street to the limits of the city. The west side-walk of market square, as far as is necessary, shall be reserved for fish carts, and fish may be sold in boats at Campbell's wharf, and from stands at the foot of the market.

2. The stalls in the market-house shall be appropriated exclusively for the use and occupancy of butchers and provision dealers for the sale of butchers' meats and provisions, at an annual rent of not less than one hundred and fifty dollars for the year, or any price which the councils may assess in December of each year. *Stalls to be used by butchers, &c. and rented annually; councils to assess rent in December*

3. The collector shall, on the first Monday in January annually, expose for rent at public auction all the stalls within the market-house, and collect the rent for the same; but in no case shall any stall be rented at a less price than the minimum price fixed by the councils. The collector shall annually collect the rent on said stalls, but in no case shall any stall be rented at less than the minimum price fixed in the preceding section; and the possession of any stall shall be forfeited if allowed to remain unoccupied for ten consecutive days without reasonable excuse to the market committee. Payment in all cases shall be made for the whole year in advance by the renter to the collector, or quarterly in advance, by giving satisfactory security to the collector for the remainder of the year. No renter shall occupy more than two stalls at the same time, nor shall he be permitted to re-rent the same to any other person; but if any renter shall not desire to use his stall it shall be surrendered to the city, and shall be rented out by the collector as prescribed in this section. *The collector to expose for rent stalls at auction; on what terms*

4. It shall be the duty of the clerk, at all times, to prevent idle and disorderly persons from frequenting the market-house, and any person who may be found sitting or sleeping within the said market-house, or upon the stalls or benches, shall pay a fine of one dollar for every such offence. And the clerk is hereby authorized to summon the police to aid him in support of his authority, who shall obey such summons, under the penalty of two dollars for every neglect to aid him, when required. Any person who shall interfere with the clerk or police in the discharge of their duties under this ordinance shall pay a fine of not less than two nor more than ten dollars. *Duty of clerk to prevent idle and disorderly persons from frequenting market-house, &c.; may require police to assist him in support of his authority; penalty*

5. It shall be the duty of the clerk to have the market-house opened and closed, and properly cleansed every day in the week (Sundays excepted). He shall prevent all unsound and unwholesome provisions from being sold, or offered for sale with the limits of the market, by seizing the same and taking such order in relation thereto as shall be directed by any two respectable housekeepers who may examine the same; he shall also decide all differences and disputes that may arise touching the weights and measures of things bought and sold *Duty of clerk to have market opened and closed and cleansed; to prevent unsound provisions from being sold, to decide differences, touching weights, penalty for selling tainted meats, &c.*

within the market. Any person selling or exposing for sale tainted or unwholesome meats or provisions of any kind shall pay a fine of not less than one nor more than twenty dollars.

Clerk shall ex-
amine fish,
oysters and
crabs 6. The clerk shall examine all fish, oysters and crabs; and if the same, in his opinion, be tainted, he shall order them to be forthwith removed out of the limits of the city; and any person having such articles, who shall fail to obey such order, shall pay a fine of five dollars.

Private mar-
ket 7. No person shall sell or expose for sale in any store, private market or other place, any tainted or unsound meats, fish, or provisions of any kind.

Any person violating the provisions of this section shall be fined not less than five nor more than twenty dollars.

Market hours
prescribed
and limited;
proviso for
sale of fresh
fish on Sunday
penalty 8. The market hours of the market shall be as follows viz: To begin at daylight in the morning and end at 12 M., except on Saturdays, on which days the market hours shall begin at daylight and end at 10 o'clock P.M., between the first day of April and the first day of October; and shall begin at daylight and end at 9 o'clock P.M. from the first day of October to the first day of April. Provided, however, that nothing in this ordinance shall prevent the sale of fresh fish within the limits assigned for that purpose on Sunday morning as late as nine o'clock. Any butcher or other person or persons offending herein, on being found at market after market hours aforesaid, shall pay a fine of not less than two nor more than twenty dollars.

Tax on per-
sons selling in
market, to be
paid by huck-
sters and ven-
ders of fish;
penalty for
selling fish
contrary to
this provision;
tax on sellers
of oysters;
penalty 9. All persons selling or exposing for sale produce of any kind, within the limits of the market, except the venders of fish, and the renters of fixed stalls, shall pay to the clerk of the market, for the use of the city, the sum of ten cents for each day; and if said produce be brought within the said limits in carts, there shall be paid ten cents for each cart. and if in wagons, fifteen cents for each wagon. Each proprietor of a huckster stand shall pay twenty-five cents per day. Every person exposing for sale fish within the limits of the market, shall pay the sum of twenty-five cents for each day; and if the fish be brought and exposed for sale in carts, for each cart there shall be paid twenty-five cents, and if in wagons, for each wagon load, forty cents; and any person refusing to pay as aforesaid, when called upon by the clerk, shall pay a fine of nor less than two dollars nor more than twenty dollars.

The occupants of the arks at Campbell's wharf, who buy and sell oysters, shall pay to the clerk of the market for the use of the city' a daily tax of fifty cents, and any such occupant refusing to pay the same, when called upon by the clerk to do so, shall pay a fine of not less than two nor more than five dollars.

Penalty for
posting bills
or hitching
horses to any
part of market
no live stock
to be retained
in market
after purchase 10. No person shall post any post-bills against any part of the market-house, nor hitch any horse, mule or other animal to any post or fixture thereof, under a penalty of not less than five nor more than ten dollars for such offense. No butcher or other person shall retain within the limits of the market space any live bullock, ox, cow, calf, sheep, hog or other cattle after the same shall have been purchased by him.

11. All bullocks, oxen, cows or other cattle brought to market for sale, shall be exposed for sale on the northwestern side of Market square; and the person bringing the same shall pay for each bullock, ox or cow the sum of twenty cents, and for each live hog, sheep or calf, the sum of five cents, to the clerk of the market, under a penalty of not less than one nor more than five dollars. *How live stock sold in market; tax on same; penalty*

12. If any person shall injure or deface any part of the market-house, or any appendage thereto, such person shall pay a fine of five dollars. *Penalty for injuring, &c., any part of the market*

13. All blocks, benches, tubs or other things used in the market for the accommodation of butchers or other persons, whilst occupying their stalls, shall be placed and kept within the limits of the stalls by them severally occupied. If any person shall violate this provision, or if any person shall make any alteration whatever to his stall, so as to injure or destroy the uniform appearance of the stalls (without first obtaining the unanimous consent of the market committee), he shall pay a fine of ten dollars. *Blocks, benches, &c., to be kept within stalls; no alteration to be made to stall; penalty*

14. No huckster or other person shall occupy more space than that assigned to him by the clerk of the market. No huckster or shipper, or his agent, shall sell or expose for sale any article or commodity whatever, in any part of the market space, other than the stall occupied by him; and no huckster or shipper, resident or non-resident, or his agent, shall buy to sell again any article which may be brought for sale, within the limits of the market, under a penalty in either offense of a forfeiture of the article so offered for sale or bought, and a fine of ten dollars. Provided, however, that hucksters or persons selling fish, oysters or crabs, may have a place other than their stalls assigned them by the clerk. *Clerk to assign place to hucksters, &c., who shall only sell at such place and shall not buy in market limits; penalty; proviso in reference to sale of fish, oysters and crabs*

15. All provisions of every kind sold by weight or measure shall be weighed or measured by weights and measures duly regulated and stamped by the sealer of the city; and if any person shall be guilty of selling by weights and measures not regulated and stamped as aforesaid, or by scales falsely balanced, he shall forfeit such measures and scales, and pay the sum of five dollars for ever such offense. And hogs, quarters of beef, and other bulky articles, may be weighed in the public scales in the market. *How provisions sold by weight or measure shall be weighed or measured; bulky articles may be weighed at public scales*

16. If any person shall offer for sale in the market any oysters, between the first day of May and the first day of September, he shall pay one dollar for every quart of opened oysters, and one dollar for every peck of oysters in the shell so exposed for sale. No oysters shall be opened at any time within the limits of the market (except on Campbell's wharf), under a penalty of five dollars for each offense. *Penalty for selling oysters in market between May 1st and Sept. 1st; or for opening them in market at any time*

17. Every butcher or other person holding a stall shall keep his stall and limits clean and in good order, under a penalty of five dollars for every failure so to do. *Butchers, &c., required to keep stalls, &c., in good order; penalty*

18. No butcher nor his agent shall cut or expose for sale

Butchers not allowed to cut or expose for sale beef, &c., out of stalls; penalty

in any part of the market, other than his stall, any beef, pork mutton, veal or lamb, nnder the penalty of five dollars for the first offense, and forfeiture of his stall for the second offense.

Each butcher required to have his own scales, &c.; proviso in case of adjoining stalls

19. Each butcher shall have and use his own scales and weights, which shall be displayed in some conspicuous place in front of or at the side of his stall, under the penalty of five dollars for each offense; provided that it shall be lawful for any two butchers having adjoining stalls to have and use one set of scales and weights in common; and provided also, that such scales shall be suspended in a conspicuous place between their stalls, and that each of the said butchers shall be responsible for the correctness of such scales and weights.

Clerk to assign places in and adjoining market to persons exposing produce, &c, for sale: penalty for failure to obey clerk

20. No person shall occupy any part of the street or market place at or near the market for the purpose of exposing for sale any garden produce or other thing, other than such part of the same as shall be assigned and set apart for that purpose by the clerk of the market; and if any person shall occupy any part of the street or market space for the purpose aforesaid, such person, on being required by the clerk to remove, and neglecting so to do immediately, shall pay a fine of five dollars for each offense; and if any person shall neglect or refuse to obey the directions of the clerk respecting the arrangement or removal of any article, cart, wagon, or other thing, in the market or street adjoining, every person so neglecting or refusing shall pay a fine of five dollars, and moreover shall be expelled from the market by the clerk.

Clerk's salary and commission

21. The clerk shall be entitled to a salary of four hundred and fifty dollars per annum, payable monthly, and also a commission of ten per centum upon all taxes collected by him under this ordinance, which commission may be allowed him by the treasurer in his settlements.

Weigher of market scales to be appointed: his fees and duties; penalties

22. There shall be appointed by the councils annually, at their first meeting in July, or as soon thereafter as practicable, a weigher at the market scales, who shall receive as a compensation for his services two cents for every hundred pounds of anything that may be weighed by him, or a like sum for any fractional part of one hundred pounds. He shall keep the scales in order, and attend strictly to them, and be under control of the market committee; and whenever he shall be sick or unable to attend, the authority to appoint a substitute shall be vested in the chairman of the said market committee. If he fail to keep the scales in good order he shall pay a tine of five dollars for every day he shall so fail.

Sale of fish after market hours

23. It shall be unlawful for any person to expose fresh fish for sale upon any public street, square or lane, or in or upon any vacant lot of land within the corporate limits of the city, after the expiration of the regular market hours provided in the ordinance concerning markets, excepting only live fish sold from boats in the county dock; and the provisions of this section shall apply to the sale from stands, or by huckstering fresh fish, in or upon the grounds belonging to Norfolk county, lying south of Water street and west of Commercial street, said grounds being within the limits of the city. Any person

violating any of the provisions of this section shall Mayor may designate places where fish may be sold after noon pay a penalty of ten dollars for each offense. And the mayor shall have authority to designate where and in what manner fish may be sold after 12 o'clock M.

24. If any person shall be convicted of any offense against General penalty this ordinance, such offender shall thereafter be prohibited from selling in the market, under the penalty of five dollars for every day or part of a day he shall be there for the purpose aforesaid, unless such person shall, after conviction, obtain permission from the councils.

25. The clerk of the market shall, on the first and fifteenth Clerk of market to make detailed reports of his collections semi-annually day of each month, make a report to the city treasurer of all his collections, showing in detail the number and kind of carts and wagons and number of hucksters and all other persons and subjects from which taxes and fees are collected by him; and he shall promptly pay over to the treasurer the amount due the city; and he shall also furnish a duplicate of said report to the auditor at the same time. The penalty for a a violation of this section shall be twenty dollars for each offense.

CHAPTER XXIII.

Nuisances.

Sec. 1. The inspector of streets shall and may enter into Inspector may enter premises to examine into nuisance and examine any building, privy or premises which he may know, or be informed, is in a state of. nuisance, and direct the cleansing and abating of all nuisances about the same, and if any person shall obstruct the inspector in the discharge of this duty, or shall refuse to abate any such nuisance when ordered so to do, he shall pay a fine of five dollars, and a further fine of five dollars for every day such nuisance shall remain after such order to remove it.

2. No person shall keep on his premises any offensive mat- Penalty for nuisance ter or thing whatever, under the penalty of five dollars for ever day such matter or thing shall remain after notice from the inspector to remove or destroy the same.

3. Any person who shall remove or transport night soil or Removal of night soil any excrementitious matter, except the same shall be removed or transported by means of some air-tight apparatus, pneumatic, or other odorless process so as to prevent the same from being agitated or exposed in the open air during said process of removal and transportation, shall be fined not less than five nor more than twenty dollars.

4. It shall be unlawful for any person to permit any pigeons, Pigeons excluded from city except carrier pigeons, to fly at large within the limits of the city, and for any violation of this ordinance, which it is hereby made the duty of the police to report, the owner or occupant of the lot or premises upon which such pigeons are kept or permitted to harbor shall be subjected to a fine of five dollars, and a further fine of two dollars each day thereafter until the nuisance be abated.

No hogs to be kept in city

5. No person shall keep a hog within the limits of the city. and any one so offending shall be liable to and pay a fine of two dollars for every hog so kept, one-half of which fine shall go to the informer; and moreover it shall be the duty of the inspector and policemen, and the right of any other citizen, to seize such hog and deliver it to the keeper of the almshouse, who shall sell the same, and after deducting expenses, and the said fine of two dollars, he shall pay to the person who seized the same (other than the inspector) one-half of the balance of the sales, and the other half to the treasurer.

Any citizen may seize hog and deliver him to keeper of almshouse

Swimming or bathing in river

6. No person shall, between the hours of five o'clock A. M., and eight o'clock P. M., swim or bathe in the waters of the Elizabeth river, or its branches, within the limits of the city, unless properly clothed. Any person violating this section shall pay a fine of three dollars.

Begging on streets

7. Any person found begging in any of the streets of the city shall incur a fine of two dollars for each offense, and in default of the payment thereof, shall be imprisoned for not less than ten days.

Drunkenness or disordly conduct

8. Any person who shall be found drunk, or who shall be found guilty of disorderly conduct, or who shall commit a breach of the peace, or any nuisance within the limits of the city, shall be fined not less than one nor more than twenty dollars.

Throwing stones or other missiles

9. If any person shall throw any stone, brick or other missile in any street, lane or square in the city, such person shall pay for every such offense the sum of two dollars, and the amount of damages occasioned by the throwing of such missile, to be recovered by warrant before the mayor or any justice of the peace of the city.

Digging holes in lots

10. If any person shall dig any hole, wherein any rain or filth may settle, or a nuisance may be created, upon any lot owned or occupied by him, he shall pay a fine of two dollars, and a further fine of one dollar for every day such nuisance may remain after notice from the inspector to abate the same.

Making bricks or burning shells in the city

11. No person shall dig pits for the making of bricks, or burn bricks or shells, within the limits of the city; and any one so offending shall pay a fine of twenty dollars, and the additional fine of ten dollars for every day he shall continue to make or burn bricks or shells.

Casting refuse matter in the streets or transporting in vessels not covered

12. No person shall cast or cause to flow any swill or other refuse matter into any street or lane, or transport through any street or lane, any swill or other liquid refuse matter, except in a covered water tight vessel; and any one so offending shall pay a fine of two dollars in each case.

Water closets in houses; how connected

13. It shall not be lawful for any builder, contractor, or workman, or other person, to introduce a water-closet into any dwelling or other building, unless the house and drain pipes from such closets shall conduct the contents into a sewer discharging into tide-water, or into water-tight sinks, which, if built of bricks, shall be laid in hydraulic cement, to prevent the escape of vitiated fluids into the earth. Any person guilty

of a violation hereof shall pay a fine of five dollars per day, so long as the nuisance shall remain.

14. No person shall carry or use within the limits of the city, or of either of the cemeteries, any sling made for throwing shot, stones or other missiles. Every person violating the provisions of this section shall pay a fine of not less than two nor more than twenty dollars, together with the amount of the damage, if any, caused by throwing such missile. Carrying slings

15. No person shall throw grape hulls or the rind of any fruit or vegetable upon any of the sidewalks of the city. Every person violating this section shall pay a fine of not less than two nor more than five dollars. Grape hulls or fruit on sidewalks

16. Whenever it shall be alleged by any two residents, or by the engineer or inspector, upon complaint to the mayor, that any building chimney or wall of any kind, hath become dangerous to citizens, or to adjoining property, by dilapidation or otherwise, the mayor shall have the owner thereof, or his agent, summoned before him, and upon proof that the said building, chimney or wall, or any part thereof, is dangerous, as aforesaid, shall order the said owner or his agent, to remove or repair the same, or so much thereof as is dangerous. And if such order be not obeyed within a reasonable time, to be fixed by the mayor in his order, he shall direct the inspector or engineer to cause such removal or repairs to be made forthwith, at the expense of the city; but the cost thereof shall be repaid to the city by the owner of said property, together with 20 per centum for damages. Dilapidated or dangerous buildings; how removed

17. Every person who shall maliciously, wantonly or carelessly mark with chalk or daub with paint, cut, break, or otherwise injure, or deface any fence, wall, post, lamp-post, lamp or lantern, tree, tree-box, house or other building, or sidewalk, in or upon any of the streets, lanes or public squares of the city, shall pay a fine of not less than five nor more than twenty dollars. Marking or daubing walls or houses and malicious injury to posts, trees, buildings, etc.

18. The inspector shall remove any obstruction or nuisance in a street, gutter or alley, at the expense of the person causing it, which expense he shall certify to the collector, who, if it be not forthwith paid, shall institute proceedings for the recovery of the same. Inspector to remove nuisance at cost of the offender.

19. If any person shall, within the limits of this city, keep a house of ill-fame or assignation, resorted to for the purpose of prostitution or lewdness, such person shall be fined not less than five nor more than twenty dollars. Houses of ill fame, etc.

20. If any person keeping a saloon, concert hall, bar-room, or other place of public entertainment, within the limits of this city, employ or harbor in such place any female of loose or doubtful character, or encourage, permit or allow any indecency or licentiousness of act. manner, dress or conversation in said place, such person shall be fined not less than five nor more than twenty dollars; and any person guilty of such indecency or licentiousness, or any disturbance of the peace, shall be fined not less than five nor more than twenty dollars. Dissolute females not to be employed in saloons or public houses

21. It shall not be lawful for any person to sell or offer for sale, at public auction, any horses or mules on any of the public Horses and mules not to be sold at auction on streets

lic streets, squares or lanes of the city, Any person violating this ordinance shall pay a fine of ten dollars.

Immoderate driving on streets
22. Any person who shall ride a horse, or drive any carriage or vehicle at an immoderate gait on the streets, shall, for every such offence. pay a fine of not less than five nor more than twenty dollars; and if any person shall ride or drive, turning the corner of any street, otherwise than in a walk, he shall pay a fine of three dollars for every offence.

Horses and vehicles not to be left standing on streets
23. No horse and cart, or horse and other vehicle, shall be left standing in any street or lane of the city by the owner or driver thereof, and no horse shall be fed on any street or lane of the city, under the penalty of two dollars for every such offence. But this shall not apply to horses fed at the market during market hours.

Flying kites
24. No person shall raise or fly any kite within the limits of the city south of Scott street, under a penalty of two dollars for every such offence.

Keeping more than two cows in one lot; beef cattle excepted
25. No person shall keep more than two cows at one and the same time in any lot or enclosure, or upon any parcel of ground of at least twenty-five feet wide and eighty feet deep, within the limits of the city. But this section shall not apply to beef cattle brought into the city for sale and impounded in a lot kept for that purpose. Any person violating this section shall pay a fine of five dollars for each offence.

CHAPTER XXIV.

Officers of the City.

Councils to meet in July to elect city officers
Sec. 1. The first meeting of the councils after their election shall be held on the first day of July, or as soon thereafter as practicable. On such day. after their separate organization, the select and common councils shall assemble in joint session, a quorum of each body being present, and proceed to elect or appoint the officers required by any law or ordinance of the

Officers to be chosen
city to be elected by the councils, viz:
The city engineer, biennially.
The auditor, biennially.
The janitor of the city hall, annually.
The messenger to the councils, annually.
The inspectors and measurers of grain, &c., annually.
The weigher at the market scales, annually.
The weigher at the platform scales on Roanoke Square, annually.
The custodian of Christ Church clock, annually.
The street sewer and drain commissioners, biennially.
The water commissioners. biennially.
The fire commissioners and the chief and assistant engineers of the fire department, biennially.
The board of health, biennially.
The justices of the peace, biennially.
The high constable, biennially.
The keeper of Calvary cemetery, biennially.

2. Every person elected or appointed to any office shall hold Officers to serve until successors appointed and qualified his office for and during the term provided by law or ordinance, and until his successor shall be lawfully appointed and quali- fied.

3. In case of the removal of the president of either branch When vice-presidents of councils to act as presidents of the councils, or of his death, resignation, absence from the city, or inability to discharge the powers and duties of the said office, the same shall devolve on the vice-president.

Salaries.

4. The several officers hereinafter named shall be entitled to receive the following salaries, per annum, payable monthly out of the city treasury, viz:

The judge of the corporation court, $3,000.
The mayor, $1,600.
The treasurer, $1,600.
The commissioner of the revenue, $800 in addition to his fees
The city engineer, $2,000 and fees not exceeding $500.
The auditor, $800.
The city attorney, $720.
The inspector of streets, $800.
The clerk of the market, $450 and ten per cent. of the amount of his collections.
The health officer, $540.
The keeper of the almshouse, $640.
The keeper of the cemeteries, $800.
The keeper of Calvary cemetery, $400.
The superintendent of public schools, $540.
The janitor of the city hall, $720.
The messenger to the councils, $600.
The mayor's clerk, $300.
The custodian of Christ Church clock, $75.
The street sewer and drain commissioners—
The president, $500.
The treasurer, $500.
The secretary, $1,000.
The clerk in the city treasurer's office, $680.
The police justice, in addition to the fees of his office, $300.

Bonds of City Officers.

5. The several city officers hereinafter named shall give Bonds with security to be given by officers bonds with sufficient sureties, to the city of Norfolk, in the penal sums following, to-wit:

The city treasurer, $50,000.
The commissioner of the revenue, $10,000.
The city engineer, $5,000.
The collector of city taxes and levies, $50,000.
The auditor, $5,000.
The inspector of streets, $1,000.
The clerk of the market, $2,000.
The keeper of the almshouse, $3,000.
The keeper of cemeteries, $1,000.

The keeper of Calvary cemetery, $500.
The weigher of hay, $1,000.
The wood measurer, $500.
The sealer of weights and measures, $1,000.
The gauger of liquors, $1,000.
Street, sewer and drain commissioners, each, $10,000.
Treasurer of the water board, $10,000.
Sinking fund commissioners, each, $5,000.

Bonds to be filed within ten days after appointment to office All officers of the city required to give bond (except when it is otherwise provided) shall file the same in the office of the treasurer of the city, within ten days after receiving notice of their appointment.

Condition of bonds 6. The bond given by each officer shall contain a condition that he will faithfully discharge the duties of his office, and **Sureties to be approved by councils** the form thereof shall be such as the city attorney shall approve; and the sureties on each bond and the bond itself shall be approved by the councils.

City officers not to deal in city securities 7. It shall not be lawful for the collector of the city, the treasurer of the city, or any member of the finance committee of the select or common councils, either directly or indirectly, to purchase or sell any of the bonds, certificates of interest or other securities issued by the city of Norfolk, under a penalty of one hundred dollars for each violation of this ordinance, one-half of said sum to go to the informer.

The Mayor.

Powers of the mayor 8. The mayor shall, in addition to the duties imposed on him by law or by the ordinances of the city, be specially required to enforce obedience to the ordinances of the city.

Mayor's fees for the use of the city 9. The mayor shall demand and receive for the use of the city, for all official acts as hereinafter mentioned, the following fees:

For each bill of health to accompany vessels on foreign voyages $4 00
For each bill of health for a vessel on a coasting or inland voyage.. 2 00
For each certificate of the execution of a deed or power of attorney to be sent within the United States (except when otherwise directed by the laws of the state) 2 00
For each certificate of the execution of a deed or a power of attorney to be sent abroad....................... 4 00
For all official acts not under the seal of the mayor the following fees—to-wit:
For each warrant in debt, detinue, trover and conversion or case, or for the penalty imposed by law or ordinance... 25
For judgment or final decision thereon......................... 25
For each warrant to apprehend a seaman deserting from a vessel... 2 00
For each warrant against a tavern or private boarding-house keeper selling liquor of any kind to, or credit-

ing or harboring such seaman............................. 1 00
For each warrant against a seaman neglecting to render
    himself on board a vessel according to agreement.... 2 00
For each warrant to commit a seaman to prison who
    refuses to proceed on a foreign voyage................ 2 00
For each warrant against a seaman for absenting him-
    self from his vessel.. 2 00
For each notice of the time and place of taking a depo-
    sition under the act of Congress......................... 1 00
For each deposition so taken................................... 3 00
    Provided that no fees shall be allowed in cases of
    felony or paupers or vagrants, nor shall fees be re-
    quired for any service in preparing or authenticating
    documents of a public nature.
On application made to the mayor to hold a survey on
    goods damaged or vessels damaged or in distress, he
    may appoint by warrant, under his hand, discreet
    and respectable merchants, carpenters and masters of
    vessels, to hold such survey, and to demand therefor,
    for the use of the city.... .... 5 00
For each warrant not hereinbefore taxed.................... 1 00
For judgment thereon.. 1 00
For an affidavit... 25
For a certificate or attestation of any special matter...... 50
For a summons for a witness.................................. 15
For administering every oath................................. 15
For a certificate of admiralty process for seamen's
    wages.. 2 00
For a mittimus not hereinbefore taxed...................... 50
For affixing the seal of the mayorality where no tax has
    been hereinbefore imposed.... .... 2 00

10. The seal commonly called the seal of mayoralty shall *Seal to remain in custody of mayor* remain in the custody of the mayor, and be by him put and affixed to all such instruments as he shall be requested to affix the same to, and as are usually certified under such seal.

11. The mayor shall keep his office in the city hall, and it *Mayor's office hours at city hall* shall be open for business between the hours of nine A. M. and one P. M. of each day (Sundays excepted), and at such other times as he may deem necessary.

Clerk to the Mayor.

12. The clerk to the mayor shall be paid a salary of twenty- *Salary to be paid when certified by mayor, police justice, &c* five dollars per month, provided, however, that no salary shall be paid unless he perform the duties of his office regularly, faithfully and intelligibly; and that such services are certified to by the mayor, the presiding justice of the police court and board of police commissioners.

City Attorney.

13. It shall be the duty of the attorney for the city to pre- *Attorney for the city to draft all instruments and appear for the city in all suits* pare all bonds, contracts, deeds and instruments of writing whatsoever which may be required by any ordinance or order

of the councils; to commence and prosecute all suits, which
at his instance or otherwise, shall be directed; and to defend
the city in all suits, which may be brought against it, or against
any officer or agent, which may involve or affect its interests,
whether the said suits be conducted in or out of the city; to
attend to any warrant or other proceeding before the mayor or
any court of the city, touching any claim or right of the city;
to furnish the councils and their committees with his opinion,
Give his opin-
ion to councils
and the
officers in writing, on any subject which they may submit to him, and
to give assistance and advice touching their duties to the
committees of the councils and the officers of the city when
they shall apply to him. and to render to the city such other
professional services as the councils may require of him.

Salary and
fees 14. The attorney for the city shall pay to the treasurer all
moneys of the city received by him, and shall be allowed a
salary of seven hundred and twenty dollars per annum, which
shall be in full for all services rendered by him, and he shall
be entitled to no further fee or emolument whatever by virtue
of his office, but the necessary traveling expenses incurred by
him in the performance of the duties of his said office, shall
be paid to him by the treasurer, after being certified to
and approved by the councils; and he shall be entitled to such
attorney's tax fees as shall be recovered against and paid by
any party other than the city in any suit to which the city may
be a party; and to demand and receive of any grantee in any
deed, to be prepared by him, and executed by the proper
authorities of the city for the sale, or for the restoration of
any land sold by the city for delinquent taxes. an appropriate
fee for such service, not exceeding in any case five dollars.

Auditor.

Councils to
elect auditor 15. The councils shall, at their first meeting in July, eighteen hundred and eighty-five, and biennially thereafter, in
joint session, appoint an auditor of city accounts, who
shall take the usual oaths of office and enter into bond, with
Oath and
bond sufficient sureties to be approved by the councils, in the penalty of five thousand dollars, with condition for the faithful
discharge of the duties of his office.

Duties of
auditor to ex-
amine ac-
counts of all
city officers
and report to
the councils 16, It shall be the duty of the auditor to examine and audit
the accounts of all the officers of the city who in any manner
or on any account receive or disburse money belonging to the
city or in which the city may have an interest. He shall make
reports to the councils monthly, showing the true condition
of the accounts of the several officers of the city, who receive
or disburse money, naming each officer and stating the amounts
Shall specially
report any
neglect of
duty received and disbursed and the balances; and shall specially
report to the councils any neglect or inefficiency or improper
conduct of any such officers, that may be brought to his
notice.

Custodian of Christ Church Clock.

Duties 17. The custodian of the Christ Church clock shall see that
the same is kept in good order and that the time is correct

according to the standard in use and generally observed in the city, being that of the seventy-fifth meridian.

Collector of City Taxes and Levies.

18. The collector of city taxes and levies shall after his election or appointment, as the case may be, qualify in the same manner and take the same oath that is prescribed for sheriff under the laws of the state; and give bond and security, to be approved by the councils, in the sum of fifty thousand dollars, conditioned for the faithful performance of the duties of his office. *Collector to take oath and give bond*

19. The collector shall collect for the city all moneys due for taxes and levies; and for assessments for paving and other purposes; and also the rents on the Town Point lots and other lands belonging to the city, and he may attach or distrain for the same, proceeding in the manner required by law; and for the collection of assessments for paving streets, opening streets and other purposes, the collector is hereby vested with all the powers which are now, or may hereafter be vested in a sheriff or collector of the State taxes for the collection of said State taxes; he shall rent out the market stalls and vegetable stands; and prosecute all persons who sell goods without having paid the tax imposed, or sell at auction without license. *Collector to collect taxes debts and demands due the city Power of sheriff vested in collector Collector to rent out market stalls To prosecute dealers selling without license*

20. The collector shall annually, in the month of July, prepare all books required for conducting the business of his office, and provide the necessary bills from time to time as may be required, said books and bills to be paid for by the treasurer of the city, and the said books shall contain full and accurate statements of all moneys received by the collector, and all books or documents belonging to or used in the office of the collector shall be the property and records of the city, and shall be at all times subject to the inspection and examination of the mayor and councils. *Collector to prepare books which shall be property of the city*

21. The collector shall on each and every Saturday afternoon, at or before the hour of 2 P. M., render to the treasurer a return of all money he shall have collected, and from what source, and pay the amount to the treasurer, taking his receipt therefor; also, once in every month, an abstract showing the sums received by him for rents of the Town Point and other lands, the names of the lessees, and the amounts and names of those in arrear. The collector, in making his weekly return, shall specify in the same the amount of cash received, and from whom, and the amount of certificates or other vouchers received in payment of taxes and from whom. *Collector to make returns to treasurer every Saturday*

22. The collector may appoint a deputy, who may be removed by him or by the councils. The deputy may discharge any of the duties of the collector, but the collector and his sureties shall be liable for any act of the said deputy. *Collector may appoint deputy*

23 In the event of the death of the collector or his disqualification from any cause, and after the appointment of his successor, the legal representatives of such deceased or dis-

In case of death all un-collected tax bills to be returned to the treasurer

qualified collector, as the case may be, shall transfer to the treasurer all the uncollected tax bills and levies which were in his hands at the time of his death or disqualification, the amount of which bills and levies the treasurer is authorized to place to the credit of such deceased or disqualified collector. Provided that nothing herein contained shall release from responsibility the securities of such deceased or disqualified collector for any amount of such tax bills which may have been paid to or collected by such deceased or disqualified collector, or his deputy, or which may have been lost through his neglect.

Council to fix compensation settlement of collector's accounts and collections when made

24. The collector shall receive for his compensation such fees and commissions as may be allowed by the councils. And he shall, within twenty days after the expiration of ten months from the time the copy of the commissioner of revenue's roll shall have been delivered to him, settle his account of the taxes therein mentioned with the treasurer, under the supervision of the committee on finance, and all other taxes, assessments, dues, rents and levies which ought to have been collected ; and if the collector shall have been unable to collect any part of said taxes by reason of the insolvency of any of the persons owing the same, or other good cause, he shall on oath deliver a list of all such insolvents, delinquents and all other tax returns uncollected, to the treasurer, to be laid before the councils, and if approved, he shall be credited with the amount thereof, or so much as may be approved. If any taxes mentioned in the commissioner of the revenue's roll book shall not be collected and paid to the treasurer by the collector for ten months and twenty days after the same shall have been delivered to him, he and the sureties on his bond shall be answerable for the same, except such as may be credited to him as before mentioned, and his bond shall be put in suit by the treasurer and the city attorney. And the collector and his sureties on his bond shall be likewise reponsible for all other taxes or levies not collected and paid over by him, which he is or may be required by law to collect.

Public notice to be gived of tax rolls for collection and when same must be paid

25. When the rolls of the commissioner of the revenue have been placed in the hands of the collector, he shall give public notice thereof in all the daily newspapers published in the city, annually, on such day as the councils shall designate and for thirty days thereafter; and shall also state in such notice the provisions of the ordinance then in force relating to the prompt payment of taxes. He shall attend at his office daily, between the hours of 9 A.M. and 6 P.M., during the period of thirty days as aforesaid, for the purpose of receiving taxes from any person charged therewith.

Penalty for failure to perform duties

26. For a failure to perform any duty required by this chapter, the collector shall pay a fine of not less than twenty nor more than one hundred dollars.

Commissioner of the Revenue.

Same commissioner of revenue for state and city

27. The commissioner of the revenue elected as such for the commonwealth, under the charter of the city or any act

of Assembly, shall be also the commissioner of the revenue for the city. Before entering upon his duties he shall take Oath and bond to city. the usual oaths of office and enter into bond in the penalty of ten thousand dollars, with sufficient securities, to be approved by the councils, with condition that he will faithfully discharge the duties of his office. He may appoint one or more deputies, May appoint deputies at his own expense, but he shall be liable to the city on his official bond for the acts of his deputies.

28. The commissioner shall apply for the official books and Must apply for books of predecessor papers of his predecessor, to the person in possession thereof, who shall deliver the same on such application; and the commissioner shall inform himself, by an application to the clerk of the court, if any alterations shall have been made therein; Penalty for refusal to deliver such person failing or refusing to deliver such books upon such application, shall pay a fine of not less than twenty dollars for every day that he shall so refuse after such application.

29. The commissioner shall proceed annually, on the first How and when assessments shall be made day of February, to make the assessments of all persons and property subject to taxation by the ordinances of the councils, in the same manner and form as required by the revenue laws of the commonwealth of Virginia; and he shall record the said assessments upon separate rolls or books of assessment for the Assessment rolls and books city, making two complete copies thereof which he shall deliver to the treasurer of the city on or before the first day of July.

The treasurer shall keep one of said copies of the assessment Treasurer to keep copy and deliver one to collector rolls in his office, and the other he shall deliver to the collector of city taxes and levies, taking his receipt therefor.

30. If the commissioner of the revenue shall fail to deliver Penalty for failing to deliver books at proper time to the treasurer of the city the copies of assessment rolls or books, on the day mentioned in the preceeding section, he shall pay a fine of ten dollars for every day thereafter that he shall so fail to complete and deliver the said rolls or books to the treasurer as aforesaid.

31. The commissioner shall annually ascertain all persons Commissioner to assess license taxes for city in the city who are engaged in any business, calling or profession prohibited without license by law, and who ought to obtain licenses; and it shall be the duty of every person so engaged, or desiring to engage in such business, calling or profession, to apply to the commissioner; but the commissioner shall assess with or without application, and it shall be the duty of the commissioner to deliver to every such person a certificate of the license to be obtained and the amount of tax to be paid by him. The commissioner shall commence his assessments of such licenses as expire on the thirtieth day of April at such time as List to be delivered to collector by May 1st will enable him to complete his assessments, and deliver to the collector a list thereof, on or before the first day of May.

32. Every certificate granting authority to engage in or Form of license exercise any business, employment or profession, unless expressly authorized elsewhere otherwise, shall designate the place of business, employment or profession at some specified house or definite place within the city; and any person engaging in or exercising any such business, employment or profession elsewhere than at such house or definite place, unless expressly author-

12

ized elsewhere otherwise by law, shall be held to be without a license. A license to an auctioneer, in addition to the place named in the license, may authorize a sale within the city for another person, at any place at which such other person is authorized to sell. Every certificate shall be produced to the collector, and his receipt for the tax written on the certificate shall be deemed a sufficient license to the person to whom the same has been issued.

When expire   33. All licenses, except such as are otherwise provided for by any ordinance of the city, shall expire on the thirtieth day of April, and if any license which expires on the thirtieth day of April be granted for a less time than one year, the tax thereon shall bear such proportion to the whole annual tax as the space of time between the granting of the same and the thirtieth day of April ensuing bears to a full year. For every certificate delivered by the commissioner to a person desiring, or who ought to obtain a license, the commissioner shall be entitled to **Fees of the commissioner** a fee of seventy-five cents, to be paid by the person to whom the certificate is delivered, and he shall receive a fee of seventy-five cents for a transfer of a license, to be paid by the person obtaining such transfer.

Commissioner to make monthly reports of licenses to treasurer   34. The commissioner shall, on or before the twenty-fourth day of every month, return to the treasurer of the city a list of all certificates for licenses issued by him, with the dates, names of parties, business and amount of taxes assessed; and the commissioner shall deliver to the collector, at intervals not exceeding fifteen days, lists of all persons to whom he has delivered certificates subsequent to the first day of May.

Penalty for giving false lists of property or making false statement to commissioner   35. If any person shall wilfully give to the commissioner a false list of persons or property subject to taxation, or make any false statement concerning his business which may be the subject of a license tax, or shall refuse to give such information to the commissioner as may be necessary to enable him to make the proper assessment, such person shall pay a fine of not less than five nor more than twenty dollars.

Penalty for failure of duty   36. If the commissioner shall fail to perform any of the duties of his office, or shall knowingly make a false or erroneous entry on any of his books, he shall pay a fine of not less than five nor more than twenty dollars for every day he shall so fail, or for every such false or erroneous entry.

Salary   37. The salary of the commissioner of the revenue shall be eight hundred dollars per annum, in addition to the fees of his office, as prescribed by law or ordinance, payable monthly, provided that his salary shall cease after the first day of July, in case he does not complete his roll at the time required by law or ordinance, unless the time for completing the same shall be extended by the councils.

Coroner.

Coroner to make detailed statement of facts in connection with his services   38. Whenever the coroner shall present any bill to the councils for the fee allowed him by law for holding an inquest and performing an autopsy on any dead body, he shall submit to the councils the name of the deceased person and a statement of the circumstances which induced him to believe that the death was caused by violence; and shall further certify under oath that the estate of said decedent is insolvent and that he cannot recover his fee from the same.

when he renders a bill to councils
Coroner to make oath that decedent's estate is insolvent

If the coroner shall fail to submit the statement as aforesaid his claim shall not be allowed.

Fee not to be paid if this ordinance is not complied with

City Engineer.

39. The councils at their first meeting in July, 1884, or as soon thereafter as practicable, and every two years thereafter, shall appoint an engineer of the city, who shall be a citizen of Virginia, and shall hold his office for two years and until his successor is appointed or he be removed. He shall give bond, with one or more sureties, approved by the councils, in the sum of five thousand dollars, with condition that he shall faithfully perform all the duties of his office; and that he will not directly or indirectly, for himself or others, or by others in trust for him, or on his account, have any interest in any purchase, lease, contract or agreement made by the city.

Engineer, when elected, term and bond

40. No person shall be eligible to the office of city engineer until he shall have been certified to be competent, after examination by a board of three competent engineers to be designated by the street committee and the presidents of the councils. The expenses of the board of examiners shall be paid by the city. Provided, that any person who has passed such an examination and served as engineer for the city shall be eligible for re-election without further examination.

To be examined before election by a board
Expense of board, how paid

41. The city engineer shall make all such surveys, plans and estimates as shall be required of him by the councils and the board of street, sewer and drain commissioners. It shall be his duty, under the direction and control of the board of street, sewer and drain commissioners, to superintend the general state of the streets, lanes, squares, culverts, and drains, and the laying out and repairs of the same. He shall have an office with the board and attend daily at the same at stated hours, except when leave of absence may be granted him by the board, and keep a record of all his proceedings. And he shall generally discharge such duties appertaining to his office as may be required of him by the councils.

Engineer to make surveys and plans when required and duties
Office with board of S., S. and D. comrs.
Duties

42. When the services of the engineer are needed by any citizen to make any survey or define the lines of any lot, or to give levels, grades, diagrams, etc., application for such services shall be made at the office of the board and entered in a book kept for the purpose. And the board shall establish reasonable rates of compensation for such services to be paid to the engineer for his use by the party for whose benefit the same may be rendered. But when the aggregate amount of such fees shall exceed the sum of five hundred dollars in any year, the excess shall be paid by the engineer into the city treasury.

Duty in defining lines
Fees

43. No person shall erect any building, bounded by any of the public streets or highways, on his ground, unless the same be previously laid out by the engineer, nor in any other manner than he, with the inspector, shall direct. Any person

Penalty for erecting building on line of any street unless line

laid out by
engineer and
Inspector

violating the provisions of this section shall pay a fine of not less than five nor more than twenty dollars.

Salary

44. The salary of the city engineer shall be two thousand dollars per annum, in addition to the fees allowed him under the forty-second section of this chapter.

Janitor of the City Hall.

Janitor to be
elected an-
nually in July

Duties

To keep city
hall and
grounds in
good order

45. The councils shall in joint session, at their first meeting in July annually, appoint a janitor of the city hall, whose duty it shall be to have the care of the city hall and the grounds in the square containing the same. He shall keep the building and its several apartments and the said public square in a neat and cleanly condition, and prevent all depredations upon the same, and shall generally perform all the duties appertaining to the office of a janitor.

Salary

He shall receive for his compensation the sum of sixty dollars per month, and may be suspended or removed at the pleasure of the councils.

Messenger to the Councils.

Duties of
messenger

To be found
al treasurer's
office

Salary

46. The councils may elect at their first meeting in July or as soon thereafter as practicable, a messenger to the councils, who shall hold his office for the term of one year, or until his successor is elected and has qualified. He shall be in attendance at all the meetings of the councils. He shall summon the councils and all their committees, and shall perform such other duties in attendance upon the councils as may be required of him by the presidents of the councils. His office shall be with the treasurer of the city, where he shall be found during business hours, except when otherwise officially engaged. and he shall be a messenger for the treasurer on city businsss and shall be ex-officio janitor of the treasurer's office. His salary shall be at the rate of fifty dollars per month.

Treasurer.

Treasurer's
duty as clerk
of common
council

Treasurer in
charge of city
real estate

Treasurer
to keep
accounts of
city

47. It shall be the duty of the treasurer or his assistant to attend every meeting of the common council, and as the clerk of the said council, to enter into its journal the proceedings thereof. The treasurer shall keep the said journal safely, receive and take into his charge and keeping all the records, papers, title deeds, bonds or evidences of debt, except his own bond of office (which shall be deposited in the clerk's office of the corporation court) transcribe in a book regularly, in the order in which they may pass, all ordinances of the councils, and keep an index of the same, and also an index of his journal. The treasurer shall also take charge of the real estate belonging to the city, and report all encroachments thereon to the councils.

48. The treasurer shall keep a regular set of books, by way of double entry, in which shall be kept an account of all moneys received and paid out. He shall cause to be opened as many accounts, under appropriate titles, as may be necessary to

show, distinctly and separately, the expenditures and receipts upon each important object, and on the thirtieth day of June in every year he shall transfer the balances to a new account, to be annually opened by him on the first day of July, and shall exhibit semi-annually an account of his receipts and expenditures, together with his bank book, his return cross checks, and the vouchers whereon such checks were drawn, which account shall be examined by the Auditor, under the direction of the finance committee. *Auditor to examine the treasurer's accouts*

49. The treasurer shall furnish to the collector accounts of all moneys due to the city; and upon default in the payment of any such money shall direct suits to be commenced, and moreover, shall report all such delinquencies to the councils. *Treasurer to place accounts and claims due the city in hands of collector*

50. The treasurer shall receive all moneys belonging to the city, and shall deposit the same in such bank at Norfolk as the councils may direct, in the name of the city, and shall draw checks for the same; and he is hereby directed to make no payment but by check on the bank. And the treasurer is hereby further directed to keep a bank book, which shall contain regular entries of all moneys by him deposited, and of all checks by him drawn, with the names of the persons in whose favor, and the account for which the same may be drawn. *Treasurer to receive city funds and shall deposit in bank*

51. The treasurer, before he shall commence the duties of his office, shall enter into an obligation, with good and suffi-cient securities, to be approved by the councils, in the penal sum of fifty thousand dollars, with the condition for the faith-ful performance of the duties of his office. *Treasurers official bond*

52. The office of the treasurer shall be open every day (Sun-days, the fourth of July, and Christmas day excepted) from ten o'clock in the morning until three in the afternoon. *Office hours*

53. In all cases where any person is indebted to the city, and such person has a claim against the city, the treasurer shall deduct the amount due to the city from such claim, and pay the balance only, if any, *How bills are paid when city has set-off*

54. The duties of the treasurer as clerk of the common council may, with the consent of that body, be performed by the assistant or clerk in the treasurer's office, as his deputy; but the treasurer shall be responsible for all of the acts of his said assistant or deputy acting as such clerk. *Treasurer may have as-sistant to act as clerk of council with its consent*

CHAPTER XXV.

Police Department.

1. The police department of the city of Norfolk shall until the first day of July, 1886, and until the successors of the present police commissioners shall have been elected and qualified in accordance with the fifty-fifth section of the char-ter of said city, be under the control and management of a board of commissioners, composed of the mayor of said city and of Washington Taylor and Robert Y. Zachary, two elec-tors of said city, who have been duly elected such police com- *Police com-missioners appointed and named*

missioners by the common council of said city. to continue in office until the first day of July, eighteen hundred and eighty-

Term of office six, and until their successors are elected and qualified; and hereafter the said police department shall be under the control and management of a board of police commissioners to be composed of the mayor, hereafter to be elected, and of two electors of said city who shall be elected biennially according to the provisions of the fifty-sixth section of the charter of

Quorum the said city, any two of the police commissioners to form a quorum for the transaction of any business.

Number of policemen authorized   2. There shall not be more than forty-three policemen, turn-keys and patrolmen, including sergeants, but excluding the chief of police and such other assistants and officers as the board of police commissioners may deem necessary, as authorized by the fifty-eighth section of the charter. All vacancies

How vacancies filled occurring among them shall be filled by the board or by a quorum thereof: but when a vacancy shall occur in the office of chief of police, or any of his assistants, the board of police commissioners, or a quorum thereof, shall, with the approval of the city councils, appoint his successor.

Oath of chief and police   3. The chief of police, his assistants and officers, and the policemen, before entering upon their duties shall take an oath, to be administered by any Justice of the Peace in and for said city, faithfully to perform their respective duties, and they shall also subscribe the same in a book to be kept for that purpose by the clerk of the common council; and each of them shall be entitled to have issued to him upon such election

Warrants of appointment or appointment and qualification, a warrant of appointment signed by the president of the board and countersigned by the clerk of the common council. Failure, from any cause on the part of the president of the board or of the clerk of the common council, to sign or countersign such warrant, or to promptly deliver the same to the person named in it as the appointee, shall be deemed misconduct, which the board of police commissioners or a quorum thereof shall report to the city councils.

Duty of chief and assistant to attend at station and also justice's court   4. The chief of police, his assistants and officers, at such times as the board of police commissioners may order, shall attend at the police station, and at the court held by the justice of the peace whom the councils may from time to to time designate as the justice, to hold the police court: and they may also, with the consent of a quorum of the board attend such court, as, under the city charter, the mayor may hold, and at such times as the regulations of the board may require. The chief shall report to the mayor, and to the board of police commissioners, neglect or violation of duty on the part of any officer or man in the police force, and he shall also make daily entries, in the record of police proceedings or

Chief to report to mayor and the board and keep record, book other book kept for the purpose, of all matters pertaining or relating to the police department that he may deem material or which may be required by the regulations of the board; and he shall be the custodian of such book, and of all the books of the police department, until a majority of the board shall order otherwise. If any person shall hereafter take or withhold any such book or record from him, or from the board, against the orders of the chief of police, or of a quorum of the board, he shall be promptly reported to the councils for their action thereon. The chief of police, his assistants and officers, and the policemen, shall promptly obey all orders issued to them in the line of their duty, by the mayor, provided the orders of the mayor do not conflict with the rules, orders or regulations of the board of police commissioners then in force. *Orders of the mayor*

5. In case of the temporary inability, or absence of the chief of police, the assistant chief shall, at the instance of the chief or of the board, take his place for the time; and the police commissioners, or such acting chief, may designate one of the sergeants to take the place temporarily of such assistant chief. *When the assistant shall act as chief*

6. The board of police commissioners shall, in addition to the regular police force hereinbefore authorized and referred to, employ other persons, who shall be qualified to serve as policemen for the time being, and the persons so added shall be denominated substitutes; and in case of the absence or sickness of any of the regular established policemen, it shall be the duty of the chief of police to supply their places with the substitutes; and such substitutes, when on duty, shall be vested with the same powers, be subject to the same regulations and orders, and be entitled to the like pay, as the regular policemen; and the board, or a quorum thereof, is further authorized to employ so many of the said substitutes, in addition to the regular force, as they shall from time to time deem proper; and all such substitutes shall be entitled to receive the pay of the policemen for whom they are thus temporarily substituted; provided a majority of the commissioners shall certify it to be due them. Additional policemen, in times of exigency, may be appointed by the board of police commissioners, or by a quorum thereof, in conformity with the fifty ninth section of the city charter. *Substitutes; how appointed; their powers and pay*

In times of exigency force may be increased

7. The chief of police shall be paid three dollars per day, and his assistants shall each be paid two dollars and seventy-five cents per day, and each of the sergeants shall be paid two dollars and fifty cents per day, and every policeman for each day shall be paid two dollars (that is, in every case, for a day of service) and all such payments to be made semi-monthly by the treasurer, on the certificate of any two of the police commissioners, audited by the city auditor. *Pay of the police.*

No member of the police force shall receive any other compensation for his services on the police force, nor as informer, from the city or any person. Nor shall any member of the police force accept any gift, or fee from any person for the performance of any duty connected with his position. *No other compensation allowed*

8. The police commissioners may arm the police force of the city in such manner as they may think proper to preserve the peace. *How armed*

9. In the case of any policemen that may be killed, wounded or otherwise disabled, while in the act of discharging his duty,

When police men killed or disabled

and as a consequence thereof, the board will submit a clear history of the affair or matter to the councils, with appropriate dispatch, for such special action thereon as the councils may, at their option, decide to take.

Private watchmen may be commissioned as policemen

10. The board of police commissioners shall have authority to confer, in their discretion, upon any person employed to patrol or protect private property and preserve order, the privilege of acting as conservator of the peace and apprehending all disorderly or riotous persons and all persons lurking about in a suspicious manner, and detain them until they can be surrendered to a roundsman of the police force of the city, or until they can be taken before the proper authority.

The board of police commissioners shall issue to all parties so privileged a commission signed by the mayor as president of said board and shall furnish such parties with a whistle and appropriate badges at their expense.

Uniform not to be worn by others

11. Any person other than a member of the police department, who shall publicly use such badges and uniforms as the board of police commissioners have prescribed or may prescribe for the use of such members, or shall make use of the whistles, calls, or other modes of signaling that are used by the police department, shall pay a fine of not less than five nor more than twenty dollars.

Repealing all previous ordinances concerning police

12. This ordinance has been adopted for the purpose of providing for the establishment of a capital police force in the city of Norfolk. It shall commence and be in force from the passage thereof, and all ordinances, or parts of ordinances, and all resolutions, or parts of resolutions, coming within the purview of this ordinance, heretofore passed or adopted at any time, shall be and are hereby repealed, whether the same were passed-by the common council of the borough of Norfolk, or by the common and select councils of the city of Norfolk.

CHAPTER XXVI.

Railroads.

Norfolk and Western

The ordinances of the councils granting the right of way, through the streets of the city, to certain railroad companies are as follows:

Norfolk and Western Railroad Company.

The franchise enjoyed by this company was granted by the city to the Norfolk and Petersburg railroad company which has been merged into the former; and can be found on the record of the common council *January 26th* 1857, as follows:

Use of streets granted to Norfolk and Petersburg R. R. Co.

Resolved, " That the Norfolk and Petersburg railroad company, be and they are hereby authorized and granted the right and privilege to enter upon, and lay the track of their road in any and upon such of the streets of this city as the directors of said company may deem fit, proper and prescribe, for their

use and purposes either in the loading or unloading of cars as
well as the transit of cars, engines and trains, on the express
condition however that the speed of their cars, engines or
trains shall not within the limits of the city exceed a rate of
five miles per hour.

Sept. 2, 1873: *Resolved,* That the A. M. & O. R. R. Co. be Matthews
allowed the privilege to run their track on Matthews street street
from Wide Water to Main and on the western extremity of
Main street so as to connect with Chamberlaine's wharf, on
the same terms as the company was allowed the said privilege
on Water street.

Sept. 14, 1874: Petition A., M. & O. R. R. Co. asking permission to place switch leading to the Baltimore wharf, was
referred to street committee with power to act.

Norfolk City Railroad Company.

1. It shall be lawful for the Norfolk City railroad company Norfolk City
R.R. Co.
to use the streets of the city of Norfolk for the purpose of (horse car
line); use of
laying out, equipping, maintaining and operating with horse streets
granted
or mule power, single or double track railroad in the said
city in manner and form, and subject to the conditions of
their Act of Incorporation, passed January the fourth, one
thousand, eight hundred and sixty-six, and subject also to the
conditions and provisions hereinafter named. The said com- Original grant
pany shall lay the said track throughout the northern portion
of Church street to Main street, and from Main street, at its
intersection with Church street, to Granby street; and shall
further have hereby the acquiescence of the city councils in
continuing the construction of said road up Granby street,
and through and upon such other streets of the city as it may
be deemed desirable and necessary to occupy. Franchise extended five
2. For the period of five years from the first day of January, years from
1884, the said railroad company may use the streets of the Jan. 1, 1884
city of Norfolk, subject to the conditions and provisions of the
charter of the said company, and the ordinances of the city,
upon the payment to the collector of city taxes of the sum of
twenty-five dollars per car, for each and every car run upon Conditions
the streets of the city during the year 1884, or any part and terms im-
thereof, and upon the payment during the succeeding four posed
years of such sums as shall be annually assessed by the councils of the city for the franchise so enjoyed, upon the express
condition that the said railroad company shall during the said
period be operated and run regularly so as to promote and
subserve the public convenience and comfort, and upon the How track
further conditions that the track shall be constructed of the maintained
Fare five cents
same style of rails and kept at the same gauge as at present,
that the fare charged shall not exceed five cents for each
passenger, and that the said company shall keep the railroad Company to
track and that part of the street on which it is laid in good keep track in
repair
repair.

3. In order to determine whether the conditions of the preceding section are performed, the councils may at any time

18

How to deter-
mine whether
conditions are
performed
require the city attorney to bring the matter before the judge of the Corporation court of the city of Norfolk, and if the court shall decide against the railroad company, the right to use the streets shall cease.

4. The use of the streets by the Norfolk City railroad company after the passage of this ordinance shall be considered an acceptance of its terms and conditions, and it is further provided that the amount annually collected from the said railroad company shall be paid into the treasury of the city to be applied to the purchase and maintenance of a park and to no other purpose whatever.

Use of streets

Acceptance of
conditions

Tax paid to be
dedicated to a
park

In force May 13th, 1884.

AN ORDINANCE

Imposing a tax upon the Norfolk City railroad company for the year commencing May 1, 1885.

Tax imposed
for 1885, $500
1. Be it ordained by the common and select councils, that for the year commencing May 1, 1885, the amount to be assessed upon and collected from the Norfolk City railroad company, for the franchise granted to said company, under the ordinance passed May 13, 1884, shall be five hundred dollars.

2. That so much of the ordinance imposing license taxes for 1885, as is inconsistent with this ordinance is hereby repealed.

3. This ordinance shall be in force from its passage.

C. C. June 2, 1885.
S. C. June 9, 1885.

Norfolk and Brambleton Railroad Company.

AN ORDINANCE

To grant certain privileges to the Norfolk and Brambleton railroad company.

Norfolk and
Brambleton
R R. Co.
Use of Queen
steeet
1. It shall be lawful for the Norfolk and Brambleton railroad company to use that portion of Queen street lying east of Church street in the city of Norfolk, for the purpose of laying out, equipping, maintaining and operating with horse or mule power, a single or double track railroad, subject to the condition of their act of incorporation, and subject also to the conditions and provisions hereinafter named.

What rails
shall be laid
and how
2. The said company shall use rails of the most approved pattern, and shall lay them five feet five inches apart between the outer flanges, and shall keep their track and two feet on each side thereof in good repair.

How long used
free of charge
Jan. 1, 1883
3. Until the first day of January, 1883, the said Company may use said portion of Queen street, subject to the conditions of their charter, and the ordinances of the city, free of the payment of any sum for the franchise so enjoyed, upon the express condition that the said railroad shall, from the time of its completion till the said first day of January, 1883, be operated and run regularly so as to promote and subserve the public convenience and comfort.

4. In order to determine whether the condition of the preceding section is performed, the councils may at any time require the city attorney to bring the matter before the judge of the Corporation court of the city of Norfolk, and if the court shall decide against the railroad company, the right to use the street shall cease. *How to determine whether conditions are performed*

5. After the first day of January, 1883, it may be lawful for the councils to require such reasonable sum as they may determine to be paid by the said railroad company, for the use of the said Queen street thereafter. Nothing herein contained shall exempt the said railroad company from keeping in repair their track and two feet on each side thereof. *Councils may require compensation* *Company to keep track in order*

6. The use of the said Queen street by the Norfolk and Brambleton railroad company shall be considered an acceptance of the terms and conditions imposed by this ordinance.

7. The rates of fare within the city limits shall not exceed five cents. *Fare not to exceed five cents*

8. This ordinance shall be in force from its passage.

Passed C. C. June 5th, 1877.

Passed S. C. June 12th, 1877.

Norfolk and Ocean View Railroad and Hotel Company.

AN ORDINANCE

To permit the Ocean View railroad and hotel company to run its tracks and trains through certain streets.

1. Be it ordained by the select and common councils of the corporation of the city of Norfolk, that it shall be lawful, and the permission of said council is hereby given, for the Norfolk and Ocean View railroad and hotel company, to lay the track and run the trains of its railroad from the limits of the corporation, at Henry street, along and through said street to its intersection with church street; provided that the said railroad company keep the streets which the road crosses or passes through, in good order along the line of said road. *Ocean View R. R.* *Use of Henry street granted* *Company to keep streets in order*

2. This ordinance shall be in force from and after its passage.

Passed S. C. July 25th, 1879.

Passed C. C. July 25th, 1879.

CHAPTER XXVII.

Sabbath Day.

1. If any person on the Sabbath day shall be found laboring at his own or any other trade or calling, or shall employ his apprentices, clerks or servants in labor or other business, except it be in the ordinary household offices of daily necessity, or in other work or duty of necessity or charity, he shall pay a fine of five dollars for every such offense. *Labor at trade prohibited*

2. If any person on the Sabbath day, or on any part thereof, shall keep open his store, shop or cellar, and shall buy or sell any article whatsoever, except in cases of sickness, or shall buy *Buying or selling from shops, boats, etc. prohibited*

or sell at any wharf, or on board of any boat, or on the streets or lanes of the said city, any article whatsoever, except in cases of sickness, such person shall pay a fine of five dollars for every such offense.

Provison as to fish and oysters
3. Nothing in this chapter shall be construed to prohibit the sale of fish in the market, or of oysters at any oyster stand in the city, on Sunday prior to the hour of nine o'clock A. M.

Sale of liquors prohibited
4. No intoxicating drink shall be sold in any bar-room, ordinary, restaurant, hotel, saloon, store, or other place within the limits of this city, from twelve o'clock on each and every Saturday night of the week until sunrise of the succeeding Monday morning; and any person violating this ordinance shall, on conviction, be fined not less than ten nor more than five hundred dollars, and shall moreover, at the discretion of the court, forfeit his license.

Extract from State law, chapter 83, Acts of 1874:—

State law
" Provided that this law shall not apply to any city having police regulations on this subject, and an ordinance inflicting a penalty equal to the penalty inflicted by this statute."

CHAPTER XXVIII.

Schools.

Two school districts established and boundaries
1. There shall be two school districts in the city entitled the eastern and western school districts, which shall be separated by the line commencing at the southern extremity of Church street at the Elizabeth river, and extending northwardly to Cove street; thence westwardly to Bank street; thence northwardly to Queen street; thence eastwardly to Cumberland street; thence in a northwardly direction along the last named street to the city limits. That portion of the city lying to the eastward of the said line shall constitute the eastern district, and that one to the westward the western district.

Board to submit annual estimates to councils to make appropriations
2. It shall be the duty of the school board once in each year in January to submit to the councils in writing a classified estimate of what funds will be needed for the proper maintenance and growth of the public free schools of the city, and to request the councils to make appropriations accordingly, and the amount so estimated shall thereupon be appropriated by the councils if the same be within the limit prescribed by law.

Treasurer to keep funds separated
3. The city treasurer shall keep the school fund (both that apportioned by the State and that apportioned by the city) in separate accounts; and the money shall be disbursed only on orders from the city school board.

Salary of superintendent
4. The city superintendent of schools appointed by the State board of education shall be allowed by the city for his services the sum of six hundred dollars per annum, payable quarterly, from any funds of the city which may be in the hands of the

treasurer subject to the order of the school board of trustees.

5. The official care and authority of the school board shall cover all the territory included in the corporate limits of the city. A majority of its members shall constitute a quorum. It may appoint a clerk, who need not be a member of the board. It may add to the pay of the clerk from any funds at its disposal other than those of the State, and may make by-laws and regulations for its own government and for the management of its official business, provided they do not conflict with the provisions of any act of Assembly. The school board of trustees shall have power, and it shall be its duty, to establish and maintain a general system of public free schools, in accordance with the requirements of the constitution and the general educational policy of the commonwealth; and it is empowered especially to make and carry out regulations for the management of public free school property and funds in the city; the location, renting, enlarging, repairing, erection and furnishing of school houses, and the proper care of the same; the attendance of pupils upon the schools; the providing of indigent children with text books; the direction of studies; the methods of teaching and government employed in the schools; the employment, remuneration and dismissal of teachers, and the length of the school term. It shall also have power to establish high and normal schools, as well as those of lower grades.

Limit of authority and care of school board

Powers and duties

6. No pupil shall be admitted into the public schools of this city unless such pupil has been vaccinated.

Pupils not admitted unless vaccinated

7. Pupils shall be admitted into the public schools free of charge, and shall be supplied by their parents or guardians with the text books of the schools; and in the event of their being unable from any cause to be thus supplied, they shall be furnished with such books as are necessary at public cost, by order of any trustee of the school in which they are pupils.

Pupils to be admitted free and books furnished in certain cases

8. In each district of the city there shall be one colored public school, which shall be under the same superintendent and trustees, and be subject to the same laws and ordinances provided for the white public schools.

Colored schools

CHAPTER XXIX.

City Small Scrip.

Concerning city small scrip issued prior to 1865.

1. Be it ordained that so much of an ordinance, passed September 7th, 1865, as authorized the funding of city small note scrip, then outstanding at the rate of seventy-five cents on the dollar, be and the same is hereby repealed.

Repealing ordinance authorizing issue of small scrip

Passed C. C. January 9th, 1877.
Passed S. C. January 9th, 1877.

CHAPTER XXX.

Sparrows and Other Birds.

1. It shall not be lawful for any person within the limits of the city to kill, maim or otherwise injure any sparrow or other

Unlawful to
kill birds in
city

bird found going at large either within the city limits or cemeteries, and any person violating this ordinance shall pay a fine of five dollars for each sparrow or other bird so killed, maimed or injured as aforesaid.

CHAPTER XXXI.

Strays.

Horses, &c.,
going at large
not allowed on
streets, &c.,
or unenclosed
lots, &c ;
penalty

1. If any horses mules. cattle, sheep or goats shall be found going at large on any street, lane, court, or any unenclosed lot or ground within the limits of the city, the owner or manager of such animal, when so found, shall forfeit not less than three nor more than twenty dollars, one-half of said fine shall go to the informer and the other half to the city, to be recovered by warrant before the mayor or any justice of the peace.

Horses, &c.,
going at large
not allowed on
enclosed
grounds;
penalty

2. If any horses, mules, cattle, sheep or goats. so running at large, shall enter into any grounds enclosed by a lawful fence, the owner or manager of any such animal or animals shall be liable for every such entry to a fine of not less than five nor more than twenty dollars, to be recovered by warrant before the mayor or any justice of the peace.

Duty of con-
stables and
policemen to
take up horses
&c., going at
large; upon
what terms
same may be
returned to
owners

3. It shall be the duty of the constables and policemen, and it shall be lawful for any other person, to take up and convey to the alms-house, or any livery stable, any horses, mules, cattle, sheep or goats found going at large on any street, lane, court or unenclosed lot of ground within the limits of the city, and deliver the same to the keepers as aforesaid, who shall immediately, by notice posted at the foot of the market and in one of the newspapers of the city, advertise the said horses, mules, cattle, sheep or goats. describing them as well as he can, and if within ten days the owner shall pay the said fine, the charges of taking up (which shall be fifty cents), and twenty-five cents per day for each day the said animal or animals shall be at the said alms-house or livery stable, then the said animal or animals shall be restored to the said owner; otherwise the said keeper shall sell the said animal or animals at public auction, at the foot of the market, and after paying the charges, and one-half of the said fine to the informer or taker-up, he shall pay over the balance of the sales to the treasurer, who, after retaining the other half of the said fine for the use of the city, shall hold the remainder subject to the order of the owner of such animal or animals.

CHAPTER XXXII.

Sale of Real Estate for Delinquent Taxes.

Real estate
delinquent
two years to
be sold ; sale
September 1,
annually

1. The collector of city taxes and levies shall annually on the first day of September. sell all real estate in the city delinquent for non payment of taxes or assessments which remain due and unpaid for two years prior to the first day of July in each year, proceeding in the manner required by law, and

especially observing the provisions of the city charter, section 45 to section 54 inclusive.

2. The collector shall annually on the first day of July, give public notice by advertisement in two daily newspapers published in the city of Norfolk, that the bills for taxes or assessments upon real estate delinquent for the non-payment thereof, have been placed in his hands for final settlement, naming the year or years for which such taxes or assessments are due; and that if said bills, be not paid on or before the first day of August next ensuing. he will proceed to advertise the said property for sale at public auction. *Collector to give public notice in July before advertising property for sale*

Treasurer to pay State taxes due July 31 on delinquent lands

3. The collector shall annually on the thirty-first day of July, deliver to the city treasurer a list of the real estate delinquent for non-payment of taxes or assessments, to be sold, and thereupon the city treasurer shall pay all the taxes due to the State of Virginia on said real estate, and deliver to the collector an account thereof, charging the same on his books to such delinquent real estate. From the proceeds of the sales made under this chapter the collector shall, in addition to the city taxes, interest and ten per centum for charges, collect the amount of said State taxes so paid and pay over the same to the city treasurer. *State taxes to be refunded to city*

Collector to advertise in August the sale of delinquent lands

4. The collector shall annually on the first day of August, and once a week for three weeks thereafter, advertise in all the newspapers published in the city the real estate delinquent for non-payment of taxes and assessments, for sale, at public auction, for cash, from the steps of the city hall, on the first day of September, describing the said real estate as required by law, and make sale of the same as provided in section 1, for the amount of said taxes or assessments, interest and State taxes, together with ten per centum for charges; and also the expenses incurred in advertising and selling the said property.

CHAPTER XXXIII.

Streets, Sewers and Drains.

1. There shall be a board of street, sewer and drain commissioners, to consist of three electors, to be chosen by the councils, who shall hold their office for two years, from July 1, 1884, and until their successors are appointed and qualified. *Board how and when appointed*

2. The councils shall designate one of said board as chairman, one as secretary, and one as treasurer; each of whom, before entering upon the discharge of the duties of his office, shall give bond with sureties to be approved by the councils, in the penalty of $10,000. *Organization; oath; bond*

3. The board shall manage the affairs relating to the streets, sewers, drains and public wharves of the city, in such manner as may be provided by the ordinances, or resolutions of the councils; and shall be entitled to receive compensation for *General powers and compensation*

their services as follows: The chairman shall receive $500; the treasurer $500 and the secretary who shall also act as bookkeeper of the board, shall receive $1,000 per annum.

Board to keep record and report to councils

4. The board shall keep a record of their proceedings and books showing the receipts and disbursements of each department under their supervision, and make detailed reports thereof to the councils annually, or oftener if required.

Board to submit annual estimates to councils

5. The board shall annually in January, submit to the councils an estimate in detail of the amounts necessary to be expended in cleaning, repairing and paving the streets and public highways, and also for keeping in repair the docks and wharves belonging to the city, and for the maintenance and preservation of the sewers and drains, together with all other matters pertaining to their department.

Monies to be expended under direction of board

All monies appropriated by the councils for the improvement, construction, maintenance and repairs of streets, sewers, drains, culverts and bridges, in or upon any of the streets or highways, or upon the public wharves and docks, shall be expended under the direction of said board.

Members not to be interested in contracts

6. Members of said board or its agents are prohibited from being interested in any way in contracts which may be made, and any bargain, contract or agreement made in violation of this section shall be void as to the city.

Councils to appoint committees to examine books of board

7. The councils shall appoint a committee to be known as the street sewer and drain committee, whose duty it shall be to examine the books, papers. accounts, contracts, and all other matters pertaining to said board and shall report to the councils. They shall specially report any irregularities in said office, or violation of duties, by any of said board.

Duty of street inspector

8. The street inspector shall report to said board of street, sewer and drain commissioners and shall perform such duties as they may require of him in accordance with existing ordinances governing his office, and under direction of said board, superintend the streets of the city, ascertain all nuisances and cause their abatement. He shall attend the meetings of the board of health as representative of this board, and receive such instructions as the board of health may give in relation to nuisances.

Street cleaning

9 It shall be the duty of the inspector to superintend the cleaning of streets under the direction of the board, and he shall report to the same for prosecution all persons offending against the provisions of these ordinances, and particularly of persons guilty of encroachments on the streets and public drains, and on the channels of the creeks within the city, provided the same is not in conflict with the authority vested in the harbor commissioners in respect to the channels of said creeks.

Encroachments on streets

Board to maintain carts, tools, &c

10. The board shall maintain and keep in repair all carts. tools, harness and other implements, purchasing whatever may be needed to efficiently perform the work on the streets. They shall carefully provide for all mules and horses. and shall dispose of any such as may be disabled. replacing same by purchase with any funds appropriated by the councils for such purpose.

11. The said board is empowered to take all legal steps *Duties of board in opening streets* when ordered to do so by the councils, in accordance with existing laws, in regard to the opening of streets and widening, extending, straightening or closing up in whole or in part any of the streets, lanes, alleys, or squares of the city.

12. Whenever proceedings shall be taken by the councils *Condemnation of lands* looking to the condemnation of lands, and the said commissioners shall therein be directed to confer with the owners of the lands sought to be acquired in relation to their purchase, it shall be the duty of the said commissioners to report the results of the conference in that behalf to the councils, before making application to the courts for the appointment of ad quod damnum commissioners.

13. The said board, its officers, agents and servants, acting *Board may enter upon lands* by authority of said board, shall have power to enter upon any land or property for the purpose of examining the same, surveying and laying out such as may be required for the opening, widening, extending, straightening or closing up in whole or in part any street. lane, alley or square, or unimproved land which may be required for above purposes.

14. No person shall break or dig up any part of any street *No street to be broken or sewer connection to be made without permit from board* or lane without the written permission of the board of street, sewer and drain commissioners, and all persons making connections either with any public or private sewer or culvert, shall first obtain permission from the board to enter the street or lane at such point and in such manner as they may direct; and shall forthwith cover the sewer or drain with earth, thoroughly consolidating the same as it was before being broken, and in ten days thereafter shall have such pavement or curbstone as was injured or removed so repaired or restored as to be in as good order as it was before. And any person failing to comply herewith shall pay a fine of not less than five nor more than twenty dollars.

15. The board of water commissioners, the city gaslight *Permits required for breaking ground in streets for water, gas, railroads, etc* company, the Norfolk city railroad company and all other corporations shall in like manner apply to the board of street, sewer and drain commissioners for written permission before breaking or digging up any portion of any street. square, lane or highway and the board shall have power to direct how and in what manner the said openings in the highway shall be made.

After said streets are torn up, and upon notification from the *Regulations and directions concerning breaking up streets and re-laying same* inspector of streets, the party or parties who caused said streets to be torn up, shall proceed at once to relay them and shall replace them in the same condition as they were before said streets were torn up.

It shall be the duty of the inspector of streets to see that all the streets torn up are properly relaid ; he shall notify all parties who caused the streets to be torn up the provisions of this ordinance. and he shall keep on file in the office of the board of street, sewer and drain commissioners a copy of the notice sent.

It shall be the duty of the street inspector as soon as a street

Duties of
inspector and
of Board has been torn up to at once notify the party or parties that they must relay the same, (but allowing sufficient time for the earth to settle), and if said party or parties shall fail to do so in four days he or they shall be subject to a fine of twenty dollars per day until the street is relaid.

Should said street settle after it has been relaid, and become uneven, it shall be the duty of the party or parties causing the tearing up of the street, to have said street taken up and relay the same and continue to do so until the street is firm and will not settle.

If after a street has been relaid the inspector of streets finds that the same has not been properly laid, and is uneven and in holes, he shall notify the party or parties who caused the laying of the same that they must take the same up and have it properly laid, and if said party or parties fail to do so in four days he or they shall pay a fine of five dollars per day until said street is properly laid.

It shall be the duty of the board of street, sewer and drain commissioners upon notification by the inspector of streets, that the party or parties who tore up the streets have failed or refused to cause them to be properly relaid (although notified and requested so to do as aforesaid) to cause the street or streets to be properly relaid in a substantial manner, and charge the cost of the work done to the party or parties causing the said streets to be torn up, and if payment of same is refused to enter suit in the name of the city against them for the cost of said pavement. It shall also be their duty to superintend the inspector of streets and see that he carries out the provisions of this ordinance, and report every violation of the same to the councils.

Pavements
injured from
defective
sewers 16. Whenever the pavement in any street or lane shall become injured by reason of any defective private sewer or drain, it shall be the duty of the person owning the same, to have the pavement properly repaired; and upon neglect thereof for five days, the engineer shall cause the repairs to be made at the expense of the said owner, to be collected by warrant before the mayor.

Penalty for
making defec-
tive sewer
under high-
way 17. Any person who shall make or cause to be made any defective private sewer or drain, where the same passes under a public highway, shall be fined not less than five nor more than twenty dollars; and the engineer shall cause the said defective sewer or drain to be shut up.

No street to be
improved
unless accept-
ed by councils
and laid out
by engineer 18. It shall be unlawful to grade, pave, light, clean, or otherwise improve at the expense of the city, any street dedicated to the public by any owners of private property, unless the same shall have been accepted by the councils, and, under their direction, laid out by the engineer as a public street.

Taking earth
away from
streets 19. If any person shall take up or carry away earth from any street he shall pay for every such offense the sum of five dollars.

Planting trees
in street 20. It shall not be lawful for any person to plant trees in any street which is less than forty feet wide, under the penalty of ten dollars for each offense; and all trees which may be

planted in any street of the width of forty feet and upwards shall be planted on the sidewalk, next to the curbstone, under the penalty of five dollars for each offense; and no person shall **Injuring trees** cut down or in any way injure any tree standing in any street under the penalty of five dollars for each tree so cut down and injured. The inspector is hereby authorized to cause any trees **Duty of inspector** to be cut down where the same may be kept standing in violation of this ordinance, and to have the sidewalks that may be injured by the removal of said tree repaired at the expense of the proprietor of the lot of land fronting thereon.

21. No piazza, porch, step, fence, enclosure or other projec- **See charter section 23** tion attached to any house or lot, shall be extended beyond the adjoining line of the side-walk.. Any person offending herein **Porches, steps &c., encroaching on streets** shall pay a fine of five dollars per day for so long a time as the same shall remain after notice from the inspector to remove said obstruction; provided that balconies may be put to any house, so as to be not less than ten feet from the ground, nor more than three feet in width, and supported otherwise than by posts and pillars from below.

Any property owner, builder or contractor, or other per- **Penalty for encroachments by owners and builders** son who shall encroach upon the line of the street in any manner, by building or otherwise, shall be liable to a fine of five dollars for every day such encroachment shall remain, after notice from the inspector to have it removed; and if the same be not taken down or removed within five days after such notice, the inspector is hereby directed to have the same removed at the expense of the person offending, and if not paid on demand, to warrant for the same. No post shall be **Posts** put up in any of the streets, without permission of the councils, under the penalty of five dollars for each offense.

22. The inspector shall order any sign or post, or any other **Duty of inspector concerning encroachments by porches, posts, etc** thing which may encumber or obstruct the street, and any cellar light, bay window or other window, shed, porch, portico, cellar door, platform or step, placed in any street contrary to this chapter, to be taken down, altered or removed; and if the person whose duty it is to obey such order shall fail to do so within five days after notice of the order, he shall pay a fine of five dollars, and a further fine of five dollars for every day he shall so fail.

23. All owners of lots on east Main street shall have permis- **Balconies on east Main Street** sion, if they elect, to place balconies in front of their houses on the said street; provided that the balconies shall be eight feet in height from the pavement and shall not project from the house more than three feet; and provided further that all persons availing themselves of this permission shall remove said balconies when required so to do by the councils, after thirty days notice.

24. No cellar openings shall be made in any street without **Cellar openings** permission of the councils, and all cellar lights shall be protected by proper grating, and no cellar light in any street shall extend from any house more than one-fifteenth part of the width of the street, nor in any case more than five feet, and no cellar door shall extend more than one-twelfth part of the

width of any street, nor in any case more than five feet.

Application for cellar openings
Every application for permission to construct a cellar opening shall state the dimensions thereof, and before commencing to construct the same the owner of the premises, or his agent, shall pay to the collector of city taxes for the use of the city fifteen cents per square foot and take his receipt for the same.

Penalty
If any person shall construct a cellar opening of greater dimensions than those allowed by the permit of councils, or otherwise violate any of the provisions of this section he shall pay a fine of not less than five nor more than twenty dollars.

Awnings.

How awnings may be placed
25. It shall be lawful to place awnings over the side-walks of any of the streets of the city, and to erect posts and pillars to support the same, under the regulations and directions contained in this ordinance, provided that no awning post shall be placed so as to obstruct the crossing on the street. All awnings shall be at least eight feet above the side-walk, and the posts or pillars to support the same shall be firmly planted on the line of the side-walk, inside of the curbstone, and shall be sufficiently high to allow at least eight feet between the lowest rail and the pavement or ground. If such posts or pillars be of wood, then the same shall not be more than five inches in diameter. All awnings shall be taken in or removed from the street every night by or before eight o'clock.

Permanent frames across sidewalks prohibited
It shall not be lawful for any person to place any slats or permanent frame-work across any side-walk for any purpose whatever, and all slats or permanent frame-work now existing across any of the side-walks shall be deemed obstructions, and the inspector of streets shall have the same removed.

Any person who shall violate any of the provisions of this section shall pay a fine of not less than five nor more than twenty dollars.

Vaults, Pits, &c.

Lights to be placed before vaults or pits at night
26. Every owner or occupant of any lot before which any vault, pit or well shall be made within the city, or the person who shall have the charge of the same, shall, during the whole of every night while such vault, pit or well shall be uncovered, cause a light to be kept at some convenient spot, so as to cast its light upon such vault, pit or well, under the penalty of ten dollars for every night on which such light shall be neglected to be placed there. And all vaults which shall be built shall be completed within three weeks after they are commenced, under the penalty of five dollars for every day thereafter during which the ground shall remain unclosed.

Snow.

Snow to be cleaned off of sidewalks
It shall be the duty of each and every person, incorporated society or public institution using or occupying in any manner, or for any purpose whatsoever, any house, store, shop, stable or tenement of any kind, and of persons having charge of churches and public buildings of any description, and of owners of unoccupied houses and unimproved lots situate on

any paved street, lane or alley in the city, within three hours after the fall of any snow (except where the snow shall have ceased to fall between the hours of 3 in the afternoon and 7 o'clock in the morning, in which case it shall be removed before 11 o'clock in the morning) to remove and clear away, or cause to be removed and cleared away, the same from the foot pavements fronting the respective houses, stores, shops, stables, churches, buildings or lots so used, occupied or owned by them or under their charge, in such manner as not to obstruct the passage of the water in the gutters, under a penalty of two dollars for any neglect besides the expense of cleaning the same away under the direction of the inspector of streets.

It shall be the duty of the inspector of streets to cause the snow and ice to be removed by the persons employed for cleaning the streets (and by additional labor when the emergency shall require it) from the footways and from the flagstones placed at the intersections of the streets, as also to remove the ice and other obstructions to the free passage of the water at the intersections of the several streets of the city, and to cause the snow and ice to be removed from the foot pavements fronting the houses, stores, stables, churches, public buildings, lots or tenements of such persons as shall neglect or refuse to remove the same at the expense of the city in the first instance to be afterwards recovered from the person or persons so neglecting or refusing. *Duty of inspector as to snow and ice*

It shall also be the duty of the said inspector of streets at the cost of the city to clear away the snow from the sidewalks and crossings in front of the public schools of the city.

It shall not be lawful for laborers who may be employed to remove and clear away snow and ice from the streets, alleys, and lanes of the city as hereinbefore provided to demand a greater price for such service than twenty-five cents per hour whilst actually employed therein. *Pay allowed to laborers cleaning off snow*

Locomotive Engines.

28. Whenever a locomotive engine, with or without a train attached, is used within the limits of the city of Norfolk, a man shall be required to ride on the front of said locomotive engine, or on the tender or car in advance of the train, as the case may be. And no locomotive engine, while being so used, shall be propelled at a greater rate of speed than four miles an hour, and all such engines shall be provided with a spark protector or other apparatus, to prevent the danger of fire from their passing through the streets. *Locomotive engines on streets how run; spark protectors*

The person or persons having charge of such locomotive engine shall ring, or cause a bell to be rung, while approaching and passing through the city. *Bell to be rung*

For a violation of any provision of this ordinance, the person or company so violating shall forfeit and pay a fine of not less than ten nor more than twenty dollars. *Penalty*

Garbage and Dirt.

29. The city shall be divided into two districts, by a line beginning at the southwest corner of Campbell's wharf; run- *Garbage districts defined*

ning thence along said wharf and the western side of Market Square to the northwest corner of said square; thence across Main street to Bank street; and along the eastern side of Bank street, and pursuing a direct course until it meets the northern limits of the city. All that part of the city which extends to the east of the line thus designated shall be called the eastern district, and all that which lies to the west of said line shall be called the western district.

Regulations as to removal of garbage

The owner or occupant of every house and lot in the eastern district shall, before the hour of nine o'clock A. M. on Monday, Wednesday and Friday of each week, from the first day of April to the first day of October of each year, and before the hour of ten o'clock A. M. on the said days from the first day of October to the first day of April of each year, cause all the offal and garbage on his premises to be put in tight barrels or boxes, and placed on the sidewalk in front of his lot; and the owner or occupant of every house or lot in the western district shall, on Tuesday, Thursday and Saturday of each week, before the said hours in the respective periods aforesaid, cause all the offal or garbage on his premises to be put in tight barrels or boxes, and placed on the sidewalk in front of his lot. All dry rubbish removed from any premises shall be deposited in one heap in the center of the street, in front of said premises, in each district, on the days and before the hours aforesaid, in the said periods of the year. For any neglect to comply herewith, the owner or occupant of any lot shall pay a fine of five dollars for each offense.

Penalty

Any person who shall cast any rubbish in the street, except as provided in this section shall pay a fine of one dollar.

Duty of inspector

30. The inspector or any person authorized by the councils, shall remove from the streets before sunset, on the days when placed there, all the offal and rubbish so collected, and at such other times as the board of health may direct; and shall also, daily, after market hours, remove the dirt and rubbish from the market and square around it. And for any violation of this section he shall pay a fine of twenty dollars.

Garbage not to be removed by person not authorized by law

No person shall carry away any manure, offal or rubbish from the streets unless authorized by the inspector, or the councils, and any one so offending shall pay a fine of two dollars.

Builders' rubbish how and when to be removed

31. Every person who may be building or repairing any house shall cause all the rubbish occasioned thereby, and all the earth, stone, sand or clay which may be cast into the street, to be removed before sunset the next day, after having received notice from the inspector to remove the same; and if any person fail to comply with this provision, he shall pay a fine of one dollar.

Sewerage.

Certain buildings to be connected with Waring system of sewerage

32. The owner of every building which shall hereafter be erected, shall before the same is occupied as a residence, or place of business, cause the said building or some portion of

the premises whereon it may be situated to be connected with the public sewer, whenever the same can be done along the line of the Waring system of sewerage and drainage, under the regulations prescribed by the board of street, sewer and drain commissioners. Any person violating the provisions of **Penalty** this section shall pay a fine of not less than five nor more than twenty dollars.

33. It shall not be lawful hereafter to erect any privy or **No privy al-** water closet upon any lot of land or in any building situated **lowed to be** on or along the line of the Waring system of sewerage and **line of Waring** drainage, unless the said privy or water closet shall be connect- **system unless** ed with the said sewerage in the manner prescribed by the **therewith** regulations of the board of street, sewer and drain commissioners. Any person violating the provisions of this section **Penalty** shall pay a fine of not less than five nor more than twenty dollars.

34. It shall not be lawful for any person to connect any privy **Freemason** or water closet with the terra cotta drain pipe leading from **street drain** Freemason street, between Brewer and Tripoli streets, to the **for connection** City Hall avenue, nor cause or permit any excrementitious mat- **with privies** ter to flow therein. Any person violating this section shall **Penalty** pay a fine of not less than five nor more than twenty dollars.

Side-walks.

35. The owner or occupant of any house or lot fronting on **Sidewalks** any street shall at his own expense or at the charge of his land- **how repaired** lord, keep in good repair with good paving brick or stone slabs, so much of the side-walk as shall front the building and lot of ground belonging to him or in his possession. The inspec- **Duty of** tor of streets shall direct such repairs to be made whenever **inspector** necessary, and if any such owner or occupant shall fail to make such repairs after having received ten days' notice so to do. the person so failing shall pay a fine of five dollars for **Penalty** each day, and after the expiration of ten days if the repairs shall not have been made by the owner or occupant it shall be the duty of the inspector to cause the repairs to be made on account of such owner or occupant and forthwith collect from the person liable the cost of such repairs and pay the amount to the person who did the work, and the inspector of streets is empowered to collect the said amount by distraint or by war- rant in the name of the city.

36. It shall not be lawful for any person to drive or back **Driving hor-** any horse or cart or wheel carriage on the foot-path or side- **ses or vehicles** walk of any street nor across any of the ditches or vacant lots **or obstructing** except where bridges are provided for that purpose. under the **same** penalty of five dollars for every such offense; nor shall any person drive or ride any horse, or wheel any handbarrow, or saw any wood, or place any wood, coal or other thing on any sidewalk, under the penalty of two dollars for every offense.

37. No person shall place any goods, wares or merchandise **Merchandise** on the sidewalk at a greater distance than three feet in front **placed on** of his house or store, unless such person be receiving or de- **sidewalks**

How long may remain

livering the same, and in no case shall such goods be allowed to remain on the side-walk longer than one hour. Any person violating this section shall pay a fine of five dollars.

Paving.

Directions as to paving streets

38. All streets within the corporation of twenty feet in width and upwards, which shall hereafter be paved, shall be paved agreeably to the following regulations—to wit: The foot-path, or side-walk, as before directed, on each side of such street, shall be paved with brown or grey square or oblong flat stones or hard brick, and secured with square and gutter stones, in conformity with the provisions of this ordinance; the middle or remaining part of every such street shall be a cart-way or passage for carriages, and shall have a gutter on each side, and next adjoining the foot-path or walk, and shall be paved with stones and arched as follows, that is to say: For every eighteen inches such cart-way shall measure from the gutter to the middle of the street, the arch or rounding of such street shall be raised one inch, to commence at the respective gutters; provided always, that if any street so to be paved shall not exactly range, the gutter or outside of the foot-path or side-walk shall be laid out, and made as nearly on a straight line as the street will admit, and that the ascent and descent of every street shall be regulated by the engineer. All streets or lanes of the width of twenty feet or less, hereafter to be paved, may be paved without curbstones if the councils shall deem it advisable.

Curbing and guttering

39. All curbstones shall be at least two feet six inches in length, four inches thick, and fourteen inches wide, and laid in the following manner—to wit: Six inches of the stone shall be laid below the gutter, and eight inches above, unless otherwise directed by the board of street, sewer and drain commissioners, and the top cut to the proper level; the ends shall be squared, so as to form close and even joints, and the front hewn, so as to present a fair surface, and the side-walks shall be raised from the curbstone in proportion of five inches in ten feet, and each gutter stone shall be at least eighteen inches in length, ten inches in width and three inches thick, with even surface, and squared so as to form close joints; and if any person shall lay any side-walk or foot-path in any other manner, or of stones of less size, or with any other material, such person shall pay a fine of ten dollars for each offense, and the further fine of one dollar for each day the same shall remain not conformable to the provisions of this ordinance, after notice from the inspector to alter the same.

Dimensions of sidewalks

40. In all streets forty feet wide and upwards, which shall be paved, the side-walks between the lines of the streets and gutters shall be of the following width: That is to say, ten feet in all streets forty feet wide; twelve feet in all streets fifty feet wide; fourteen feet in all streets sixty feet wide; and in all streets between forty and sixty feet, and not of any of the widths herein above mentioned, the side-walks shall be in proportion to the width of those above specified.

41. Private cartways crossing the side-walks shall be paved at the expense of the person requiring the same with square or oblong flat stones, hewn and laid close together, in such manner as the board of street, sewer and drain commissioners may direct. *Private cart ways*

Public Drains.

42. Any person who shall fill up or in any manner injure or obstruct any of the public drains or sewers in any part of the city shall pay a fine of not less than five dollars nor more than twenty dollars. *Filling up or obstructing public drains or sewers*

Inspector of Plumbing.

43. The board of street, sewer and drain commissioners may appoint a competent person as inspector of plumbing, who shall obey the orders of the board and be specially charged with the duty of enforcing the rules and regulations of the board concerning the public sewers and the connections made therewith. The inspector of plumbing shall receive a salary at the rate of one thousand dollars per annum until the first day of January, 1886, and after that period such compensation as the councils may determine. He shall be subject to removal by the board or the councils at any time. *Inspector of plumbing to be appointed by board* *Salary*

Local Assessments.

44. Whenever any street shall be laid out or a street graded or paved or otherwise improved and the councils shall determine and order that a local assessment shall be levied upon the owners of real estate benefited thereby in the manner provided by section 25 of the city charter, such assessment shall be made as follows—viz: One-half of the cost of such improvement shall be paid by the owners of real estate so benefited—that is to say: One-fourth the cost thereof shall be paid by the owners of the real estate abutting on said street on each side thereof, to be charged on the basis of frontage. And this proportion shall be the rule in making local assessments unless the councils shall especially otherwise determine in their order directing any improvement to be made. Whenever there is a dispute between property owners as to the number of feet owned on any street, the assessment shall be equally divided between them. *How local assessments made for cost of paving, &c.* *What proportion paid by owners of lots*

45. The board of street, sewer and drain commissioners shall cause bills of assessment to be made out in accordance with the preceding section from the plans of the city engineer, and deliver the same to the city treasurer. It shall be the duty of the treasurer forthwith to record the same in a book kept in his office for that purpose, and place the said bills in the hands of the city collector for collection. And the said bills of assessment shall be a charge against the property specified therein as other taxes and levies are made by law, and shall be collected in the manner prescribed by law for the collection of taxes upon real estate. *Duty of board of S. S. and D. in making out bills for local assessments* *Duty of city collector*

Changes made in the names of Streets since 1865.

Catharine to *Bank.*

Ordinances of Jan. 30, 1871 *Boush,* between Wood and Mosely to *Queen.*

Boush, between Princess Anne road and Calvert to *Henry.*

Union, between Church and Hawk to *Smith.*

William, between Granby and Chamberlaine's wharf to *Randolph.*

Washington, between Fayette and Matthews to *Jackson.*

Washington, between Newton and Chapel to *Pulaski.*

Wide Water changed to *Water.*

Little Water	"	*Elizabeth.*
Gray	"	*Atlantic.*
Amelia	"	*Boush.*
Princess	"	*Duke.*
Second Cross	"	*Reilly.*
Third Cross	"	*Walke.*
First North	"	*Willoughby.*
Second North	"	*Suffolk.*
Third North	"	*Kent.*
Marsh	"	*Cove.*
Wolf	"	*Washington.*

The foregoing passed select and common councils January 30th, 1871.

AN ORDINANCE

Changing the name of Metcalf's Lane to Chesapeake Street.

Metcalf's lane to Chesapeake street Sec. 1. Be it ordained, by the common and select councils of the city of Norfolk, that Metcalf's Lane, which is twelve feet wide, and runs from Main to Cove street, be, and the same is hereby changed to Chesapeake street, and the treasurer is directed to give ten days' notice of the fact in the official paper of the city.

2. This ordinance shall be in force from and after its passage.

Passed S. C., June 7th, 1879.

Passed C. C., June 24th, 1879.

A portion of Washington changed to Wolf.

Wolf street Be it ordained, that the last paragraph of the ordinance entitled an ordinance changing the name of certain streets, passed in January, 1871, be amended so as to provide that the name of the section of the street running from Granby street east, to Cumberland street, shall be changed from Washington to Wolf its original name by which it shall hereafter be known.

July 18th, 1880.

AN ORDINANCE

To change the name of the extension of Reilly street so that the same shall be known as Clay street.

Reilly to Clay Sec. 1. Be it ordained by the common and select councils that all that portion of the extension of Reilly street, leading from Bute street extended to Queen street, shall be hereafter called and known by the name of Clay street, and shall be so designated upon the map of the city.

2. That the city treasurer shall cause this ordinance to be published for thirty days in the official newspapers.

3. This ordinance shall take effect from its passage.

March 19th, 1884.

AN ORDINANCE

Designating the Avenue in front of the City Hall by the name of City Hall Avenue.

Sec. 1. Be it ordained, by the select and common councils City Hall that the Avenue now being opened and graded running from Avenue Bank to Granby street, be and the same is hereby named and designated City Hall Avenue.

2. This ordinance shall be in force from and after its passage.

Passed the select council October 1st, 1884.

Passed the common council January 6th, 1885.

AN ORDINANCE

Changing the name of Hawk street to that of St. Paul street.

Sec. 1. Be it ordained, by the select and common councils Hawk to that the street which is now known as Hawk street, shall be St. Paul known hereafter under the name of Saint Paul street.

2. That this ordinance shall be in force from and after its passage.

Passed August 11th, 1885.

Ends of Streets.

The following resolution was adopted by the select council, July 12th, 1881, and was concurred in by the common council August 2d, 1881.

Whereas, frequent applications have been made to this and former councils, for the use and occupation of the ends and other portions of the public streets of the city, for railroad and other purposes, and whereas, in view of the common public right in the streets thereof, no permit for the use and occupancy of the same can be granted individuals or others for such purposes, inconsistent with the rights of the public therein, as defined by various decisions of the courts of this and other states, therefore

Resolved, that all such permits heretofore or hereafter granted, being beyond the power of the councils, and in res- Defining the traint of the free use of the streets by our people, shall be which the construed as conferring on the benificiaries thereof, such use ends of the or occupation only as does not interfere with the free and used. unobstructed access to and enjoyment thereof, at all times by the public; and when any street named in such permit ends on the river or the tributaries thereof, the like free access to and use of the said end shall be regarded as embraced in the rights of the public.

Closing of Parker Street. Lease of same and Kelly Street.

September 4th, 1883.   Record of Common Council, page 135.

The common council concurred in the action of the select council of July 10th, 1883, in the passage of the following resolution:

Whereas, the consent of the owners of the property on both sides of Parker street, between Water and Main street, has been obtained to the closing of said street, between Water and Main streets; and whereas the board of street, sewer and drain commissioners have recommended the closing of the said street, as aforesaid; and whereas in the judgment of this body no damage would result to any individual or to the public by the closing of said street as aforesaid, therefore be it

Resolved, that Parker street, between Water and Main streets, be and the same is hereby closed.

Also, the following resolution:

Resolved, that a lease be made by the city to the Baltimore Steam Packet Company, for ninety-nine years, renewable forever, of the piece of land between Water and Main streets, heretofore known as a part of Parker street (but closed by the city as such) of the western end of Kelly street, and of the dock between the same and the Port Warden's line, for the sum of $20,000, cash, and the yearly rent of $5; and upon the further terms embodied in the draft of a lease now before the councils, which lease is hereby approved.

Regulations governing Plumbing, House Drainage and the Ventilation of House Sewers.

(Established by the Board of S., S. and D. Commissioners.)

Sec. A. It shall be the duty of every person doing business as a plumber, or engaged in conducting plumbing or house drainage, in the city of Norfolk, to register his name in a book to be provided for that purpose, at the office of the board of of street, sewer and drain commissioners, giving full name, residence, and place of business, and in case of removal from one place to another in said city, to make corresponding change in said register accordingly; and it shall be the further duty of every such person to give good and sufficient bond, in the sum of three hundred dollars (300) dollars, to be approved by the board of street, sewer snd drain commissioners, conditioned upon the observance of these regulations.

[margin note: Plumbers to be bonded, registered and display a sign]

It shall be the duty of every such person to display at his place of business, in a conspicuous place, a sign with full registered name and words '*Registered Plumber,*' in letters not less than three inches in size.

Sec. B. Before any portion of the drainage system of any building shall be laid or constructed, there shall be filed by the owner, with the city engineer, for the inspector of plumbing, a plan thereof showing the said drainage system entire from its connection with the curb end of the house drain to its terminus in the house, together with the location of all traps, ventilating pipes, &c. The name of the plumber who

[margin note: Plan of plumbing work to be filed at office of city engineer.]

is to perform the work shall be given on said plan, which must be approved by the inspector of plumbing before any portion of the work shall be executed. A permit shall not be given for the connection with the sewer until such plan shall have been presented and approved.

Sec. C. No plumber or any other person shall be allowed to uncover the public sewer or any of its branches for any pur- pose, or to make connections therewith, unless and except by consent of the board of street, sewer and drain commissioners, or their duly authorized agent or agents, whose duty it shall be to insure a full compliance with these regulations in relation to house connections; and no such connections shall be made except by skilled and competent mechanics, duly licensed to do such work by the board of street, sewer and drain commis- sioners. *No persons except skilled and licensed mechanics to make connec- tions with public sewers, &c.*

Sec. D. Each and every plumber engaged in plumbing a building, shall at all times, before any portion of his work is covered up or hidden from sight, and before making connec- tion with fixtures, fill the pipes to be inspected with water, and send a written notice to the inspector of plumbing to the office, asking an official inspection of his work, and upon the final completion of his work, shall ask for a final inspection thereof in accordance with the rules of the board. *Written re- quest to be made for in- spection be- fore work is covered, and at completion*

Sec. E. It shall be the duty of the inspector of plumbing, under the direction of the city engineer, to sign and issue all notices and certificates, to keep a daily record of his work, including all notices and applications received, violations of these regulations, and all other matters pertaining thereto; to make daily, weekly and quarterly reports of his operations to the city engineer, and when not engaged in inspecting, to per- form any other duty the city engineer may assign him. *Duties of in- spector of plumbing* *Reports to be made*

Sec. F. He shall inspect all houses in course of erection, alteration or repair as often as may be necessary, and shall see that all plumbing, drainage, and sewerage work is done in ac- cordance with the provision of these regulations. *House to be inspected*

Sec. G. It shall be the duty of the inspector of plumbing, immediately upon notification by the plumber, to proceed to inspect and pass upon the work, and all inspections shall be made within twenty-four hours after such notification. *The inspector shall proceed within twenty- four hours after notifica- tion to inspect*

He shall promptly condemn and order the removal of any defective material, or any work done other than in accordance with these regulations, and the specifications to govern the connecting houses with the public sewers of the city; and upon a complete and satisfactory inspection of any work shall grant a certificate of approval. *Defective work and material to be condemned* *Certificate of approval*

Sec. H. He shall take and subscribe an oath or affirmation that he will faithfully perform the duties of his office, and shall, before entering upon his duties, execute a bond to the city of Norfolk in the sum of five hundred (500) dollars, with two sureties, to be approved by the board of street, sewer and drain commissioners, conditioned upon the faithful performance of the duties of his office, and for the benefit of all persons aggrieved by his acts or neglect. *Oath to be taken and bond entered into*

Applications to be signed by owners

Sec. I. Blank forms of application will be furnished to plumbers. All applications must be signed by the owner of the premises and his or her address written under his or her signature. Signing by agents will not be accepted if the owner resides in the city of Norfolk.

Fee for permit required

Sec. J. A fee of one dollar is required to be paid as permit fee for each house connected, the receipt of which must be endorsed upon application; the fee to be paid to the clerk of the street, sewer and drain commissioners.

General.

Sec. K. No plumber or any other person shall make connections from any house with the public sewer except in strict accordance with all of the foregoing regulations and the following specifications.

SPECIFICATIONS

To govern the Plumbing and connecting houses with the Public Sewers of the City of Norfolk, Va.

Every house to be separately connected

Sec. 1. Every house or building must be separately and individually connected with the nearest sewer.

Laying of pipes, grades, connections, &c.

2. The drain and soil pipe must be laid as direct as possible, and to a uniform grade, with a fall of not less than one foot in thirty-six, if possible, and all changes in direction must be made with curved pipes, and all connections with Y branches and one eighth bends. The drain pipe must be laid at a sufficient depth to protect it from breakage or freezing.

Terra cotta pipes may be laid outside a building.

3. The house drains, when not entering into or underlying a building, may be of salt glazed vitrified stoneware pipe, laid so as to have a uniform space between each spigot and socket end, the joints to be made with oakum gaskets well caulked

How joints are to be made

in, and finished with good strong fresh hydraulic cement mortar, composed of one part of cement and one of clean sharp sand; the joint to be out-wiped carefully and well pointed on the

Iron pipes must be laid inside and under buildings

outside. But where drains enter and underlie a building the pipe must be of cast iron, to extend to and form part of the soil pipe, and extend at least four (4) feet above the roof, or

Height above roof to carry pipes

top of the highest window, of undiminished size, and terminate with a wire basket.

Where iron pipe shall begin and how terra cotta pipes shall be laid

The iron drain pipe must extend at least five (5) feet outside of every building, and all terra cotta pipe inside of the building line of the street must be laid upon a foundation of hydraulic cement concrete, unless otherwise specially permitted by the city engineer.

Relieving arch to protect pipes from settling walls

4. When a pipe passes through or under the walls of a building there shall be a relieving arch turned over it to protect it from breakage by the settling of the wall.

Pipes to be coated with coal tar

5. The iron soil and drain pipe must be full four (4) inches in interior diameter at every point, to be coated inside and outside with coal tar, applied hot. The horizontal portions of all iron pipes used under ground shall in no case weigh less than—

Weight of iron pipe under ground

For four-inch pipe, 13 lbs. per lineal foot.

For three-inch pipe, 9½   "   "

For two-inch pipe, 5½   "   "

The joints are to be made with gaskets of picked oakum, *Joints, how made* and hot lead at one pouring, thoroughly caulked in so as to render them impermeable to gases.

Waste pipes or lateral drains from bath tubs, basins, or other *Waste pipes may be 2 inches in diameter* fixtures, with the exception of water-closets, may be of two (2) inch diameter pipe.

6. No trap or any manner of obstruction to the complete *Flow of air through drain not to be obstructed* and perfectly free flow of air throughout the entire course of the drain or soil pipe will be permitted. No brick, sheet metal *Brick, sheet metal and earthenware prohibited as ventilators* or earthenware flue shall be used as a sewer ventilator, nor shall any chimney flue be used for this purpose.

Pipes must be concentrated as much as possible, and where *Pipes to be concentrated and covered with wood work* placed within walls they should be covered with wood work, fastened with screws, so as to give ready access to the pipes for inspection and repairs.

7. All joints in waste pipes, except where screw joints are *Joints in waste pipes* used, must be made like those in the soil and drain pipes, with oakum gaskets and lead well caulked so as to render them gastight.

All connections of lead with iron pipes must be made with *Connections of lead with iron pipes* a brass sleeve or ferrule of the same size as the lead pipe; the sleeve to be put in the hub of the iron pipe and thoroughly caulked with lead, and the lead pipe to be attached to the sleeve or ferrule by a wiped lead joint. *Connections of lead with lead pipe*

All connections of lead pipes must be by wiped lead joints.

8. Every sink, basin, W. C. wash tray, bath, safe, urinal, and *Every fixture to be separately trapped* every tub or set of tubs, must be separately and effectively trapped; the traps to be of suitable and approved pattern, and to be placed as near the fixture as practicable.

All exit pipes, except in the case of W. C's, to be provided *Exit pipes to have strainers* with strong metallic strainers.

9. Every trap must be separately ventilated, and protected *Ventilation of traps and size of vent pipes* from syphonage by a special vent pipe not less than two (2) inches in diameter for W. C's, nor less than one and one-quarter (1¼) inches for other fixtures; but if exceeding fifteen (15) feet in length, this pipe shall not be less than one and one-half (1½) inches in diameter.

These vent or air pipes should extend four (4) feet above the *Vent pipes to extend above roof or inlet of highest fixture* roof, and terminate with a wire basket, but if they are branched into the soil pipe, it must be above the inlet pipe of the highest fixture.

They may be continuous by branching together these which *Vent pipes may be branched together* serve several traps, provided they are branched into a vent pipe not less than two (2) inches in interior diameter.

These vent or air pipes must always have a continuous slope *Vent pipes to have continuous slope* to avoid collecting water by condensation.

10. Every lead safe under a wash basin, bath, urinal, refrig- *Safes not to connect directly with soil pipe, &c.* erator, or W. C. must be drained by a special pipe not *directly* connected with any waste pipe, soil pipe, drain or sewer, but must be discharged into a open sink or drain outside the house.

11. Waste pipes from wash tubs, wash stands and sinks shall *Connection of waste from bath tubs, &c.* not be connected with the trap of a W. C.

W. C. to be of improved patterns

12. W. C.'s must be of the hopper or approved pattern, [pan closets being absolutely prohibited] and should be supplied from a special tank placed over them, in which case the

Supply of W. C.

waste or overflow from the tank must discharge into the open air, or the basin of the closet, and not into the soil pipe directly.

If above kitchen or hydrant, direct service is prohibited

Direct service of a W. C. is always objectionable, and in case the W. C. is in a second or third story of a building, and above the supply to a kitchen or hydrant, it is absolutely prohibited.

Wooden wash trays and sinks prohibited

13. Wooden wash trays and sinks are prohibited inside of buildings; they shall be of non-absorbent material.

Lead, zinc and galvanized iron linings for cisterns prohibited

14. Lead, zinc or galvanized iron linings for house cisterns are prohibited, but wood, iron or tinned copper may be used. In every instance the overflow must be trapped into the open air.

Overflow to be trapped, &c.

Materials and workmanship to be approved by city engineer and inspector of plumbing

15. All materials must be of good quality, and free from all defects; the work must be executed in a thorough and workmanlike manner, and subject to the approval of the city engineer and the inspector of plumbing.

Regulations, &c., may be amended

16. The foregoing regulations and specifications will be altered, amended and added to, whenever it may be deemed by the board of street, sewer and drain commissioners proper to do so.

How prosecution shall be instituted

17. Prosecution for infringement upon the provisions of these regulations and specifications shall be made by information filed in the mayor's court, in the city of Norfolk, Virginia.

Approved by board of S., S. and D. Commissioners, 1883.

General Provision.

If any person shall violate any provisions contained in this chapter, entitled streets, sewers and drains, or hinder or obstruct any officer of the city in the proper discharge of his duty in relation to the same, such person shall, where no other penalty is imposed, pay a fine of not less than five nor more than twenty dollars.

CHAPTER XXXIV.

City Seal.

Description of city seal

Sec. 1. The seal of the city of Norfolk is as follows, viz:

Around the margin of the same a raised circle, containing the words "Seal of the City of Norfolk, Incorporated 1736," within which circle, a shield, bearing the representation of a steamship.

Treasurer to keep seal

The city treasurer shall be the keeper of the city seal.

Mayor's seal

2. The seal of the mayoralty, to be kept by the mayor, is as follows:

Around the margin of the same a raised circle, containing the words "Mayor's office, Norfolk," within which circle, a shield, bearing the representation of a ship under sail.

CHAPTER XXXV.

Special Appropriations of Revenue for 1885.

AN ORDINANCE
Making Appropriations to meet Deficiencies.

Sec. 1. Be it enacted by the common and select councils of the city of Norfolk, that the following amounts hereinafter named be appropriated to the several departments of the city, to make good the deficiencies in said departments incurred prior to July 1st, 1885 ; and the treasurer of the city is hereby authorized to cause the said accounts to be placed to the credit of said departments as named below:

Almshouse	$3,564 27
Court allowance	439 96
Expense account	944 19
Public printing	377 32
Elections	380 95
Public buildings	651 07
Fire department	1,782 67
Cemeteries	478 59
Lights	2,149 87
Juries	145 00
Board of health	260 00
Markets	220 40
Interest to pay interest on coupons and registered stock due prior to July 1, 1885, and not yet called for	1,000 00
	$12,394 29

2. This ordinance shall be in force from and after its passage.
Passed C. C., August 4th, 1885.
Passed S. C., August 11th, 1885.

AN ORDINANCE

Making extra Appropriations for the fiscal year 1885.

Sec. 1. Be it ordained by the common and select councils of the city of Norfolk, that the following amounts be, and they are hereby appropriated for the purposes as named below, and the treasurer of the city is hereby authorized to pay the same whenever the same shall be provided for by the councils, viz:

Codifying and printing city ordinances	$ 878 00
Policeman Buchanan	188 00
R. D. Doyle	50 00
The board of street, sewer and drain commissioners to pay Donoghue & Co., and other items incurred prior to July 1, 1885	6,225 78
	$7,341 78

2. This ordinance shall be in force from its passage.
Passed C. C., August 4th, 1885.
Passed S. C., August 11th, 1885.

CHAPTER XXXVI.

Taxes on Property, &c., 1885.

AN ORDINANCE

Imposing Taxes on Property, Persons and income, for the payment of interest on the City Debt, including the special water tax, and to meet the general appropriations for the year 1885.

Sec. 1. Be it ordained by the common and select councils of the city of Norfolk, that for the year beginning the first day of February, 1885, and for each year thereafter, the taxes on lands, lots, persons and incomes, shall be as follows:

Water tax, 30 cents

General tax $1.50 on $100

2. Upon all lands, wharves and lots, and the improvements thereon, and upon all personal property of every description, except such real and personal property as is exempted from taxation by the State of Virginia or any ordinance of the city, and except the bonds issued by the city of Norfolk, thirty cents on every hundred dollars of the assessed value thereof, shall be the special water tax required to be levied by the laws and ordinances concerning the Norfolk water works, and one dollar and fifty cents on every hundred dollars of the assessed value thereof for general purposes, as stated in the ordinances concerning appropriations.

Income.

Income tax $1.80 on $100

3. On the salary or income received by any person during the year ending February 1st, one dollar and eighty cents upon each one hundred dollars value thereof in excess of six hundred dollars; provided, that the salary of a Minister of the Gospel and the salary of officers paid out of the city treasury shall be exempt from taxation; and provided further, that no income is hereby taxed which may be derived from any business, calling or profession, or subject of taxation otherwise taxed in the ordinance imposing license taxes, except as therein provided.

Personal Tax.

Capitation tax 50 cents

4. On every male inhabitant who has attained the age of twenty-one years, fifty cents, except those who are by law exempt from taxation.

Collector to give notice of taxes when due

5. The collector shall give public notice by advertisement in all of the daily newspapers published in the city, on the first day of October, and for thirty days thereafter, that the rolls of the commissioner of the revenue, containing the list of taxes, have been placed in his hands for collection, and also state in such notice the provisions of law relating to the prompt payment of taxes.

Office hours of collector

He shall attend at his office daily between the hours of nine A. M., and six o'clock P. M., from the first to the thirty-first day of October, inclusive, for the purpose of receiving from any person charged with said taxes the whole amount thereof.

Any person who shall fail to pay the collector on or before *When taxes payable; penalty for non-payment* the thirty-first day of October the taxes assessed against him for that year, shall be subject to a penalty of three per centum for the first month, and a further penalty of one per centum per month thereafter until the penalty shall have reached five per cent., according to the State law. After the penalty shall have reached five per centum, all persons failing to pay their said taxes shall pay in addition to the penalty, pay interest on their bills at the rate of six per cent. per annum.

The collector may collect the taxes herein imposed by distraint at any time.

6. The collector shall receive 1½ per cent. for his compensation on all moneys collected by him. *Collector's commission*

7. Nothing herein contained shall be construed to repeal the taxes imposed by ordinances upon licensed hacks and other vehicles, or tax upon dogs or upon persons, property or subjects not herein mentioned. *Other taxes in force*

8. The lessee of any lease-hold property, when required to do so by his lease, shall have the right to pay the city taxes on any piece or pieces of real estate, not assessed to the lessee, under a statute of the State of Virginia, approved March 20th, 1877, and the collector shall make out separate bills for each piece or pieces of real estate, and settle the same with the lessee upon the same terms as prescribed in this ordinance for the settlement of other bills. *Taxes may be paid by lessee*

9. This ordinance shall be in force from its passage, and all ordinances or parts of ordinances in conflict herewith, are hereby repealed.

C. C., August 11th, 1885; adopted by an aye and nay vote unanimously.

[Signed],   BARTON MYERS,
                                President C. C.

S. C., August 11th, 1885; adopted by an aye and nay vote unanimously.

[Signed].   ANDREW MARTIN,
                                Vice-President S. C.

Teste: W. W. HUNTER,
                                City Treasurer.

CHAPTER XXXVII.

Transfer and Redemption of Delinquent Lands.

Resolution of the Councils.

Resolved, that the treasurer be authorized to receive from any delinquent tax payer whose lands have been sold and purchased by the city, for delinquent taxes, the amount of the tax bill charged thereto, and interest at the rate of six per cent., to the day of payment, and allow the same in full settlement of the claim of the city and in redemption of the property; and that upon the payment of the same to the treasurer by the delinquent tax payer, or in case of his neglect to pay the same by the remainderman or reversioner expectant, upon the deter- *Treasurer may receipt tax bills and interest due on lands sold prior to Nov. 1882*

Mayor and
treasurer to
execute deed

mination of any life or other estate therein, the mayor and treasurer of the city of Norfolk shall execute a deed reconveying such real estate as may have been sold for delinquent taxes, and bought by the city, to the delinquent tax payer or to the remainderman or reversioner, as the case may be as aforesaid; and the treasurer shall give notice by advertisement, or postal card, that all such bills may be settled and the property reconveyed, provided, such delinquent taxes are paid before the city has acquired absolute possession to such property as provided by law.

Treasurer to
give notice

Passed common council November 9th, 1882.
Passed select council November 16th, 1882.

CHAPTER XXXVIII.

Vagrants.

Police to report all vagrants and obtain warrants for their arrest

1. The police of the city shall be and are hereby empowered and required upon discovering any vagrant or vagrants within the city, to make information thereof to the mayor or any justice of the peace of the city, and require a warrant for apprehending such vagrant or vagrants, to be brought before the mayor or such justice, to be dealt with as prescribed by law.

The following described persons shall be liable to the penalties imposed by law upon vagrants:

Who declared
to be vagrants

First. All persons who shall unlawfully return to the city after they have been legally removed.

Second. All persons who, not having wherewith to maintain themselves and their families, live idly and without employment, and refuse to work for the usual and common wages given to other laborers in the like work in the city.

Third. All persons in the almshouse who shall refuse to perform the work allotted to them by the keeper of the almshouse.

Fourth. All persons going about from door to door or placing themselves in the streets, highways, or other places to beg alms, and all other persons wandering and begging, unless disabled or incapable of labor.

Fifth. All persons who shall come to this city and shall be found loitering and residing therein, and shall follow no labor, trade, occupation or business, and have no visible means of subsistence, and can give no reasonable account of themselves or their business.

CHAPTER XXXIX.

Wards, Registration Precincts and Voting Places.

1. The city is divided into four wards, bounded as follows:

FIRST WARD.

Boundaries 1st
ward

Beginning at the eastern end of Queen street, at Newton's creek; thence westwardly, on the south side, to Church street; thence southwardly down Church street, eastern side, to the

Elizabeth river ; Thence eastwardly along the Port Warden's line to the Draw Bridge ; thence northwardly along the channel of Newton's creek to the place of beginning.

SECOND WARD.

Beginning at the south end of Church street, on the Eliza- 2d ward beth river, thence northwardly, on the west side of Church street, to Freemason street; thence westwardly, on the south side of Freemason street, to Yarmouth street; thence south-westwardly, down the east side of Yarmouth street, to the Port Warden's line at Chamberlaine's wharf; thence following the Port Warden's line to the place of beginning.

THIRD WARD.

Beginning at the northwest corner of Freemason and Church 3d ward street; thence northwardly, along the west side of Church street, to Queen street; thence westwardly, along the south side of Queen street, to James street; thence across James street; thence northwardly, along the west side of James street, to Armistead's bridge ; thence southwardly, down the channel of Smith's creek, to the Port Warden's line ; thence southeast-wardly, down the Port Warden's line, to Chamberlaine's wharf; thence northeastwardly to the west side of Yarmouth street ; thence up the same to Freemason street; thence eastwardly, along the north side of Freemason street, to the place of beginning.

FOURTH WARD.

Beginning at Armistead's bridge ; thence southwardly, along 4th ward the eastern side of James street, to Queen street; thence east-wardly, along the north side of Queen street, to Church street ; thence across Church street to the north side of Queen street; thence eastwardly, along the north side of Queen street, to Newton's creek, at the county line; thence north and west, and southwest, along the county line, to the place of beginning.

2. Each of said wards is divided into two precincts, bounded Boundaries of as follows:—See Acts of Assembly of Virginia, 1883-'84, voting pre-Chapter I. cincts

1. Be it enacted by the General Assembly of Virginia, that each of the wards of the city of Norfolk, as now established and defined, be and the same is hereby subdivided into two voting precincts as follows, to-wit :

That part of the first ward of said city which is included Precinct No. 1 within the following boundaries, to-wit: Beginning at the first ward intersection of the Port Warden's line, on the Elizabeth river, with the eastern line of Church street; and running thence along said eastern line of Church street to Holt street; thence, along the south line of Holt street, to Newton's creek ; thence along Newton's creek and the eastern boundary of the city, in a southerly direction, to the said Port Warden's line ; and thence, along the Port Warden's line, westerly, to the point of beginning, shall constitute precinct number one of the said first ward.

Precinct No. 2 first ward That part of the first ward which is included within the following boundaries, to-wit: Beginning at the northeast corner of Holt and Church streets; and running thence, along the east line of Church street to Queen street; thence, eastwardly, along the south line of Queen street to Newton's creek; thence, southerly, along Newton's creek to the northern line of Holt street; and thence, along the northern line of Holt street to the point of beginning, shall constitute precinct number two of said first ward.

Precinct No. 1 2d ward 2. That part of the second ward of said city which is included in the following boundaries, to-wit: Beginning at the intersection of the Port Warden's line, on the Elizabeth river, with the west line of Church street; and running thence, along the west line of Church street, to Freemason street; thence, along the south line of Freemason street to Bank street; thence, along the east line of Bank street, to Main street; thence, across Main street, to the east side of Roanoke avenue; thence, along the east line of said avenue, extended, to the Port Warden's line; and thence, along the Port Warden's line, to the point of beginning, shall constitute precinct number one of the second ward.

Precinct No. 2 2d ward That part of the second ward which is included within the following boundaries, to wit: beginning at the intersection of the Port Warden's line, on the Elizabeth river, with the west line of Roanoke square; and running thence, along the west line of said square and Roanoke avenue, to Main street; thence, across Main street to the west line of Bank street; thence, along the west line of Bank street, to Freemason street; thence, along the south line of Freemason street, to Yarmouth street; thence, south, along the east side of Yarmouth street, extended, to the Port Warden's line, on Elizabeth river, at the Boston (formerly Chamberlaine's) wharf; and thence, along said Port Warden's line to the point of beginning, shall constitute precinct number two of the said second ward.

Precinct No. 1 3d ward 3. That part of the third ward, of said city, which is included within the following boundaries, to-wit: beginning at the northwest corner of Freemason and Church streets, and running thence along the west line of Church street, to Queen street; thence, along the south line of Queen street, to Brewer street; thence, along the east line of Brewer street, to Freemason street, and thence, along the north line of Freemason street, to the point of beginning, shall constitute precinct number one of the said third ward.

Precinct No. 2 3d ward That part of the third ward, which is included within the following boundaries, to-wit: beginning at Armistead's bridge, at the west line of James street, and running thence along the west line of James street, to Queen street; thence, across Queen street, to the southwest corner of Brewer and Queen streets; thence south, along the west line of Brewer street to Freemason street; thence along the north line of Freemason street to the west line of Yarmouth street; thence southwardly, along the west line of Yarmouth street, extended, and southwest-wardly to the Port Warden's line, on the Elizabeth river, at the Boston (formerly Chamberlaine's) wharf; thence, along the said Port Warden's line to the mouth of Smith's creek, and thence, along Smith's creek, to the point of beginning, shall constitute precinct number two, of the said third ward.

4. That part of the fourth ward, of said city, which is included in the following boundaries, to-wit: Beginning at Armistead's bridge, at the east end of James street, and run-ning thence along the east line of James street, to Queen street; thence, along the north line of Queen street, to Hawk street; thence, along the west line of Hawk street, to the city limits, and thence, westerly along the line of the northern boundary of the city, to the point of beginning, shall constitue precinct number one of the fourth ward. *Precinct No. 1 4th ward*

Name of Hawk street changed to St. Paul

That part of the fourth ward, which is included within the following boundaries, to-wit: Beginning at the intersection of the northern line of Queen street, with Newton's creek, and running thence along the north line of Queen street, to Hawk street; thence, along the east line of Hawk street, to the nor-thern boundary line of the city; thence, along said boundary line eastwardly, to the stone in Princess Anne road at the head of Newton's creek, and thence, along Newton's creek, to the point of beginning, shall constitute precinct number two, of the said fourth ward. *Precinct No. 2 4th ward*

3. The voting places appointed by ordinance of the coun-cils in pursuance of the Act of Assembly approved December 21, 1883, are as follows: *Voting places*

FIRST WARD. *First ward*

Precinct Number one—At Hunter Woodis Clubhouse, on Fenchurch street, formerly known as the Union Hook and Ladder company's house. *1st precinct*

Precinct Number Two—At Beale & McGuire's shop, on Falkland street, between Fenchurch and Chapel streets. *2d precinct*

SECOND WARD. *Second ward*

Precinct Number One—At the city hall. *1st precinct*

Precinct Number Two—Lawrence's shop, on Granby street, near the stone bridge. *2d precinct*

THIRD WARD. *Third ward*

Precinct Number One—At Cannon's corner, northeast cor-ner of Bute and Brewer streets *1st precinct*

Precinct Number Two—At Hozier's corner, southwest cor-ner of Brewer and Charlotte streets. *2d precinct*

FOURTH WARD. *Fourth ward*

Precinct Number One—At Williams' hall, northwest corner of Jefferson and Willoughby streets. *1st precinct*

Precinct Number Two—At Spann's shop, on Church street. *2d precinct*

4. The committee of the councils on public buildings are

Committee on public buildings to make all arrangements for holding elections — empowered to provide from time to time such ballot boxes as may be required for holding elections in the city according to law, and further to make all necessary, suitable and proper arrangements at the several voting places for the convenience of the voters and the officers of the election. No person or persons except the said committee on public buildings shall assume to do or perform any act in this section required to be done by said committee, under a penalty of twenty dollars for each offense.

5. The judges, clerks and commissioners of elections shall each receive two dollars as a compensation for their services in any and every election held in the city, to be paid out of the treasury·

CHAPTER XL.

Wharves.

Wharves at ends of street public — 1. All wharves made out into the harbor in front of any street, or part of any street, and which street was heretofore laid out in the plan of the city as extending to the water, are hereby, as heretofore, declared public wharves, and subject to the regulations and management of the councils.

Digging holes near wharves prohibited — 2. No person shall dig a hole for any purpose whatever outside of any stone wall on the banks of the river or creeks in the harbor, within thirty feet of such wall, under a penalty of five dollars for each offense.

The Norfolk City Water Works.

CHAPTER XLI.

The Norfolk City Water Works.

Cʜᴀᴘ. 65.—An ACT to authorize the City of Norfolk to Construct Water Works for the use of the people of the said city.

Passed January 14, 1867.

1. Be it enacted by the general assembly, That it shall be lawful for the city of Norfolk tó construct suitable works to convey a supply of water from some point in the Dismal swamp in Norfolk county, or such other place as the said city may select, into the said city; and the said city may acquire and hold for that purpose a slip of land not exceeding one hundred feet in width, and other lands at the termini and stations of their works, in the city and county of Norfolk, not exceeding one hundred acres; and shall have the same rights and powers in respect to obtaining right of way, and lands for their pipes, aqueducts and other suitable structures and fixtures for securing and conveying water, as are conferred upon railroad and other internal improvement companies by the Code of Virginia; and may hold, use and employ such machinery, boats, apparatus and other appliances as they may deem proper for supplying the said city with water, and for the transaction of the attendant business. City of Norfolk may construct water works
Amount of land to be acquired for this purpose
Right of way, &c.
Machinery, apparatus, &c.

2. The councils of the said city may make such ordinances and regulations for the government and management of the said water works, and may establish and collect such rates of charges for the use of the water as they may deem proper; and may open streets, lanes, alleys and public squares of the said city, for the purpose of laying down water pipes and other fixtures for the distribution of water. Ordinances, &c.
Water rates
May lay pipes and fixtures

3. Any person who shall open a communication with the main or other pipe of the said water works, without authority from the said councils or the the superintendent of the said works, or shall wilfully let on the water after it has been stopped by order of the said councils or superintendent, for repairs or any other purpose; or shall put up any pipes in addition to the pipes originally put up and inspected, or introduce water into them without authority as aforesaid; or shall wilfully do or cause to be done any act whereby the said works or any portion thereof shall be obstructed, injured or destroyed, such person shall forfeit for each offence not less than ten nor more than fifty dollars, to be recovered before the mayor of the said city or any justice of the peace, one-half to the informer and the other half to the said city; and shall, moreover, forfeit and pay to the said city double the amount of damages sustained by reason of such offence or injury, to be recovered by action or motion in any court of record. Penalty for interfering with works

4. In order to provide for payment for the said works, the said city may issue bonds bearing interest not exceeding eight City may issue bonds for this

per centum per annum; which bonds shall be known as the "Norfolk city water bonds"--the proceeds of which shall not be applied or used for other purposes—and all the net revenues or income derived from the said works and for the use of the water, shall be applied exclusively to the payment of the interest and principal of the said bonds; and the councils of the said city are authorized to levy a special tax, to be known as the "water tax," on all real and leasehold property situated on such streets, lanes and squares in the said city as the main or other pipes of the said water works may pass along; the proceeds of which tax shall also be applied exclusively to the payment of the interest and principal of the said bonds.

5. This act shall be in force from its passage.

Acts of Assembly of Virginia, 1870–71, *pages*, 254, 255.

CHAP. 172.—An ACT to amend and re-enact the first and fourth sections of an act entitled an act to authorize the city of Norfolk to construct Water Works for the use of the people of said city. Passed January 14th, 1867.

Approved March 22d, 1871.

1. Be it enacted by the General Assembly, that the first and fourth sections of the act entitled an act to authorize the city of Norfolk to construct water works for the use of the people of the said city, passed January 14th, 1867, be amended and re-enacted so as to read as follows:

It shall be lawful for the city of Norfolk to construct suitable works to convey a supply of water from some point in Dismal Swamp, Norfolk county, or such other place as the said city may select, into the said city; and the said city may acquire and hold for that purpose a slip of land not exceeding one hundred feet in width, and other lands at the termini and stations of their works in the city and county of Norfolk, and in any other county and counties in this Commonwealth, not exceeding one hundred acres; and shall have the same rights and powers in respect to obtaining right of way, and lands for their pipes, aqueducts and other suitable structures and fixtures for securing and conveying water, as are conferred upon railroad and other internal improvement companies by the Code of Virginia; and may hold, use and employ such machinery, boats, apparatus, and other appliances as they may deem proper for supplying the said city with water and for the transaction of the attendant business.

4. In order to provide for payment of said works, the said city may issue bonds, bearing interest not exceeding eight per centum per annum; which bonds shall be known as the "Norfolk city water bonds," the proceeds of which shall not be applied or used for other purposes, and all the net revenues or income derived from the said works and for the use of the water, shall be applied exclusively to the payment of the interest and principal of the said bonds; and the councils of the said city are authorized to levy a special tax, to be known as the

"water tax," upon all property in the said city, real and personal, and on such other subjects as may be assessed with State taxes against persons residing in the said city; the said levy to be made in the mode prescribed by law and the Constitution of this State for the levy of other taxes by the said city.

2. This act shall be in force from its passage.

AN ORDINANCE

Concerning the erection of the Norfolk City Water Works and the maintenance of the same, as provided for in the act of the General Assembly of the State of Virginia, entitled an act to authorize the city of Norfolk to construct Water Works for the use of the people of the said city. Passed January 14, 1867.

1. Be it enacted by the select and common councils of the city of Norfolk, that five persons be appointed, who shall be residents thereof, to be known as the board of water commissioners of the city of Norfolk, who shall serve in that capacity until the completion of the works therein provided for, unless removed by the councils for incompetency or malfeasance in said office. Should a vacancy occur from any cause the councils shall have power to fill the vacancy. Ordinance Jan. 14, 1867 Organization of board

2. Said commissioners shall be appointed at a joint meeting of the councils to be called for that purpose, and the parties so appointed shall be declared the board of water commissioners of the city of Norfolk. The salaries of the commissioners shall be hereafter provided for by the councils. How elected

3. It shall be the duty of the said board of water commissioners to manage the affairs and business of said water works, to employ labor, to receive proposals, and to award contracts. They shall appoint a competent scientific engineer, who shall make all requisite surveys and specifications for all portions of the works, and who shall report and be subject to the control of said board; and also appoint such other officers as they may deem necessary for the construction of said works. And the said board of water commissioners are prohibited from being interested in any way with the contracts which may be made, either pecuniarily or otherwise. Powers and duties of board

4. The said board are hereby authorized to enter upon any land or water for the purpose of making surveys, and to agree with the owner or owners of any property which may be required for the purposes of said works, as to the amount of damage and compensation to be paid said owner or owners, as provided for in the act of General Assembly. And further, the said board, in behalf of the corporation of the city of Norfolk, and all persons acting under their authority, shall have the right to use the ground or soil under any street, road or highway, within the county or city, for the purpose of introducing water into the city, on condition that they cause the surface of said street, road or highway to be restored to its original state, and all damage caused by introducing said water be repaired. Board may enter upon lands

5. It shall be the duty of the city councils at the expiration of ever quarter to appoint a committee of one from the select Councils to appoint a

committee on water   and two from the common council, whose duty it shall be to examine works, contracts, &c., entered into by the water commissioners, and if said committee shall find that any excessive or exorbitant prices have been allowed for any damage to property, or for any property purchased, or for work or labor done, said committee shall have power to prefer charges of incompetency or malfeasance, as provided for in section one, and shall report the same to the councils.

Board authorized to draw on treasurer   6. The said board of water commissioners are hereby authorized to draw upon the treasurer of the city of Norfolk for any purpose authorized by this ordinance. Such drafts shall specify the objects for which they may be drawn, and shall be countersigned by the chairman and one other member thereof. It is hereby made the duty of the said treasurer to pay such drafts out of the funds herein provided for, and from no other source.

Bonds   7. The said water commissioners, each and every one of the same, before entering on the execution of the duties hereby imposed upon him or them, shall execute to the city of Norfolk a bond, with sufficient securities, in the penalty of twenty thousand dollars, for the faithful performance of the duties of the office.

Contracts; how made   8. All contracts for materials, or for the construction of the works, shall be made in writing. Public notice shall be given of the time and place at which sealed proposals will be received for entering into contract. Every person who shall enter into contract for the supply of materials, or the performance of labor, shall give satisfactory security to the commissioners for the faithful performance of his contract according to its terms.

City attorney to act for board   9. It shall be the duty of the corporation attorney to attend to all legal business for the said board of commissioners, and under their direction prepare all deeds, contracts, and other legal writings required by them. For so doing, the said corporation attorney shall be entitled such remuneration as shall be certified to by said water commissioners, to be paid by the treasurer upon such certificates.

Work to be paid for with bonds   10. All work contracted for, and material furnished for the construction of the works, shall be paid for in the said water bonds, or the proceeds of the same. The said water commissioners shall quarterly, or at any time required by the councils, report to the said councils a general exhibition of the state of the works, including a full detail of the moneys or bonds expended.

Issue of bonds authorized   11. Be it further ordained by the select and common councils of the city of Norfolk, that the treasurer of the city be authorized and empowered, under the directions of the said commissioners, to issue twenty year coupon bonds to the amount of five hundred thousand dollars, bearing an annual rate of interest of six per cent. per annum in gold, and payable semi-annually at the Park Bank of New York. The said bonds to be delivered to said water commissioners as the work progresses, they giving their receipt for the same. These bonds shall be known as the Norfolk city water bonds, and shall be countersigned by the chairman of the board of water commissioners. And be it further ordained, in order to meet the interest of the said bonds, a specific *ad valorem* tax of one half of one per cent. shall be assessed on all lands or property in the city of Norfolk as now, or hereafter may be assessed, to have the like operation and effect upon said lands or property —the said tax to be collected by the city collector as other city taxes now are, or hereafter may be collected. All moneys derived from the taxes thus assessed shall be set apart as a fund inviolate, for the express purpose of liquidating the interest and principal of the said bonds, and it shall in no case whatsoever be used or appropriated for any other purpose than the above mentioned. *(margin: Special water tax to be levied)*

This ordinance shall be in effect from its passage.
July 21 and July 28, C. C., 1870; S. C. July 28, 1870.

AMENDMENT.—Eleventh section amended to read as follows: To strike out six per cent., payable in gold, and make the same eight per cent. currency, payable at the National Park Bank, New York.

Common council, September 6th; Select council, 9th.

NOTE,—The above ordinance appears to be practically repealed by the following:.

AN ORDINANCE

To amend an ordinance passed on the 28th day of July, A. D. 1870 entitled an ordinance concerning the erection of the Norfolk City water works and the maintenance of the same, as provided for in the act of the General Assembly of the State of Virginia, entitled an act to authorize the city of Norfolk to construct water works for the use of the people of the said city. passed January 14, 1867.

1. Be it enacted by the select and common councils of the city of Norfolk, that the ordinance concerning the erection of the Norfolk city water works and the maintenance of the same, passed on the 28th day of July, 1870, be amended and re-enacted so as to read as follows: *(margin: Amendment)*

"1. Five persons, residents of the city of Norfolk, shall be appointed water commissioners by the councils, in joint meeting assembled, called for that purpose. The persons so appointed shall constitute a board, to be called 'The board of water commissioners of the city of Norfolk.'" *(margin: Board organized)*

2. The said commissioners shall hold their offices for two years from date of election, unless removed by the councils, in joint meeting assembled, for incompetency or malfeasance in office, at the expiration of which time three commissioners shall be appointed which shall constitute the said board. Each of the said commissioners shall, before the presidents of the two councils of the said city, with surety deemed sufficient by the said presidents, give bond in the penalty of twenty thousand dollars, payable to the city of Norfolk, and with condition for the faithful discharge by him of the duties of his office, and shall receive a salary of five hundred dollars per annum during his continuance in office, payable quarterly, out of any *(margin: Term of office / Official bonds)*

funds provided for by this ordinance, which shall commence on the 28th day of July, 1871.

Powers and duties of board

3. It shall be the duty of the said board to employ labor, receive proposals and make contracts; to appoint a competent scientific engineer, whose duties shall from time to time be prescribed by the said board; to appoint such other officers as they may deem decessary, and to govern and manage the said water works, and all business and affairs relating thereto or connected therewith. But no member or members of the said board shall be personally interested, directly or indirectly, in any contract made by the said board.

Board may enter upon lands

4. The said board, and its officers, agents and servants acting by the authority of the said board, shall have power to enter upon any lands for the purpose of examining the same and surveying and laying out such as may seem fit to any officer authorized by said board, provided no injury be done to the owner or possessor of the land; to agree in the manner prescribed by an act of the General Assembly passed January 14, 1867, with those entitled to lands wanted for the purposes of the said water works; and, in behalf of the corporation of the city of Norfolk, to use the ground or soil under any street, road or highway within the county or city of Norfolk for the purposes of the said water works, but to restore the surface of such street, road or highway. as near as may be, to its original condition, and repair all damage caused by such use thereof.

Councils to appoint water committee quarterly

5. It shall be the duty of the city councils, at the expiration of every quarter, to appoint a committee of one from the select and two from the common council, whose duty it shall be to examine work, contracts, &c., entered into by the water commissioners, and if said committee shall find that any excessive or exorbitant prices have been allowed for any damage to property, or for any property purchased, or for work or labor done, said committee shall have power to prefer charges of incompetency or malfeasance, as provided for in section two, and shall report the same to the councils.

How board shall be organized

6. The said board shall appoint from their own body a chairman, secretary and treasurer, and the duties of each shall be prescribed by the said board; and the treasurer, in addition to the bond required of him as a member of the said board by section two of this ordinance, shall, before entering upon the duties of his office of treasurer, before the presidents of the common and select councils of the city of Norfolk, with surety deemed sufficient by the said presidents of the select and common councils of the city of Norfolk, give bond in the penalty of fifty thousand dollars, payable to the city of Norfolk, with condition for the faithful discharge by him of the duties of his said office of treasurer of said board.

Contracts; how made

7. All contracts for materials or for the construction of the said works, or any part thereof, shall be in writing. Public notice, in one or more newspapers printed in the city of Norfolk and elsewhere, at the discretion of the said board, shall be given of the time and place at which sealed proposals for

such contracts will be received ; and the contractors shall, under the direction of the said board, with surety deemed sufficient by the said board, give bond in such penalty as the said board may require, payable to the city of Norfolk, and with condition for the faithful performance by them of such contract.

8. All work contracted for, and material furnished for the construction of the said water works, shall be paid for in water bonds herein provided for, or the proceeds of the same; and the said board shall monthly report to the councils the state of the said water works, and an account specifying the bonds and moneys received and disbursed by them. *Work paid for in bonds*

9. Coupon bonds of the city of Norfolk, which shall be known as the Norfolk city water bonds, to the amount of five hundred thousand dollars, bearing interest at the rate of eight per centum per annum, payable semi-annually, shall be issued. The said bonds shall be in such form as may be prescribed by the said board, and be signed by the mayor and treasurer of the city of Norfolk, and countersigned by the chairman of the said board, and each shall be for such sum as may be directed by the said board. The said bonds, when and as they may be so signed and countersigned, shall be delivered to the said board by the treasurer of the said city, and the said board shall deposit their receipts therefor with the said treasurer, signed by the chairman and countersigned by the treasurer of the said board. The said bonds shall, from time to time, be sold by the said board, at their discretion, for the best price or prices the said board can obtain for the same; and such bonds, or the proceeds of such bonds, shall be used by the said board for payment for the said works, and all expenses attending the same, and shall not be applied or used for other purposes ; and the said city shall convey by deed of trust to three persons—to-wit: Captain James Cornick, Thomas J. Corprew, of Norfolk, and H. C. Hardy, of New York city—the said water works, together with all the lands, buildings, machinery, pipes, and appurtenances to the said water works belonging, then or thereafter to be acquired or connected therewith, and all the revenues and income which may be derived from the said works or for the use of water, in trust, to secure the payment of the interest and principal of the said bonds, and the said deed of trust shall, on the part of the said city, be executed by the presidents of the select and common councils, and sealed with the seal of the said city; and a special tax, to be known as the water tax, of one-half of one per centum of the assessed value of all real and lease-hold property situated on such streets, lanes and squares in the said city as the main or other pipes of the said water works may pass along, shall be levied annually, on such real and leasehold property, and collected as other taxes levied by the said city shall be collected; and the proceeds of said water tax shall be applied exclusively to the payment of the interest and principal of the said bonds. The said board shall, with all convenient dispatch, designate in such manner as they may deem expedient, such streets, lanes and squares in the said city, as the main or other pipes of the *Coupon bonds to be issued ; $500,000; 8 per cent.* *Deed of trust to secure bonds* *Special tax to be levied*

said water works shall pass along. The city collector shall pay monthly to the treasurer of the said board all the proceeds of the said water tax collected by the said collector, and the said proceeds shall be applied by the said board exclusively to the payment of the interest and principal of the said bonds; and any and every year when the proceeds of the said water tax, together with the net revenue and income derived from the said works, shall exceed the annual interest payable on the said bonds, such excess shall be set apart by the said board as a sinking fund, and invested by them in said bonds, or otherwise, as they may deem most expedient; and such sinking fund shall be applied to the payment of the principal of the said bonds when they shall fall due. And the said board shall pay out of any moneys which may come to their hands the interest of the said bonds, half yearly, as the same shall accrue. The persons heretofore appointed water commissioners shall continue in office, and hold the same under the same tenure prescribed by section two of this ordinance, as amended; and all acts which have been done by them in pursuance of the ordinance passed on the 28th day of July, A. D. 1870, shall be valid and **Repeal of prior ordinances** effectual. All the provisions and parts of the provisions of said ordinance, passed on the 28th day of July, 1870, inconsistent with this ordinance, or not hereby re enacted, are hereby repealed.

This ordinance shall be in force from and after the passage thereof.

Passed common council March 2, 1871; select council, February 14, 1881.

NOTE.—Sections one, two, four and nine are amended by subsequent ordinances.

AN ORDINANCE

To amend the fourth and ninth sections of an ordinance passed on on the 2d day of March, 1871, amending an ordinance passed on the 28th day of July, A. D. 1870, entitled an ordinance concerning the erection of the Norfolk City Water Works, and the maintenance of the same as provided for in the act of the General Assembly of the State of Virginia, entitled an act to authorize the city of Norfolk to construct Water Works for the use of the people of the said city, passed January 14th, 1867, "which act" has been subsequently amended by an act of the General Assembly of the State of Virginia, passed at the session of 1870-'71.

Amending section 4

Be it enacted by the select and common councils of the city of Norfolk, that the fourth section of the ordinance passed March 2d, 1871, be amended so as to read as follows:

Board may enter upon lands, &c

4 The said board, and its officers, agents and servants acting by the authority of the said board, shall have power to enter upon any lands for the purpose of examining the same and surveying and laying out such as may seem fit to any officer authorized by the said board, provided no injury be done to the owner or possessor of the land; to agree in the manner prescribed by an act of the General Assembly passed January 14th, 1867, as amended by an act of the General Assembly passed

at the session of 1870 and 1871, with those entitled to land
wanted for the purposes of the said water works, and in behalf
of the corporation of the city of Norfolk, to use the ground
or soil under any street, road or highway within the county or
city of Norfolk for the purposes of the said water works, but
to restore the surface of such street, road or highway, as near
as may be, to its original condition, and repair all damage
caused by such use thereof.

Section nine to be amended so as to read as follows: Amending
9. Coupon bonds of the city of Norfolk having thirty years section 9
to run from the 1st day of May. 1871, which shall be known Coupon bonds
as the Norfolk City Water Bonds, to the amount of five hundred $500,000. 8 per
thousand dollars, interest payable at the National Park Bank, cent.; 1901
city of New York, and bearing interest after the rate of eight
per centum, payable semi-annually, shall be issued. The said
bonds may be in such form as may be prescribed by the said
board, and be signed by the mayor and treasurer of the city of
Norfolk, and countersigned by the chairman of the said board,
and each shall be for such sum as may be directed by the said
board. The said bonds, when and as they may be signed and
countersigned, shall be delivered to the said board by the
treasurer of the said city, and the said board shall deposit
their receipts therefor with the said treasurer, signed by the How bonds to
chairman and countersigned by the treasurer of the said board. be prepared
The said bonds shall, from time to time, be sold by the said and issued
board, at their discretion, for the best price or prices the said
board can obtain for the same. And such bonds, or the proceeds of such bonds, shall be used by the said board for payment for said works, and all expenses attending the same, and
shall not be applied or used for other purposes; and the said
city shall convey by deed of trust to three persons. to-wit:
Chas. H. Rowland. Thomas J. Corprew and Henry C. Hardy, Trustees
of the city of Norfolk, the said water works, together with all named
the lands, buildings, machinery, pipes and appurtenances to
the said water works belonging, then or thereafter to be acquired or connected therewith, together with the rights and franchises of the city in said water works, and all the resources
and income which may be derived from said works and for the
use of the water, in trust to secure the interest and principal
of said bonds. The said deed of trust shall be in such form
and shall contain such usual provisions and conditions as shall
be approved by the board, and shall be executed on the part of
the city by the presidents of the select and common councils.
and sealed with the seal of the city. A special tax shall also Special tax to
be levied annually until the whole principal sum of said bonds be levied
is paid, to be known as the water tax, one-eighth of one per annually
cent. upon all property in the city, real and personal, and on
such other subjects as may be assessed with State taxes against
persons (residing in the said city, the said levy to be made in
the mode prescribed by law and the constitution of the State,
for the levy of other taxes by the said city, and collected as
other taxes levied by the city shall be collected, in current
funds, and the proceeds of the said water tax shall be applied

exclusively to the payment of the interest and principal of the said bonds. The city collector shall pay semi-monthly to the treasurer of the said board all the proceeds of the said water tax collected by the said collector, and the said proceeds shall be applied by the board exclusively to the payment of the interest of said bonds, and the surplus, if any, after the payment of the interest, to the payment of the principal; and any and every year when the proceeds of the said water tax, together with the net revenue and income derived from the said water works shall exceed the annual interest payable on the said bonds, said excess shall be set apart by the said board **Sinking fund to be established by board** as a sinking fund, and invested by them in said bonds or otherwise, as they may deem most expedient, and such sinking fund shall be applied to the payment of the principal of the said bonds when they shall fall due. And the said board shall pay out of any moneys which may come to their hands the interest of the said bonds half-yearly as the same may accrue. The persons heretofore appointed water commissioners shall continue in office and hold the same under the same tenure prescribed by section 2 of this ordinance as amended, and all acts which have been done by them in pursuance of the ordinance passed on the 28th day of July, A. D. 1870, shall be valid and effectual. All the provisions and parts of the provisions of the said ordinance passed on the 28th day of July, A. D. 1870, as amended and re-enacted March 2d, 1871, inconsistent with this ordinance, or not hereby re-enacted, are hereby repealed. This ordinance shall be in force from and after the passage thereof.

Passed select council, August 31, 1871; common council, August 21, 1871.

Note subsequent amendment to section nine.

AN ORDINANCE

To amend section one of an ordinance concerning the erection of the Norfolk City Water Works, and the maintenance of the same.

Number of commission'rs changed from 5 to 3

1. Be it enacted by the select and common councils that section 1 of an ordinance concerning the erection of the Norfolk city water works, be amended so as to read in place of the word *three*, the word five.

2. This ordinance shall be in force from and after its passage.

Passed common council, November 15, 1871; select council, November 15, 1871.

AN ORDINANCE

To amend an Ordinance passed on the 1st day of September, 1871, entitled an Ordinance to amend the fourth and ninth sections of an Ordinance passed on the 2d day of March, 1871, amending an Ordinance passed on the 28th day of July, 1870, entitled an Ordinance concerning the erection of the Norfolk City Water Works, and the maintenance of the same, as provided for in the act of the General Assembly of the State of Virginia, entitled " An Act to authorize the city of Norfolk to construct Water Works for the use of the people of the said city, passed January 14th, 1867, which act has been subsequently amended by an act of the General Assembly of the State of Virginia, passed at the session of 1870-'71.

1. Be it enacted by the select and common councils of the city of Norfolk, that the ninth section of the ordinance passed March 2d, 1871, as amended by the ordinance passed September 1st, 1871, as set out above in the title of this ordinance, be and the same is hereby amended so as to read as follows: *Amending section 9*

9. Coupon bonds of the city of Norfolk having thirty years to run from the 1st day of May, 1871, which shall be known as the "Norfolk City Water Bonds," to the amount of five hundred thousand dollars, interest payable at the National Park Bank, city of New York, and bearing interest at the rate of eight per centum per annum, payable semi-annually, shall be issued; the said bonds shall be in such form as may be prescribed by the said board, and be signed by the mayor and treasurer of the city of Norfolk, and countersigned by the chairman of the said board; and each shall be for such sum as may be directed by the said board; the said bonds, when and as they may be so signed and countersigned, shall be delivered to the said board by the treasurer of the said city, and the said board shall deposit their receipts therefor with the said treasurer, signed by the chairman and countersigned by the treasurer of the said board; the said bonds shall be sold by the board, at their discretion, for the best price or prices the said board can obtain for the same; and such bonds, or the proceeds of such bonds, shall be used by the said board for payment for said works, and all expenses attending the same, and shall not be applied or used for other purposes; and the said city shall convey by deed of trust to three persons, to-wit: Charles H. Rowland, Thomas J. Corprew and Henry C. Hardy, of the city of Norfolk, the said water works, together with all the lands, buildings, machinery, pipes and appurtenances to the said water works belonging, then and thereafter to be acquired or connected therewith, together with the rights and franchises of the city in said water works, and all the resources and income which may be derived from said works and for the use of the water, in trust to secure the interest and principal of said bonds. The said deed of trust shall be in such form and shall contain such usual provisions and conditions as shall be approved by the board, and shall be executed on the part of the city by the presidents of the select and common councils, and sealed with the seal of the city. A special tax, sufficient to pay the interest on said bonds, shall also be levied annually until the whole principal sum of said bonds are paid, to be known as the water tax, upon all property in the city, real and personal, and on such other subjects as may be assessed with State taxes against persons residing in said city, the said levy to be made in the mode prescribed by law and constitution of the State, for the levy of other taxes by the said city, and collected at the same time and in the same manner as other taxes levied by the said city shall be collected, in current *Coupon bonds authorized; $500,000, 8 per cts.; due May 1, 1901* *Trustees' deed* *Special tax to be levied annually to pay interest*

funds, and the proceeds of said water tax shall be applied exclusively to the payment of the interest and principal of the said bonds. The city collector shall pay semi-monthly to the treasurer of the said board all the proceeds of the said "water tax" collected by the said collector, and the proceeds shall be applied by the said board exclusively to the payment of the interest of said bonds, and surplus, if and, after the payment of interest, to the payment of the principal; and any and every year when the proceeds of the said water tax, together with the net revenue and income derived from the said water works shall exceed the annual interest payable on the said bonds, such excess shall be set apart by the said board as a sinking fund, and invested by them in said bonds or otherwise, as they may deem most expedient, and such sinking fund shall be applied to the payment of the principal of said bonds when they shall fall due. And the said board shall pay out of any moneys which may come to their hands the interest of the said bonds half-yearly as the same shall accrue. The persons heretofore appointed water commissioners shall continue in office and hold the same under the same tenure prescribed by section two of this ordinance as amended, and all acts which have been done by them in pursuance of the ordinance passed the 28th day of July, A. D. 1870, shall be valid and effectual. All the provisions and parts of the provisions of the said ordinance passed on the 28th day of July, A. D. 1870, as amended and re-enacted March 2d, 1871, inconsistent with this ordinance, are hereby repealed.

2. And be it enacted, that nothing contained in the said ordinance passed September 1st, 1871, shall operate a repeal of any previous ordinances or parts of ordinances except so far as incontistent therewith, and all the said ordinance of March 2d, 1871, with the amendments under said ordinance passed September 1st, 1871, shall be operative to the same extent as though the language of the ninth section under said ordinance passed September 1st, 1871, had been the same as prescribed by this ordinance for said ninth section; and this ordinance shall be in force from and after the passage thereof. Passed April 2, 1872.

(Marginal notes: Duty of city collector; Sinking fund; Amending clause; Explanatory of ordinance Sept. 1, 1871)

AN ORDINANCE

To provide for the payment of the interest on the bonds issued by the city of Norfolk, for the purpose of erecting water works and for the maintenance of the same.

1. Be it ordained by the select and common councils of the city of Norfolk, that the special tax for the year 1872, and for each succeeding year, to be called the "water tax," shall be at and after the rate of twenty-five cents on each hundred dollars valuation of all real and personal property which is taxed generally by the said city of Norfolk, and the said tax shall be assessed and collected at the same time and in the same manner as the general tax levied for the use of the said city,

(Marginal note: Water tax for 1872)

except that current funds only shall be receivable for the said tax.

2. Be it further ordained, that the duties of the commis- *Duties of* *commissioner* sioner of the revenue and the collector of the said city shall *of revenue* in all respects be the same in making out and collecting and *and collector* making returns of the said special tax roll, as is provided for by law or ordinance in respect to the general tax levy of the said city; and the same fees *pro rata* shall be allowed to them, and the same penalties for any neglect of the duties hereby imposed upon the said officers, or either of them, are hereby provided for.

3. This ordinance shall be in force from and after its passage, and all ordinances and parts of ordinances in conflict with this ordinance are hereby repealed.

Passed common council, May 10th, 1872; select council, May 10th, 1872.

AN ORDINANCE

To provide for the registration, at the option of the owners and holders thereof, of any of the bonds issued by the city of Norfolk for the purpose of erecting water works, and for the maintenance of the same.

Whereas, Under and by virtue of certain ordinances here- *Preamble* tofore passed by the select and common councils of the city of Norfolk, the city of Norfolk hath issued its coupon bonds, payable to the bearer thereof to the amount of five hundred thousand dollars, known as the Norfolk City Water Bonds, for the purpose of erecting and and maintaining water works for said city, and in order to secure the payment of the principal and interest of the said bonds, hath executed to a board of trustees a mortgage of all the property to be used for such purpose, and the revenues and income to be derived therefrom; and, whereas, it is now represented to the select and common councils of said city that, in order to avoid certain risks attendant upon the ownership of bonds payable to the bearer of the same, certain of the holders of the same may from time to time desire to procure such a registration of the bonds as will prevent the same being thereafter, or until endorsement to that effect, payable to bearer, and will make the same transferable only upon certain books to be kept as herein provided.

1. Be it ordained by the select and common councils of the *Treasurer of* city of Norfolk, that it shall be the duty of the treasurer of *water board* the board of water commissioners of the city of Norfolk to *to keep a book* procure and keep a book, which shall be the property of the *for registra-* *tion of bonds* said board in the city of Norfolk, and upon presentment to the said treasurer of any of said bonds and coupons known as the Norfolk City Water Bonds, issued as aforesaid, and payable to the bearer, and at the request of the bearer of the same, the said treasurer shall register and enter in said book the

number and amount of such bond or bonds, but not the coupons; the name of the bearer who hath so presented the same, the date of such presentment, and the name of the party or parties in whose name such bond or bonds shall be registered as the owner thereof; and he shall cause the bearer of the said bond or bonds to sign his name in said book, with a designation of the capacity in which he acts, whether as attorney of the owner or as owner of said bond or bonds; and the said bond or bonds, and the said book, shall be so prepared as to admit conveniently of such entries from time to time in columns; and the said treasurer shall thereupon endorse upon the back of each of said bonds the words following: " Registered on the books of the treasurer of the board of water commissioner of the city of Norfolk to —— ——, on the — day of ——, and transferable only on the said books "; and he shall date the same and sign the same as such treasurer, and thereafter the said bond or bonds, but not the coupons, shall be transferable only upon said books upon the presentment of said bond or bonds by such registered owner, his personal representatives under the appointment of the proper authority, at the residence of such owner, or by his or their duly constituted attorney in fact.

Transfer of bonds 2. And be it further ordained, that whenever any bond or bonds which hath or have been so registered shall be presented for transfer to the said treasurer, it shall be his duty to enter in the book before mentioned, or in another book to be kept by him for the purpose at the said office, and as the property of the said board of water commissioners, the amount or amounts, number or numbers of such bond or bonds, the name of such registered owner or owners, the date of the presentment for transfer, and the name of the party or parties to whom the same is or are transferred; and he shall cause the said owner, his personal representative, or his or their attorney in fact to sign such transfer in said book, and he shall caresully preserve and file all evidences of administration and power of attorney upon which transfers may be based; and said treasurer shall thereupon endorse on the said bond or bonds the words following; "Transferred on the books of the treasurer of the water commissioners of the city of Norfolk to —— ——," and he shall date and sign the same as such treasurer.

May be transferred to bearer 3. And be it further ordained, that any registered owner of a bond may transfer the same in the manner aforesaid to the bearer, when the endorsement shall be made upon the bond as follows: " Transferred on the books of the treasurer of the water commissioners of the city of Norfolk to and now payable to the bearer," dated and signed by the said treasurer as aforesaid, and thereafter the said bond shall pass by delivery in the same manner as though the same had never been registered, until the same shall be thereafter again registered in the manner stated in the first section of this ordinance.

4. Be it further ordained, that the endorsement before mentioned may be printed upon the said bonds, with the excep-

tion of the date and signature of the treasurer.

Passed common and select councils, February 14, 1873.

AN ORDINANCE

For the regulation and protection of the Norfolk City Water Works.

1. It shall be unlawful for any person except the engineer or superintendent to take water from any public or private hydrant (except such free hydrants as may be opened), plug, street-washer, draw-cock, hose-pipe or fountain (except for fire purposes or for the use of the fire department in case of fire), or in any way use or take any water for private use which is furnished by the water works, unless such person shall first pay for the same and receive the usual permit from the register of the water works so to do. *No person to take water from works without permit*

2. No person shall open any fire hydrant or remove or obstruct the stop-cock cover of any hydrant, private stop-cock of any street washer, place or deposit any dirt or other material in such stop-cock boxes, or turn any public or private stop-cock, or commit any act tending to obstruct the use thereof, or injure in any manner any building, machinery, pipe, apparatus, tools, or fixtures of the water works. *Opening hydrants. Injuring or obstructing water works*

3. No person shall put any filth, animal or vegetable matter, chips, shavings, or any other substance on the water works property, or do any injury thereto. *Filth, chips, &c., not to be put on water works property*

4. No person but the properly authorized agents of the board of water commissioners shall tap or make any connection with the main or distributing pipes of the water works. *Taps; by whom made*

5. The superintendent and the proper officers of the board shall have free access, at all reasonable hours, to all parts of any premises to which water is or may be supplied, to make necessary examinations. *Officers to have access to private premises*

6. The board shall have the right to apply a meter to any service pipe where they may deem it advisable. *Meters*

7. In all cases where any servant, apprentice, minor, or employee shall be guilty of any breach of the preceding rules and regulations, the master, mistress, employer, parent, or guardian of such guilty person shall be responsible for and subject to prosecution for such violation if in any manner authorizing or tolerating the same. *Persons responsible for acts of employees, &c.*

8. Any consumer who shall habitually permit others not members of his family to use water from his pipe, and any one who shall thus obtain water shall be fined in a sum not less than five and not exceeding twenty dollars. *Consumer not to permit others to use water from his pipe*

9. No water shall be taken or used from hydrants at curbstone except for sprinkling purposes and washing front of house or houses unless by special permit from the office, and any one violating the requirements of this section shall be fined in a sum not less than five and not exceeding ten dollars for each offense. *Water not to be taken from curb except by permit*

10. Any person violating either of the provisions of the foregoing regulations shall, upon conviction thereof, be fined *Penalty*

not less than five nor more twenty dollars, unless otherwise herein provided, and be liable to all damage and costs accruing from such violation and prosecution.

Board may establish regulations

11. That the board of water commissioners are hereby authorized to make such by-laws and regulations as they may deem necessary for the safe, economical and efficient management and protection of the works.

Passed common council April 22, 1874; select council April 22, 1874.

[Note.—In obedience to section 69 of the city charter of 1884, the councils, in July, 1884, elected three persons to constitute the board of water commissioners and serve for two years. The salary of the treasurer is $500 per annum, but no compensation is allowed to the other commissioners].

Rules and Regulations of the Norfolk City Water Works.

Adopted by the Board of Water Commissioners.

1. All applications for the introduction of water into any premises, or for the extension of any water pipe, shall be made to the board in writing, (if by a tenant, with the written con. sent of the owner,) stating fully all the purposes for which it is required, and the locality of the premises to be supplied : the applicant shall sign the rules and regulations of the board and pay the sum of $5.00 in advance to cover the expense of service pipe, &c., to the curbstone.

2. No private hydrant will be permitted on the sidewalk or alley, or in front of a building, or on a vacant lot. If there be no yard in the rear of the building, it may be set six feet from front of the house, for which a special permit will be required, and if standing in a yard attached to a dwelling or building, it must be situated two feet from any wall or line of the lot, and must not be permitted to be left running when not in actual use ; and if the drip or waste from such hydrant becomes a nuisance to the adjacent property, or overruns the sidewalk, the supply will be shut off, and kept off until the evil is satisfactorily corrected.

3. No horse watering fixtures will be permitted in the streets or on the sidewalks, except upon a license taken out for that purpose. The license must be annually renewed.

4. No addition to or alteration whatever of any tap, pipe, water-cock, or any other fixture shall be made, or caused to be made, by persons taken water, except by permission first had and obtained from the office.

5. Persons taking water must keep their service pipes and all fixtures connected therewith, in good repair and protected from frost at their own expense, and must prevent all unnecessary waste of water.

6. The superintendent, or other proper agent of the department, shall have free access, at all reasonable hours of the day, to all parts of the premises to which water is supplied, to make the necessary examination.

7. Service pipe intended to supply two or more distinct premises, or tenements, must be provided with separate and distinct stop-cocks for each tenement on the outside of the same; or, when only one stop-cock is used by more than one consumer, if any one of them shall violate the rules the water shall be turned off from all. The party controlling the stop-cock must pay the water rent of all parties who are thus supplied, as separate accounts will not be kept.

8. No water taker will be allowed to supply water to others, except by special permission from the office. If found so doing without a permit, the supply will be stopped and the water rent already paid forfeited, and the city ordinance strictly enforced.

9. No claim shall be made against the city by reason of the breaking of any pipe or service cock, or from damage arising from shutting of water to repair mains.

10. In sprinkling streets each water taker must confine himself to the front of his premises, and half the width of the street in front thereof. Hose larger than ¾ inch will not be permitted, except upon an additional charge, and sprinkling without a nozzle, or a larger opening than ¼ inch. is forbidden. If a street washer or sprinkler is allowed to run when not used by a person engaged in sprinkling, the supply will be cut off without previous notice. Parties may obtain a permit for one year from the office to use their neighbor's wash pave, with their permission, provided they pay the year's rent in advance. Permits are to be annually renewed.

11. The Department reserves the right to apply a Meter to any service pipe when they may deem it advisible.

12. All water rents are due in advance, quarterly, commencing on the 1st of January. If not paid within fifteen days, 10 per cent. to be added; and if not paid in thirty days, the water shall be turned off.

13. The consequence of a violation of any of the preceding rules will be the stoppage of the supply of water, without preliminary notice, and forfeiture of rent paid, and it will not be restored except under payment of damages, and upon satisfactory understanding with the party that no future cause of complaint shall arise.

14. Any person wishing to discontinue the use of the water must notify the board thirty days before the expiration of the last quarter of his year.

15. In all cases where the water is turned off for violation of the rules, the owner or occupant of such premises shall pay fifty cents for turning the water off and on.

16. Steam boilers taking a supply of water directly from the service pipe, depending upon the hydraulic or hydrostatic pressure in the pipe system of the water works for supplying such boilers under working pressure, are required to have tanks erected that will contain an ample quantity of water for supplying such boiler or boilers for at least 10 hours, in case the water is shut off for necessary repairs or extensions, as the board will not be responsible for any accidents or damages to which such devices are frequently subject.

19

17. No lease of water will be made for a shorter period than one year.

RATES.

A house containing 1 or 4 rooms $6 00 per annum, fifty cents for each room over 4 to 10. No charge for unoccupied attics or cellars.

Houses containing more than 10 rooms to be charged at the rate of twenty-five cents for each additional room over 10.

Dwellings, bath tubs in connection with other supply in
 house... ......$ 3 00
Dwellings, water closets, self-acting, each............ 3 00
 " urinal, each.. 1 50
 " wash pave of every description, each.......... 6 00
A screw nozzle on a hydrant will be charged as wash pave, unless already charged.
Stores, hydrants in yard or basin in store.................. 6 00
 " " each basin or sink additional 2 00
 " water closets, double-acting, self-acting........... 3 00
 " urinals, self-closing........... .... 2 00
Public Buildings, hydrants.... .... 12 00
 " " each basin or sink...................... 3 00
 " " water closets, double-acting, self-clos-
 ing...... .... 5 00
Public Buildings, urinals, self-closing....................... 5 00
Hotels, family keeping hotel, boarding houses, each room 1 20
 " hotel bars, water in or not........................ 15 00
 " slop sinks, each................................. 8 00
 " water closets, double-acting, self-closing.......... 5 00
 " urinals......... .'... .... 5 00
 " bath tubs for use of boarders.................... 25 00
 " horse trough, for watering horses................ 10 00
 " stable, each stall................................. 1 50
Stable, livery for each stall.. .... 1 00
 " " " vehicle...................... 1 50
 " private, for each horse, (carriage additional).... 1 50
Family Bakers, additional.................................. 12 00
All Bakeries and Confectioneries, additional............ 12 00
Wholesale Rectifiers and liquor stores...................... 25 00
Bars or restaurants, exclusive of dwelling............ 15 00
Slaughter houses.. 25 00
Daguerreian rooms.. 15 00
Barber shop, for one basin.............................. 6 00
 " " each additional basin........ .... 1 20
 " " bath tubs, for first tub..... .... 20 00
 " " " for each additional........... 5 00
Drug stores, one sink...................................... 8 00
 " counter fountain, not exceeding 1-16 inch 6 00
Counter fountains and tumbler washers exceeding 1-16
 inch, subject to assessment.
Printing offices... 6 00
Offices generally.. 6 00
Blacksmith shops, one fire................................. 6 00

Blacksmith shops, each additional fire................... $1 00
Shops generally...................................... 6 00
Building purposes, brick per 1,000.......................... 10
    "   "   stone per perch...... 6
Plastering, for each 30 sqr. yds...................... 10
Fountains, not exceeding 6 hours, 1-8 in. nozzle, during
   the season.................................... 5 00
Fountains, not exceeding 6 hours, 1-16 in. nozzle, during
   the season............................... 12 00
Fountains, not exceeding 6 hours, 1-4 in. nozzle during
   the season............................... 25 00

SPECIAL RATES.—Steam engines, provision and meat stores, breweries, and purposes not above enumerated, subject to assessment.

METER RATES.—Where the average daily consumption is 1,000 gallons or less, 4 cents per 100 gallons; over 1,000 less than 5,000 gallons, 3 cents per 100 gallons; over 5,000 gallons, 2 cents per 100 gallons.

METERS.

When a consumer shall prefer to pay the cost of such a meter as shall be approved by the commissioners, together with the cost of putting in and of maintenance, rather than to pay schedule rates, or for the quantity estimated, a meter will be put in; provided, however, that in no case where a meter is used shall the annual charge be less than $10 00

The commissioners reserve the right to put in a meter at the cost of the city, in any case, and charge for measured water, instead of being governed by the above schedule.

For all amounts to any single consumer over 15,000 gallons per day shall be charged such special rates as may be fixed by contract with the superintendent, provided no such contract shall be made to extend over one year from the date thereof.

The city will set meters upon any premises where the superintendent determines so to do; and on all premises where the meters are set, the owner of the premises will be held thereafter to pay the rate according to the schedule for the entire amount of water used, irrespective of all under leases, or any individual consumer or individual consumers, upon such premises.

All meters set on private premises shall be subject to the inspection and control of the water commissioners, or such agent or officer as they shall designate to have the care and supervision of meters.

The officer whose duty it is to care for the meters in the city, or his agent, shall have free access at all times upon the premises of the owner thereof for the purpose of reading the meter, or he may remove a meter at any time for the purpose of testing the accuracy of its measurement, and when any meter shall be found incorrect in measurement and unworthy further use, such meter so condemned will be replaced at once by one which is approved by the superintendent at the expense of the owner thereof.

Whenever any consumer selects to pay rate by meter, he shall ever after be held to pay rate thereby, until released therefrom by the water commissioners.

Where the rate to any single consumer by any mode of assessment is over fifty dollars per annum, the commissioner may set on such premises a meter at the expense of the owners.

The rate by meter measurement in all cases where they are used shall take precedence of other modes of rating named in these rules.

No meter will be allowed to be set or used on any connection of the water works, unless approved by the superintendent.

By-laws and Regulations adopted by the Board of Water Commissioners, May 19, 1874.

FOR PLUMBERS.

1. No person, except the tappers employed by the water board, or person in their service and approved by them, will be permitted, under any circumstances, to tap the distributing pipes, or insert stop-cocks or ferrules therein, under penalty as prescribed by city ordinance. Any plumber or pipe fitter wishing to do business in connection with the water works, shall, before receiving a license to do so, file in the office of the water works his petition in writing, giving the name of the firm and each member thereof, and place of business, asking to become a licensed plumber or pipe fitter, stating his willingness and consent to be governed in all respects by the by-laws and regulations of said water works. The said petition must be signed by two responsible citizens, vouching for the worthiness of the applicant to receive license. On receiving his license, he shall have recorded his actual place of business, the name under which his business is transacted, and shall immediately notify the board of every change of either thereafter. A plumber will not be deemed to have a place of business unless a sign bearing his name and business be publicly exposed at the premises occupied by him for this purpose. Removal of place of business from the city shall act as a forfeiture of license.

2. No plumber or other person shall make any attachment to an old pipe or other fixture which has been shut off by the rule of the works, or which is out of use, without having first obtained a permit; nor shall any plumber or other person make any alteration in any of the conduit pipes or other fixtures attached to the water works, so as to conduct water into the adjoining premises, without a written permit so to do, signed by the proper officer of the works.

3. In removing pavements for the purpose of inserting ferrules, making attachments or repairs, the earth, stone and gravel must be deposited in such a manner as to guard against inconvenience to the public, by obstructing streets, alleys or sidewalks; nor shall the hole in any street be left open during the night. The flagging or pavement must be restored to at least as good condition as previous to excavation, and all dirt,

stones and rubbish removed immediately after the completion
of the work. If the flagging disturbed by any plumber be
not restored to as good order as it was at the time said plumber commenced his work, and all dirt, &c., carted away, and
if the plumber shall neglect or refuse to do such work within
forty-eight hours after notice thereof from the water commissioners, or their authorized agent or officer, then proper repairs
or work will be done by the said water commissioners, and the
cost thereof charged to said plumber. After the service of
such notice, no permits will be granted to such plumber until
the cause of complaint is removed.

4. All applications for the introduction of water into any
premises, or for the extension of any water pipe, shall be made
to the board in writing, (if by a tenant with the written consent of the owner) stating fully all the purposes for which it
is required, and the locality of the premises to be supplied, and
the applicant shall deposit $5.00 for the expense of service to
the curb, and sign the rules and regulations of the board.

5. All plumbing work required in a building, or for other
purposes, must be completed before application is made for a
tap, and the service pipe laid complete to the stop-stock before
making the connection at the main.

6. All service pipes, boilers and other water appertenances
shall be constructed of sufficient strength to bear the highest
fire pressure. A stop and waste or draw cock must be provided
for the purpose of emptying the pipes.

7. All plumbers shall make full returns of the ordinary and
special uses to which the water is designed to be applied under
any permit granted from the office, with a description of all
the apparatus and arrangements for using the water, in every
case. The return is to be made by the plumber who obtained
the permit, and shall be filed at the office of the water works,
and for any misrepresentation in the statement of work done,
or appurtenances set, through which there may be water used,
the plumber may be suspended, and if it appear to be wilful,
his license will be revoked.

8. The water will not be turned into any house, or private
service pipes, except by the superintendent, upon receiving
notice from the registrar that the applicant has paid his rent
for the current term; and plumbers or pipe fitters are strictly
prohibited from turning the water into any service pipes except
upon the order or permission of the superintendent. This
rule shall not be construed to prevent the superintendent from
allowing plumbers or pipe fitters to test their work by letting
water into the pipes. But they will be allowed to do it for
this purpose only, upon receiving permission from the superintendent. A violation of this rule will subject the plumber or
pipe fitter to the forfeiture of his license.'

9. No plumber shall allow his name to be used by any other
person or party, directly or indirectly, either for the purpose
of obtaining permits, or doing any work under his license.

10. Whenever a licensed plumber shall make misrepresentation in reference to his plumbing work to an officer of this

department, or its authorized agent, or if any extensions or alterations be made in the service without previously obtaining a permit from the proper officer or upon failing to make a return of his work within forty-eight hours after being served with a notice so to do, at his place of business, the license of such plumber so offending shall be suspended.

11. The ferrule to be inserted in the distributing pipe will be of the size in the permit and order. The serve pipe must be placed not less than two feet below the surface, and in all cases to be so arranged as to prevent rupture from freezing.

12. Any plumber who shall be guilty of a violation of any of the rules adopted by the water commissioners will be immediately deprived of his license.

13. Galvanized iron pipe of size not less than ¾ inch, or lead pipe, shall be used from the curb across the side-walk in every instance.

14. Separate lines and separate stops at the curb are required for each house, and a stop and waste in each line.

15. Extension permits must be obtained for the following plumbing work, when removed or put in buildings where the city water is used or intended to be used—viz: Baths, water-closets, urinals, hydrants, street washers, sinks or faucets in bars or soda fountains, engines, or for any work for which an extra rate may becharged, and failure to report such extension will make the plumber liable for any additional rent accruing therefrom from the date the work was done.

16. All water-closets or outside fixtures shall have a stop and water cock at least 12 inches below ground to protect same from the frost and so arranged as to be accessible at all times in order that it may be easily cut off in case of breakage or leaky pipes.

Table, showing the discharge of water in gallons, per minute, from different sized orifices, under the domestic pressure of the Norfolk city water works, and the size of street service pipes and the weight per foot of lead pipe necessary in plumbing houses.

Average pressure, 35 pounds.

Size of ferrule or opening in disk.	Discharge in gallons per hour.	Size of Pipe Required.	Weight of street service pipe used, per ft., ex. strong.	Weight of house service pipe per foot strung.
1-16 inch.	30			
⅛ "	120			
3-16 "	270			
¼ "	480			
5-16 "	750			
⅜ "	1080	½ Inch.	2 lbs., 7 oz.	1 lb., 6 oz.
½ "	1920	⅝ "	3 " 7 "	2 "
⅝ "	3000	¾ "	3 " 10 "	2 " 8 "
¾ "	4320	1 "	4 " 12 "	3 "
1 "	7680	1¼ "	6 "	4 "

SIZE OF ATTACHMENTS.

All attachments for ordinary service shall be made by means of brass ferrules of one-half (½), five-eights (⅝). three-quarters (¾), or one inch diameter of water way, and in order to provide an ample supply, with a minimum tax upon the capacity of the works, and at a minimum cost to the consumer, ferrules will be allowed as follows :

½ inch for all houses of 18 rooms and less.
⅝ inch for all houses above 18 rooms.
¾ inch for all stores and offices.

Extra supplies to be determined by the board of commissioners upon special application.

Five per cent. Bonds for New Main for the Water Works.

1. Be it ordained by the common and select councils of the city of Norfolk, that for the purpose of enlarging the capacity of the Norfolk city water works by laying a new main iron pipe from the pump house to the city, and other pipes of greater dimension than those now in use, coupon bonds of the city of Norfolk, to the amount of $90,000, shall be issued, payable on the first day of May, 1914, bearing interest payable semi-annually, namely, on the first days of May and November, at the rate of five per centum per annum. *$90,000 five per cents, due May 1, 1914*

Interest, May and November

2. Full power and authority are hereby given to the finance committee of said common and select council to prepare and issue the said bonds in such form and each for such sum as the said committee shall prescribe, and each of said bonds shall be signed by the presidents respectively of the said councils and countersigned by the treasurer of said city, with the corporate seal of the said city affixed thereto, and each of the coupons shall have name of said treasurer affixed thereto. *Power to finance committee to prepare bonds*

3. The said bonds when executed as provided in the preceding section shall be delivered to the board of water commissioners of the city of Norfolk by the treasurer of said city, and the said board shall deposit their receipt therefor with the said treasurer, signed by the chairman and countersigned by the treasurer of said board. *Bonds to be delivered to water board*

4. The said bonds shall be sold by the board of water commissioners at their discretion for the best price that the board can obtain for the same, provided, that none of said bonds shall be sold for less than their par value and accrued interest, and such bonds or the proceeds of the sales thereof, shall be used by the said board of water commissioners for the payment of the cost of said iron pipes and the laying of the same, according to the contracts to be made and entered into in pursuance of the resolution and order of said select and common councils, adopted March, 1884, and all expenses attending the same, and shall not be applied or used for other purposes. *Water board to sell bonds* *Proceeds ; how applied* *See amendment*

5. The said bonds shall be exempt from any and all taxation by the said city, and the said coupons shall be received in payment of all dues to the said city and of all taxes levied or assessed by the said city. *Exempt from taxes* *Coupons receivable for all dues to city*

Board to pay interest out of special tax

6. The board of water commissioners shall pay the interest of said bonds half yearly as the same shall accrue, out of the proceeds of the special water tax levied by the councils, subject to the payment first of the sums due from time to time for interest and sinking fund of the Norfolk city 8 per cent water bonds, issued May 1, 1875, and if the funds in the hands of said board be at any time insufficient to meet the payment of interest on the bonds herein authorized as the coupons shall become due and payable, then, and in that case, the said interest shall be paid by the treasurer of said city out of the general fund.

Proviso

C. C., March 20, 1884; S. C., March 20, 1884.

Amending 4th Section of Ordinance authorizing issue of

Water Bonds.

Amendment to section 4

4. The said bonds shall be sold by the board of water commissioners at their discretion for the best price that the board can obtain for the same, provided that none of said bonds shall be sold for less than ninety six cents on the dollar of principal, and the accrued interest.

And such bonds or the proceeds of the sales thereof shall be used by the said board of water commissioners for the payment of the cost of the said iron pipe and the laying of the same; according to the contracts to be made and entered into in pursuance of the resolution and order of the said common and select councils, adopted March   , 1884. and all expenses attending the same, and not be applied or used for any other purpose.

August 19, 1884.

Amending and Re-enacting 4th Section of Ordinance Concerning Water Bonds.

Section 4 further amended

4. Full power and authority are hereby vested in the joint finance committee of the councils to make sale of the residue of the five per cent. coupon bonds issued for the improvement of the Norfolk city water works, or as many of them as in their judgment is necessary, or to hypothecate the same, and borrow money for the purpose of meeting the pressing payments for the objects for which the bonds were issued. The joint finance committee are further authorized and empowered if in their judgment they decide it to be for the interest of the city to sell said bonds, or hypothecate said bonds and borrow money to turn the proceeds of either the sale or the hypothecation over to the treasurer of the city of Norfolk, who, upon receiving the same, shall immediately pay the same over to the treasurer of the board of water commissioners, taking his receipt for the same.

The treasurer of the board of water commissioners shall use the money so received by him for the payment of the cost of the iron pipe and laying the same, according to the contract made and entered into in pursuance of the resolution and order of said common and select councils, adopted March, 1884, and all expenses attending the same, and it shall not be applied to any other purpose.

September 26, 1884.

AN ORDINANCE

Authorizing the issue of bonds for the improvement of the Norfolk City Water Works.

1. Be it ordained by the common and select councils of the city of Norfolk, that for the purpose of enlarging the capacity of the Norfolk city water works, by laying a new main iron pipe from Lake Bradford to Lake Lawson, coupon bonds of the city of Norfolk, to the amount of fifty thousand dollars, ($50,000) shall be issued, payable on the first day of May, A. D. nineteen hundred and fifteen, bearing interest payable semi-annually, namely, on the first days of May and November, at the rate of five per centum per annum. *$50,000, five per cents.; due 1915; to connect Lake Bradford*

2. Full power and authority are hereby given to the finance committee of said common and select councils to prepare and issue the said bonds in such form and each for such sum as the said committee shall prescribe; and each of said bonds shall be signed by the presidents respectively of said councils and countersigned by the treasurer of the said city, with the corporate seal of the said city affixed thereto, and each of the coupons shall have the name of the said treasurer affixed thereto. *Finance committee to prepare bonds*

The said bonds when executed as provided in the preceding section, shall be delivered to the board of water commissioners of the city of Norfolk, by the treasurer of said city, and the said board shall deposit their receipt therefor with the said treasurer signed by the chairman and countersigned by the treasurer of said board. *Bonds to be delivered to water board*

4. The said bonds shall be sold by the board of water commissioners at their discretion for the best price that the board can obtain for same, provided that none of said bonds shall be sold for less than 95 per cent. and accrued interest, and such bonds, or the proceeds of the sales thereof, shall be used by the said board of water commissioners for the payment of the cost of said iron pipe and the laying of the same, according to the contracts made and entered into, (in pursuance of a resolution adopted by said common and select councils) and all expenses attending the same, and shall not be applied or used for other purposes. *Board shall sell bonds* *Proceeds; how applied*

5. The said bonds shall be exempt from any and all taxation by said city, and the said coupons shall be received in payment of all dues to the said city, and of all taxes levied or assessed by the said city. *Exempt from taxes; coupons receivable for all dues*

6. The board of water commissioners shall pay the interest of the said bonds half yearly, as the same accrues, out of the proceeds of the special water tax levied by the councils, subject to the payment, first, of the sums due from time to time *Interest to be paid by board out of special tax*

for interest and sinking fund of the Norfolk city eight per cent. water bonds, issued May 1st, 1871

Proviso

And if the funds in the hands of said board be at any time insufficient to meet the payments of interest on the bonds herein authorized as the coupons shall become due and payable, then, and in that case, the said interest shall be paid by the treasurer of said city out of the general fund.

7. This ordinance shall be in force from its passage.

C. C. August 11, 1885.

S. C. August 11, 1885.

CHAPTER XLII.

Weights and Measures.

Sealer of weights and measures appointed by councils: his official bond and oath

1. The sealer of weights and measures shall keep the standard of weights and measures belonging to the city. He shall give bond to the city in the sum of one thousand dollars, conditioned for the faithful discharge of the duties of his office, which bond shall be filed in the office of the treasurer.

Penalty for selling or using weights, &c., not sealed and marked by sealer

2. All persons selling weights, measures or scale beams, by retail, or using weights, measures or beams in weighing or measuring any article for sale, shall cause such weights, measures or beams to be sealed and marked by the sealer; and if any person shall sell any weight, measure or scale beam by retail, or in weighing or measuring any article for sale, shall use any weight, measure or beam not so sealed or marked, such person shall pay a fine of ten dollars.

How weights, &c., sealed and marked; penalty for using weights, &c., not conformable to standard, or for using broken, changed or condemned weights, &c.

3. All weights, measures and beams sealed or adjusted by the sealer shall be made conformable to the act of congress, and shall be marked by him with the initials of his name, and the year in which the same shall be marked and sealed; and if any person shall use in weighing or measuring any weight, measure or beam which shall not be conformable to such standard, every such person shall pay a fine of twenty dollars; and if any weight or measure which has been stamped according to the requirements of this ordinance shall be broken or changed, or condemned by the sealer, and found thereafter in the use of any person, such person shall pay a fine of twenty dollars.

Sealer's duty in the inspection and examination of weights, &c.

4. It shall be the duty of the sealer to inspect and examine, at least once a year, and more frequently when he may think proper, all weights, measures and beams used in weighing and measuring; and if any person shall refuse to exhibit his weights, measures and beams, or any of them, for the purpose of being inspected and examined, such person shall pay a fine of twenty dollars. If the sealer shall be informed, or have reason to suspect that any person is using, or has in his possession, with a fraudulent intention, any false beam, scales, weights, or measures, it shall be his duty to examine the same, and if he finds them false, to seize the same, and after having the same adjusted, to sell them at public auction, and the proceeds to pay over to the treasurer.

Sealer's fees

5. The sealer shall be entitled to receive for his services in

sealing and marking: For every two-bushel measure, fifty cents; for every bushel measure, twenty-five cents; for every half bushel, peck, half peck, and five-gallon measure, fifteen cents; for every gallon, half gallon, quart, pint, half pint, gill or half-gill measure, five cents. For every fifty-six, twenty-eight, fourteen, or seven-pound weight, ten cents; for every set of weights from four pounds to half an ounce weight, twenty-five cents; for every single weight under seven pounds, five cents; for every yard measure, ten cents; for every scale beam not exceeding eighteen inches, fifteen cents; above eighteen inches and not exceeding thirty-six inches, twenty cents; above thirty-six inches, twenty-five cents; over and above, a reasonable compensation for making them conformable to the standard established by law, to be paid by the person requiring the same to be inspected. Provided, that the sealer shall not be entitled to any fee for examining and inspecting any weight, measure or beam which shall have been already sealed, unless upon such examination such weight, measure or beam shall be found not to be conformable to the standard.

6. The sealer shall keep a book in which he shall register the names of the persons whose beams and scales, weights and measures, he shall have had adjusted, together with the month and year, and the number and description of the same so adjusted, which book he shall submit to the inspection of the mayor once in every year, or more frequently, if the mayor shall require it; and if the sealer shall be convicted of having stamped any weight, measure, scale or beam, without having accurately adjusted the same, he shall pay a fine of twenty dollars for every such offense. *Sealer's duty to keep register of beams, scales, weights and measures adjusted, &c.; penalty for stamping weights, &c., inaccurately*

Grain, Produce, Etc.

7. There shall be appointed by the councils annually, at their first meeting in July, or as soon thereafter as practicable, as many measurers as may be necessary to measure all salt, charcoal, wheat, Indian corn, rye, barley, oats, flaxseed, peanuts, beans, peas, dried apples, dried peaches, and dried cherries, bought and sold within the city. The standard weight of the above articles, except salt and charcoal, shall be, at wholesale or retail, as follows: *Measurers to be appointed; standard weight of grain, &c.; provision where weight is above or below standard*

Wheat	60 lbs.	per	bushel
Indian corn	56 "	"	"
Rye	56 "	"	"
Barley	48 "	"	"
Oats	32 "	"	"
Flaxseed	56 "	"	"
Peanuts	22 "	"	"
Beans	60 "	"	"
Peas	60 "	"	"
Dried apples	28 "	"	"
Dried peaches, peeled	40 "	"	"
Dried cherries	50 "	"	"

and in all cases of sales of wheat, Indian corn, rye, barley, or oats, by the bushel, if the same shall exceed the standard weight, the buyer shall pay a proportionally greater price, and if the same shall be less than the said standard, the buyer shall pay a proportionally less price; provided that this regulation shall not extend to any special contracts respecting sales of wheat, Indian corn, rye, barley or oats, whatever may be the weight thereof.

Fixtures for weighing to be furnished by measurers; fines and penalty for neglect or violation of duty

8. The necessary fixtures for weighing shall be provided by the measurers at their own cost. If any of the measurers, on application to measure any of the aforesaid articles, shall not comply with such application within one hour, he shall, unless he be elsewhere engaged in the line of his duty, pay a fine of five dollars; and if any measurer shall be detected in any fraud in the execution of his office, or shall demand higher or less fees for his services than are allowed by this ordinance, he shall pay a fine of twenty dollars, and be disqualified from serving in the said office, or in any other municipal office.

How weight ascertained; measurer's certificate and report; fees

9. In order to ascertain the weight, the measurer shall weigh one bushel out of every hundred measured by him; but whenever the buyer or seller may require a bushel to be weighed, the measurer shall do so; provided, however, that he shall not weigh more than one bushel in every twenty-five so measured. The measurer shall make an estimate of the quantity weighed according to the standard provided in section one; and give a certificate of the number of bushels so weighed to the buyer and seller, and make a monthly report thereof to the auditor. The measurers shall receive fifty cents for every hundred bushels of the aforesaid articles they may measure, one-half of which shall be paid by the buyer and one-half by the seller.

Directions for measuring

10. It shall be the duty of the measurers to see that the measure of charcoal be well heaped, and that all salt and grain be measured with a half bushel, having a bar of iron at the top, secured by another passing through the centre at the bottom of the standard measure of the city, which shall be so filled in measuring, and being on a level, as to strike off not less than three pints, and shall be stricken with a straight striker rounded on the edges, of at least three-quarters of an inch in thickness, and not less than four inches broad; and the measurer shall have always on hand for measuring three or more half-bushel measures, and at least two two-bushel tubs (in which alone charcoal shall be measured and delivered) their own property, and regulated every six months by the sealer, according to the standard.

When weighing may be dispensed with; fines for sales without attendance of measurer; proviso in favor of charcoal

11. When any article is delivered to any person in quantities less than fifty bushels, the buyer and seller consenting thereto, may dispense with the attendance of a measurer. But if either of the persons require that one shall be called, then the expense of one cent per bushel shall be paid by the person requiring the same. And if the seller receive or deliver the same (unless the quantity be less than fifty bushels) without the attendance of a measurer, for every such offense he shall

pay a fine of ten dollars; provided, no seller of charcoal, brought to this city by land or in casks, shall be compelled to cause the same to be measured, unless thereto required by the purchaser of the same.

12. When the measurers engaged in measuring any corn or other grain shall perceive a difference in the kind or quality, they shall stop all further measurement, and give notice immediately of such difference to the purchaser and await his directions in the matter. If any measurer shall fail to comply with this provision he shall pay a fine of five dollars; and it shall be the duty of the measurer, when engaged in measuring any corn or other grain, to notice if any dirt, such as cobs, silk, gravel, or any matter other than fine chaff, be mingled with the corn or other grain, and in his returns to the buyer and seller of the same he shall state what quantity of dirt or other matter was passed in the measurement, which shall be allowed by the seller and deducted as refuse. If any measurer shall fail to comply with this provision he shall pay a fine of five dollars. *Duty of measurer when there is any difference in kind or quality, cobs, gravel, &c, in article measured*

Grain Elevators and the Regulation of the Same.

13. Be it ordained by the common and select councils of the city of Norfolk, that at any steam elevator, for the purpose of handling or transferring grain of any kind, located in the city of Norfolk, or at any floating elevator in the harbor of Norfolk, where all the grain handled is weighed, it shall be necessary to employ two or more weighers or tally keepers, who shall be appointed as hereinafter provided for, and be subject to such rules and regulations as may be prescribed. *Weighers to be employed at elevators*

14. It shall be the duty of the councils, immediately after the passage of this ordinance, and thereafter at their first joint meeting in July of each year, to appoint a board, consisting of five persons, who shall be receivers and shippers of grain. They shall be authorized and empowered to appoint two or more weighers or tally keepers, to render service at the elevators in their official capacity, and who shall qualify under oath before the mayor of the city, to faithfully perform the duties of their office; and should they prove incompetent or unfit to fill the position, the said board, or a majority thereof, shall have the power to remove them, and to fill the vacancy or vacancies. The fee for weighing and other official duties, shall be one-eighth of a cent per bushel, and shall be paid by the owner. *Councils to appoint board; board to appoint weighers* *Fees*

15. The owner or owners of any elevator, whether permanent or afloat, shall make a monthly report to the city auditor, showing the quantity of each kind of grain weighed, and the number of bushels, and jointly with the weigher, shall furnish the buyer and seller with a certificate of the number of pounds of grain and the number of bushels weighed for them, as per the following standard of weights: *Owners to make reports*

Wheat, 60 lbs. per bushel; Indian corn, 56 lbs. per bushel; rye, 56 lbs. per bushel; barley, 48 lbs. per bushel; oats, 32 *Standard of weights* lbs. per bushel; flaxseed, 56 lbs. per bushel; beans, 60 lbs. per bushel; peas, 60 lbs. per bushel; and for such certificate, the owner of the elevator may charge and receive fifty cents per hundred bushels, one half to be paid by the seller, and the other half by the buyer.

Duties of weigher

16. When the weigher or tally keeper engaged in weighing grain at an elevator shall perceive a difference in the kind or quality of the grain then being received, and differing in any particular from sample or article purchased, he shall stop the further weighing, and give notice of such difference to the purchasers, and await his or their directions in the matter; and should the owner or owners of the elevator refuse to comply with the order of the weigher, and continue the delivery of the rejected grain, he or they shall be subject to a fine of fifty dollars for every such offence.

Duty of weigher

17. The weigher or tally keeper shall notice if any dirt, such as cobs, silk, gravel, or any matter be mingled with the grain, and he, together with the owner, in granting a certificate of quantity to the buyer and seller, shall deduct the proper quantity of dirt or other matter contained therein; and should the said weigher and owner fail to comply with this provision, the weigher, with the owner of such elevator, shall be fined ten dollars each for every such offence.

Scales; how furnished

18. Every scale used in the weighing of grain at any elevator, shall be furnished by the owner or owners of said elevator, and tested by the sealer of weights and measures, and the board or a majority thereof, upon a complaint of the weigher or any receiver or buyer of grain, that in their opinion the said scales are not in good order, shall be empowered to order an immediate examination and correction of the same, the cost to be paid by the owner or owners of said elevator, and should the owner or owners persist in using said scales, declared and shewn to be out of order, they shall be subject to a fine of twenty dollars for every such offence.

Scales to be examined

Fines and penalties

19. The fines or penalties herein imposed may be recovered, by warrant before the mayor or any justice of the peace of the city, as in other cases of fines and penalties, and one half of said fines shall go to the informer, and the other half to the city, except when the weigher or tally keeper is the informer, in which case the whole of such fine or fines shall go to the city.

Passed C. C., December 17, 1878.
Passed S. C., December 17, 1878.

Weighing of Coals.

Coals to be sold by weight; weigher's duty; proviso

20. All coals, except charcoals, sold for consumption within this city, shall be sold by weight, to be ascertained by weighing at the platform scales on Roanoke square, and it shall be the duty of the weigher at the said scales to weigh all coals brought there in carts or otherwise, and to give certificates thereof to the seller or purchaser when required to do so; provided, however, that any dealer in or seller of coals, who may

be provided with the proper scales, may have the same weighed in his yard under the inspection of a sworn measurer, appointed by the councils annually at their first meeting in July, or as soon thereafter as practicable, who shall be entitled to the compensation provided for in the third section of this ordinance, and to be paid as therein directed.

21. The weight of a ton of coal shall be two thousand two hundred and forty pounds. *Standard weight of ton of coal*

22. The weigher at said scales shall be entitled to demand and receive the sum of twelve cents for every ton of coals weighed by him, and in that proportion for any less quantity, to be paid one half by the buyer and one half by the seller. *Weigher's fees*

23. It shall be the duty of the said weigher to see that all carts with coals coming to the said scales to be weighed are provided with good and sufficient tail-boards, so as to prevent the coals from escaping or dropping therefrom, and he is hereby authorized to refuse to weigh any cart deficient therein. *Carts to be securely made*

24. It shall be lawful for any dealer in coals to discharge coals from any vessel into his yard, free from any weighing or measurement, unless he shall think proper to have the same weighed or measured--in which case he shall employ a sworn measurer or weighmaster, whose fee shall be ten cents per ton of two thousand two hundred and forty pounds. But any vender who shall deliver coals from any vessel, or his coal-yard, for consumption within the limits of the city, without having the same weighed as provided for in the first section of this ordinance, shall pay twenty dollars for each offense, one half of which shall go to the informer and the other half to the use of the city, except where the weigher shall be the informer, in which case the whole of such fine shall go to the city. *Dealers in coals may discharge coals from vessels free from weighing, &c but venders delivering the same for consumption in city must comply with section 1.*

Hay in Bales or Blocks.

25. All hay in bales or blocks, brought to the city for sale, whenever required by the buyer or seller, shall be weighed by the weigher of hay in a just and equitable manner. *When hay required to be weighed*

The weigher shall make allowance for moisture, as well as for mud and all other foreign substances, and shall mark the weight on each bale or block of hay so weighed, and shall be entitled to receive three and one half cents for each bale and one and three quarter cents for each block so weighed, one half to be paid by the buyer and one half by the seller; provided that nothing herein contained shall be construed as rendering the weighing of hay in bales or blocks compulsory except when required by the buyer or seller; *provided*, further, that the buyer and seller may unite in an agreement with the weigher of hay as to his fees for weighing hay in bales or blocks in any case, and such agreement shall be binding on all the parties thereto; but in the absence of any such agreement between all the parties concerned, the fees shall be as hereinbefore provided. *Duties of weigher* *Fees allowed weigher* *Private agreement may be made as to fees*

Wood for Fuel.

Firewood to be corded

26. All fire wood brought to the city for sale and consumption therein, shall be corded on some wharf between posts, and measured; and for each cord of wood so measured, the

Fee of measurer

measurer shall be entitled to ten cents, to be paid by the seller; and the measurer of wood shall be entitled to ten cents for each cord of wood measured by him for shipment, or for consumption by steam boats or other vessels, to be paid by the seller and purchaser in equal portions. The cord of wood shall be eight feet in breadth, four feet in length and four feet in height, and every log shall be sound, free from projecting knots and four feet long; and any person who shall sell, or offer for sale, fire wood in violation of this provision, shall pay

Certain dealers exempted

a fine of two dollars, unless it be sold as refuse wood; provided that the keepers of wood yards in the city, who pay a license as other merchants, shall not be required to have the wood bought or sold by them, at their yards, measured by the wood measurer, except in those cases where the purchaser or seller shall require it; and in such case the said measurement shall be at the cost and expense of the person selling.

Measurer not to deal in wood

27. No inspector and measurer shall buy more wood than may be necessary for his own use, nor shall he sell for any person, nor make any bargain in relation thereto, under a penalty of four dollars for each offense.

Wood dealers must sell ¼ cord

28. Every person who shall bring firewood into the city for sale, shall sell the same in quantities as small as one-eighth of a cord, if required; and any person refusing so to do shall pay a fine of five dollars, one half of which shall go to the informer.

Penalty for dealing in certain cases

29. Any person who shall purchase fire-wood within the city to sell again therein, shall pay a fine of five dollars, one half of which shall go to the informer.

Duty of measurer

30. The measurer shall render under oath a quarterly return to the auditor of all wood measured by him, with the amount of fees charged or received, and pay five per cent. thereon to the treasurer; and for any failure to comply with this provision the measurer shall pay a fine of twenty dollars, and may be dismissed from office.

Weigher at the Public Scales on Roanoke Square.

Weigher at public scales appointed by councils; his official bond; monthly reports

31. There shall be appointed by the councils annually, at their first meeting in July, or as soon thereafter as practicable, a weigher at the public scales at the head of Roanoke square. The weigher shall give bond in the sum of two hundred dollars for the faithful performance of the duties of his office, and shall make a report, certified under oath, to the Auditor, at the end of every month, of the amount of fees, received by him.

Hay, &c., to be weighed; weigher's duties and fees; penalty on sel-

32. All hay, straw or fodder brought to the city of Norfolk for sale, either by land or water, except hay in bales or blocks, shall be weighed when the value of the same shall be more than two dollars, at the said scales, and at no other place, and

by the weigher appointed as aforesaid, at the rate of one hundred pounds to the hundred weight; and it shall be the duty of the said weigher to make a reasonable allowance for the moisture of the said hay, straw or fodder, as well as for any mud or other substance attached to the wagon or cart containing the same; and the said weigher shall make out his certificate for every net hundred pounds weight; and every twenty hundred pounds net weight shall be considered a ton, and he shall be entitled to receive three cents, to be paid by the seller, for every hundred weight of hay, fodder or straw thus weighed, until the weight or load amount to twenty hundred pounds; but in no case shall he receive more than forty cents for any one load of hay. straw or fodder so weighed; and if any seller of hay, straw or fodder shall neglect or refuse to have the same weighed on the day of the delivery thereof, he shall pay a fine of five dollars. ler for neglect or refusal to have hay, &c. weighed

33. If any person bringing hay, straw or fodder to the city for sale, except hay brought for sale in bales, and in quantities of less value than that mentioned in the thirty-second section, shall neglect or refuse to have the same weighed in the manner hereinbefore provided for, or shall in any manner be guilty of fraud in weighing or selling the same, he shall pay for each and every offense a fine of five dollars; and if any person, after having his hay, straw or fodder weighed, and having obtained the weigher's certificate specifying the quantity thereof, shall sell or dispose of any part thereof, or in any manner diminish the quantity, to defraud or deceive the purchaser, such person shall pay for each and every such offense a fine of twenty dollars. Penalty on persons bringing hay, &c., to city for sale, who neglect to have same weighed, or are guilty of fraud, &c

34. The weighing apparatus shall be adjusted at least once in every six months by the standard weights for the city of Norfolk, the expense of which, together with all expenses for repairs, shall be incurred by the city. Weighing apparatus to be adjusted every six months

35. The weigher at the public scales may at all times, when required. weigh hemp, cotton, cables, anchors, dye-woods, bark, live stock, or any other heavy articles in bulk, and shall be paid according to the rate provided in section thirty-two; a monthly report of which he shall also make to the auditor. Weigher may weigh hemp cotton, &c.; his fees and reports

36. One half of all fines imposed by sections 32 and 33 shall go to the informer. and the other half to the city, except when the weigher is the informer, in which case the whole of such fine or fines shall go to the city. How fines appropriated

Gauging and Inspecting Liquors.

37. The Gauger and Inspector of liquors shall give bond in the sum of one thousand dollars, with security, to be approved by the councils, conditioned for the faithful performance of the duties of his office. Gauger and inspector appointed ; his official bond

38. Once in every three months—to wit, on the twenty-fourth day of September, on the twenth-fourth day of December, on the twenty-fourth day of March, and on the twenty-fourth day of June in each year, the gauger and inspector shall make a return to the auditor of the city of the number of casks Gauger and inspector to make reports to auditor

of oil, molasses or liquor inspected and guaged, distinguishing foreign from domestic distilled liquors, and the number of gallons, and enumerating such of the said articles as may have been distilled within the city. Such return shall set forth the sums received or charged by the gauger and inspector for gauging and inspecting, and shall be verified by affidavit before the mayor or some justice of the peace.

Fees of gauger and inspector

39. The gauger and inspector shall be entitled to receive the following fees for his services—to wit: For all casks containing oil or molasses, not exceeding forty gallons, eight cents per cask; and for all casks containing more than forty gallons, twelve and a half cents per cask; and for all spirituous liquors, the casks thereof not exceeding forty gallons, six and a quarter cents per cask; and for all casks containing more than forty gallons, eight cents for each cask; and for proving all casks of spirituous liquors, or liquid merchandise of any kind, three cents for each cask; and in every case where the ullages only of a cask or casks are to be taken, for each cask four cents, and no more, all fees to be paid by the seller.

Duties of gauger and inspector

40. It shall be the duty of the said gauger and inspector, when required, to gauge, oil, wine, rum, molasses, and other liquid merchandise (malt liquor excepted) imported or brought to this city, to mark and set down the number of gallons which each cask or vessel shall contain, with his mark, all of which casks, with the marks and numbers and the owners' names, shall be entered in a book kept for that purpose; and in case of spirituous liquor, he shall mark the proof it may be found to bear on each cask. And if any cask or vessel gauged or marked by the gauger and inspector of liquors shall be found lacking or exceeding one or more gallons in every quarter cask, or two or more gallons in casks of a larger size, the quantity so numbered and marked, the said gauger and inspector shall pay two dollars for every gallon so lacking or exceeding the number set down on each cask.

Penalty for altering mark of gauger, &c., or for putting false mark

41. If any person shall alter any mark or number marked by the gauger and inspector, or shall put any false mark or number on any cask of oil, wine, rum, molasses, or other liquid merchandise, such person shall pay a fine of ten dollars for every such offense.

Reports of Measurers, Inspectors, Gaugers and Weighers.

Measurers, &c. to make quarterly reports to auditor; penalty; auditor to report delinquencies to councils

42. The measurers, inspectors weighers and gaugers shall keep accurate accounts of the several articles imported into or exported from the city, and measured, weighed, inspected, received or delivered by them respectively, together with the market prices, and places from whence imported, and report the same, on oath, in the last week of every quarter, to the Auditor of the city; and if any such person shall neglect or refuse to make such report he shall pay twenty dollars for each week's failure, to be recovered as in other cases of fines, and if such person shall refuse or neglect to make such report

for one month after it shall be required of him by the auditor, or shall give in any false or fraudulent reports, he shall be dismissed from office, and it shall be the duty of the auditor, from time to time, to report to the councils the delinquency of all and every one of the said officers.

43. It shall be the duty of the auditor to collate the said reports and make quarterly an aggregate return thereof to the committee on statistics, to be laid before the councils. The original reports shall be filed by the auditor.

Auditor to make quarterly report to committee on statistics

CHAPTER XLIII.

Powder.

1. No person shall keep in any house or store any quantity of gunpowder exceeding two kegs or vessels thereof of the weight of twenty-five pounds each, and before such person shall have this privilege he shall make an application in writing to the mayor for permission to do so, to be approved by the chief engineer of the fire department. The chief engineer shall keep a list of all permits granted, and for any violation of this section such person shall pay a fine of twenty dollars, one-half of which shall go to the informer; and the person offending shall not be permitted to keep the said amount of powder thereafter without the consent of the councils; provided, that nothing contained in this section shall be construed to prevent any person from keeping in any one house as much as two pounds of powder for such private purposes as may be proper.

Amount of gunpowder allowed to be kept, application to the mayor for permission to keep same, duty of chief engineer of fire department, penalty, proviso

2. No person shall carry in any dray or other carriage, or in any other manner, any quantity of gunpowder exceeding two pounds in or through the city, unless the same shall be first secured in good bags, and covered with a sail or other cloth, under a penalty of five dollars for every barrel, half-barrel, cask, bag, or keg so carried. One-half of all fines and penalties incurred under this ordinance shall go to the informer, and the other half to the city.

How gunpowder to be transported through the city, fines and penalties

CHAPTER XLIV.

The Map of the City.

Resolution of the Councils, December 6, 1881.

Resolved, That the report of the street committee, dated November 15, 1881, upon the report of Thomas Bernard, city engineer, submitting the topographical map of the city, made by him, in pursuance of a former resolution of the councils, be received, approved and adopted; and the said topographical map be received as the official map of the city.

Rules of Order of the Common and Select Councils of the City of Norfolk.

—·◆·—

MONTHLY MEETING DAYS.

1. The common council shall meet on the first Tuesday and the select council on the second Tuesday in every month, at such hour as may be designated by the president.

DUTIES OF THE MESSENGER.

2. The messenger shall summon the members to attend the regular or special meetings by a written or printed notice delivered to each member or left at his dwelling, and shall make a return of the members summoned to the treasurer before the appointed meeting; and if he shall fail to perform any duty herein assigned to him he shall forfeit and pay two dollars for every such failure.

JOINT SESSIONS OF THE COUNCILS.

3. The select and common councils shall meet together in joint session on the first day of July of each year, (and if the first day of July shall fall on Sunday then on the day following) for the purpose of electing such officers as are, or may be, by law, or by any city ordinance, required to be elected at their first meeting in July, and may adjourn such meeting from day to day.

4. It shall be the duty of the presidents of the select and common councils to convene the councils in joint session for the election of officers of the city whenever a vacancy occurs or when in any case such election is required to be held at any other time than the month of July, by any law or ordinance. In all joint sessions under this rule a president *pro tempore* shall be chosen by the members present.

ORDER OF BUSINESS.

5. The order of business at all meetings of the councils shall be as follows:

Upon the appearance of a quorum the president, or, in his absence, the vice-president, shall open the business of the meeting, which shall have priority over all other business. In case the president and vice-president shall both be absent, a president *pro tempore* shall be appointed by the meeting.

Regular Meetings.

1. Reading proceedings of previous meetings of both branches of the councils.
2. Reports of standing committees.
3. Report of special committees.

4. Special orders for business.
5. Unfinished business of previous meetings.
6. Introduction of ordinances, resolutions, or new business.
7. Presentation of petitions, claims, &c.

Special Meetings.

1. Reading proceedings of previous meeting.
2. Special business for which meeting is ordered. No other business shall be in order at a special meeting except by consent of two-thirds of the members present, and if so allowed, shall be introduced in the order prescribed for regular meetings.

HOW MEMBERS MAY RETIRE.

6. No member, after his name shall have been duly entered, shall absent himself without permission of the presiding officer.

DUTY OF CLERK WHERE THERE IS NO QUORUM.

7. In the absence of a quorum, the clerk shall, at the expiration of half an hour from the time appointed for the meeting, enter upon the journal the names of the members present.

COMPELLING MEMBERS TO ATTEND, FINES, &c.

8. The president shall have power to send a messenger to summon members to attend to form a quorum for business; and if after such notice a member fail to attend, he shall be fined two dollars, for the use of the city, unless excused by the council.

POWERS OF THE PRESIDENT.

9. The president shall in all cases be entitled to one vote He shall preserve order and decorum, and decide all questions of order, subject to an appeal to the council. He shall appoint all committees, unless otherwise ordered by the councils; and may express his opinion upon any subject under discussion.

INTRODUCTION OF RESOLUTIONS.

10. No questions shall be debated or taken on any resolution or motion unless it be first reduced to writing and seconded; and when a motion is seconded it shall be stated by the president before debate.

DEPORTMENT IN DEBATE.

11. All debate shall be regular, without altercation or personal invective, each member addressing himself to the chair, and rising when doing so; confining himself to the subject in debate, and preserving order without interruption or hindrance.

LIMITATION TO SPEECHES.

12. No member shall speak upon the same question more than twice without leave from the council.

HOW MOTIONS MAY BE WITHDRAWN.

13. After a motion is stated by the president it shall be deemed to be in possession of the council, but may be withdrawn at any time before decision or amendment.

MOTIONS ALLOWABLE UPON QUESTIONS UNDER DEBATE.

14. When a question is under debate, no motion shall be received, unless—first, to offer a substitute; second, to amend; third, to commit; fourth, to postpone to a certain day; fifth, for the previous question; sixth, to lay on the table, or to adjourn.

MOTIONS FOR ADJOURNMENT.

15. A motion to adjourn shall be always in order, and shall be decided without debate.

VOTING BY THE MEMBERS—OBLIGATORY.

16. Every member who shall be present when any question is put or ballot taken, shall vote or ballot, as the case may be, unless personally interested or excused by the council.

DECIDING THE "PREVIOUS QUESTION"

17. The previous question, until it is decided, shall preclude all amendments and debate of the main question, and shall be in this form: "Shall the main question now be put."

HOW QUESTIONS SHALL BE PUT.

18. All questions shall be put in the order they are moved, except that in filling blanks, the largest sum and the longest time shall be first put.

THE YEAS AND NAYS.

19. Upon every question, any member may require the yeas and nays to be taken and recorded.

CALLING MEMBERS TO ORDER.

20. A member called to order shall immediately sit down, unless permitted to explain, and the council, if appealed to, shall decide the case, but without debate. If there be no appeal the decision of the chair shall be submitted to.

DISSENT TO A VOTE OR DECISION.

21. Any member may have recorded upon the minutes his dissent to any vote or decision of the council.

MOTIONS FOR RECONSIDERATION.

22. No motion for a reconsideration shall be in order unless made at the same meeting, or in pursuance of notice then given for the next meeting after that on which the decision proposed to be reconsidered took place, except by unanimous consent.

HOW APPOINTEES TO ÓFFICE SHALL BE VOTED FOR.

23. Every appointment to office by the councils shall be by ballot, where more than one person is in nomination, otherwise by *viva voce* vote.

SIGNING OF THE ORDINANCES.

24. All ordinances shall be signed by the presidents of the select and common councils, or, in the absence of either, by the vice-president, and attested by the treasurer.

RESOLUTIONS APPROPRIATING MONEY AND ALL ORDINANCES TO LIE OVER.

25. No resolution appropriating money, nor any ordinance, shall pass on the day on which the same shall be introduced; nor shall any appropriation of money be made, nor any indebtedness be incurred, nor any bond authorized to be issued, in the name of the city, except by a majority vote of all the members elected to each council.

HOW ORDINANCES MAY BE CHANGED.

26. No ordinance shall be amended, suspended or repealed, except by ordinance regularly introduced and passed; nor shall any section of an ordinance be amended unless the whole section be re-enacted.

REMISSION OF FINES.

27. No application for the remission or repayment of a fine shall be considered, unless the facts in regard to such a fine be at the same time reported by the mayor or justice who imposed it.

DUTY OF THE TREASURER AS TO MATTERS REFERRED.

28. It shall be the duty of the treasurer to furnish without delay to the chairman of every committee a copy of every resolution or motion, petition or other matter, referred to such committee, with a list of his colleagues; or, where the matter is referred to any officer of the city, the copy shall be in like manner furnished to such officer. Any matter which may be referred by either branch of the councils to any committee, or to any officer of the city for investigation, information and report, shall be at once, by the treasurer, laid before such committee or officer without concurrence of the other branch, and the report in such cases shall be returned to the branch which shall first meet thereafter, but no reference under this rule shall authorize "*power to act.*"

DUTIES OF COUNCIL CLERKS.

29. The clerk of each council shall deliver to the clerk of the other council a fair copy of such proceedings as shall have been finally disposed of immediately after every meeting.

HOW QUESTIONS ONCE DECIDED MAY AGAIN BE INTRO-DUCED.

30. No question decided by the council shall be again brought forward during the term for which the council was elected, unless on a motion *for reconsideration* there be votes equal to or greater than the majority of the members present when the question was before decided.

DISPOSING OF UNFINISHED BUSINESS.

31. All unfinished business at the expiration of the term for which the councils were elected, shall be considered as laid upon the table, and may be acted on thereafter at the pleasure of the councils succeeding.

APPOINTMENTS OF STANDING COMMITTEES.

32. As soon as convenient after the organization of the councils, there shall be appointed by the presidents the following standing committees, viz:

1st. The committee on finance, to be composed of the vice-president of the common council, the vice-president of the select council, together with two members from the common and one from the select council. Also the following which shall consist of two members from the common and one from the select council, viz:

2d. The committee on Ordinances and Police.
3d. The committee on Almshouse.
4th. The committee on the Fire Department.
5th. The committee on Streets, Sewers and Drains.
6th. The committee on Light.
7th. The committee on Markets.
8th. The committee on Water.
9th. The committee on Wharves and Docks.
10th. The committee on Schools.
11th. The committee on Public Buildings and Grounds.
12th. The committee on Statistics.
13th. The committee on Cemeteries.

DUTIES OF CHAIRMEN OF COMMITTEES, AND THEIR MEETINGS.

33. When any matter is referred to a committee the chairman shall cause the members thereof to be summoned as soon thereafter as practicable, and make report to the next meeting of the councils; provided, that a quorum shall not be deemed present unless the select council is represented in every meeting of a committee, and all meetings shall be held at the office of the city treasurer, and no bills or claims against the city shall be approved except at a meeting of the committee.

PENALTY FOR DELINQUENCY.

34. If any member shall fail to attend three meetings of the council to which he may belong, in succession, without a good excuse, he may be fined not exceeding five dollars. And if any member shall from any cause absent himself from the meetings of the council for three months together, the council may by resolution declare the seat of such member to be vacant, and proceed to fill the vacancy. And if any member appointed on a committee shall fail to attend the meetings thereof and to discharge his duty thereon, his name shall be reported by the committee to the councils in open session and entered on the journal.

PETITIONS AND COMMUNICATIONS.

35. Every petition, communication or address to the councils, from any person not a member thereof, shall be in writing, unless otherwise specially allowed.

SUSPENSION OF RULES.

36. Any rule herein adopted may, at any particular time, be suspended for a special purpose, by a vote of two-thirds of the members present at the time, except the extracts from the city charter.

COMMITTEE OF THE WHOLE.

37. Any motion, resolution or pending ordinance may by a majority vote of both councils be referred to a committee of the whole, which shall consist of a majority of the members of each council.

Extracts from City Charter.

Councilmen; election and duties

15. There shall be elected on the fourth Thursday in May, eighteen hundred and eighty-four, and on the fourth Thursday in May biennially thereafter, thirty councilmen, who shall be apportioned to the several wards, as follows: To the first, second and third wards eight each, and to the fourth ward six, and the same number of councilmen shall be so elected until a reapportionment shall be made according to law. The councilmen shall proceed at the first meeting after their election, or as soon thereafter as practicable, in such manner as they may deem proper, to elect eleven of their number to constitute a select council, which select council shall hold its meetings separate and apart from the remaining nineteen councilmen, who shall constitute the common council. The councils after their separate organization, shall in such manner and at such time as may be prescribed by ordinance, proceed to appoint all officers, clerks and assistants, whose election or appointment is not otherwise provided for by law.

Select council; duties and rights

16. The select council shall elect its officers, to consist of a president, vice president and clerk; and the common council shall elect its officers, to consist of a president and vice presi-

dent; the city treasurer shall be ex-officio clerk of the com- *Treasurer to be clerk of common councils, and shall have an assistant. The select and common coun- common councils, respectively, may elect such other officers cil and clerks as they may deem necessary, which officers shall be *Each council may elect liable to be removed by the councils respectively, each acting clerks, &c. for itself in this regard, with power to the respective councils, each acting for itself, to supply any vacancy occuring. The president or the president pro tempore, who shall preside when the proceedings of a previous meeting are read, shall sign the same. The president shall have the power, at any *Power of time to call a meeting of his council, and in case of his ab- *president sence from sickness, disability or refusal, the councils may be convened by the order in writing, of any five members of the common council, or three of the select council.

17. Ordinances and resolutions may originate in either the *Ordinances of select or common council, to be approved or rejected by the *council other, and may be amended by either council with the consent *How ordinances and reso- of the other. But when the councils cannot agree upon any *lutions passed and disagree- ordinance or resolution, the same shall be referred to a com- *ments settled mittee of conference, to be appointed by each council.

18. The councils shall have authority to compel the attend- *Power of councils as to ance of absent members; to punish members for disorderly *misconduct of behavior, and by a vote of two-thirds of the council to expel *members a member for malfeasance or misfeasance in the office. They shall keep a journal of their proceedings; and their meetings shall be open. A majority of the members of the councils shall constitute a quorum for the transaction of business. *Quorum But on all ordinances or resolutions appropriating money, im- *How appro- priations of posing taxes, or authorising the borrowing of money, the yeas *money to be and nays shall be entered on the journal, and a majority of *made or debt incurred all the members elected to each council, shall be necessary to give them the force of law. No vote shall be reconsidered or *Reconsidera- rescinded at a special meeting, unless at such special meeting *tion of votes there be present as large a number of members as were present when such vote was taken.

Statement of the Leases to Various Parties of the Ends of Streets and Town Point Lots.

Commerce street, leased for five years from July, 1883; expires July, 1888; leased to J. B. Camp, for $100 per annum.

Yarmouth street, leased for twenty years to John L. Roper, for $5 per year; lease expires January, 1905.

West Main street, leased to Boston Wharf and Warehouse Company, at $25 per annum; lease expires October, 1886.

Lee street, leased to the Seaboard Cotton Compress Company, at $120 per annum; no time specified, but to be vacated whenever ordered by councils on thirty days' notice.

Fayette street, leased to Seaboard Cotton Compress Company for five years; lease expires July, 1888; at $100 per annum.

Parker and Wide Water streets, leased to J. Manson Smith for ten years from July, 1876; expires July, 1886; at $150 per annum.

Church street, leased to Old Dominion Steamship Company for fifteen years from July, 1877; expires July, 1892; at $200 per annum.

Parker street, leased to the Baltimore Steam Packet Company for ninety-nine years, renewable, a $5 per annum.

Tobacco Warehouse, leased to Messrs. Vaughan & Barnes for $3,755 per year, for one year, with the privilege of a three years' lease, provided the city does not sell, and if sold, the parties to vacate the premises on the first day of July succeeding such sale; lease commenced July 1, 1885, and includes whatever rights the city may have in the ends of Jackson and Matthews streets.

Newton street, leased to Boston Wharf and Warehouse Company for ten years from July, 1881; at $25 per annum.

Town Point Lots.

Lot No. 1—Minnie L. Norcop, 99 years, ground rent and renewable.... ....$ 111 12

Lot No. 2, 3 and 4—Reynolds Bros., 99 years, (transferred to Seaboard Cotton Compress Company), renewable...................................... 8 25

Lot No. 2, 3 and 4—E. T. Summer's estate, 10 years, January, 1894.............................. 135 00

Lot Nos. 2, 3 and 4—Phoebe Williams' estate, 99 years, and renewable............................ 0 00

Lot No. 9—Phoebe Williams' estate, 99 years, and renewable............................ 124 58

Lot Nos. 6, 7 and 8—McCullough, A. A., & C. W. Grandy, 99 years, and renewable.................. 179 25

Lot Nos. 10, 11, 32 and 33—R. H. Hare, 99 years, and renewable..................... 76 91

Lot Nos. 16 and 17 Worthington & Shepherd. 99 years, and renewable......................... 43 06

Lot Nos. 18, 19, 20 and 21—E. Truxel, 99 years and renewable............................. 29 23

Lot Nos. 26 and 25—Boston Wharf and Warehouse
    Company, 99 years, and renewable.............   36 11
Lot Nos. 22, 24, 23 and 34—Baltimore Steam Pac-
    ket Company, 99 years, and renewable..........   13 05
Lot Nos. 27, 28 and 29—C. B. & W. W. Gwathmey,
    99 years, and renewable................... ....   157 77
Lot No. 29—Baltimore Steam Packet Company, 99
    years, and renewable.............................   39 58
Lot No. 12—T. W. Thompson, 99 years, and renew-
    able..   222 33

Total rents,.....................................$1,176 24

Old Fair Grounds, on Tanner's Creek road, unoccupied.

CHAPTER XLV.

Enacting and Repealing Ordinance.

1. The Ordinances of the City of Norfolk, as they have been revised, codified and compiled by CHARLES G. ELLIOTT, and printed at the office of the Norfolk Landmark Publishing Company, shall be in force from and after the passage of this ordinance, and all ordinances and parts of ordinances of a general nature, in force at the time of passing this ordinance and not included in the foregoing ordinances, shall be repealed from and after the passage of this ordinance, with such limitations and exceptions as are hereinafter expressed.

2. Such repeal shall not affect any act or offense committed or done, or any penalty or forfeiture incurred, or any right accruing or accrued, or acquired or established, or remedy for any injury thereto, or any prosecution or proceeding pending, at or on the day of the passage of this ordinance; or of any order or resolution of the councils hereafter made levying any special assessment or tax for any improvement begun but not now completed.

3. No ordinance which has heretofore been repealed shall be revived by the repeal contained in this chapter of the ordinances hereby repealed.

4. This ordinance shall be in force from its passage.

Passed common council September 1, 1885.

Passed select council September 8, 1885.

Laws of Virginia Relating to the City.

—•◆•—

THE HARBOR.

Acts of Assembly, 1874.

CHAP. 229.—An ACT to repeal Section 3 of an Act passed in 1801, entitled an Act Concerning the Docks and Wharves in the Borough of Norfolk.

Approved April 22, 1874.

1. Be it enacted by the general assembly, That section three of an act passed in the year eighteen hundred and one, entitled an act concerning the docks and wharves in the borough of Norfolk, be and the same is hereby repealed.

2. This act shall be in force from its passage.

———

CHAP. 266.—An ACT to authorize the Councils of Norfolk City to drain, or otherwise improve, certain low or marsh lands, and to change Back Creek in said City.

Approved April 28, 1874.

1. Be it enacted by the general assembly, That the councils of the city of Norfolk, shall have full power and authority to make such orders as they may deem proper, not inconsistant with the laws of the State, for the purpose of filling reclaiming, draining, or otherwise improving the low lands or marsh lying between Bank street in said city and the Elizabeth river, which are left uncovered by the recession of the tide, and known as Back creek, and may change the dimensions and direction of the said creek, or the channel thereof, so as to provide for the proper drainage of the said lands, and improvements of the same.

2. This act shall be in force from its passage.

———

BOARD OF HARBOR COMMISSIONERS.

Acts of Assembly, 1874–'75.

CHAP. 104.—An ACT to create a Board of Harbor Commissioners of Norfolk and Portsmouth, and for the Preservation and Improvement of the Harbor of Norfolk and Portsmouth.

Approved February 18. 1875.

1. Be it enacted by the general assembly, That for the purpose of preserving and improving the harbor of Norfolk and Portsmouth, seven commissioners shall be appointed by the governor—three residents of the city of Norfolk, two of the city of Portsmouth, and two of the county of Norfolk. The commissioners from Norfolk and Portsmouth shall be nominated to the governor for his appointment by the chamber of commerce of Norfolk, and if there should be no chamber of commerce, then by the Norfolk and Portsmouth Cotton Ex-

change, at a meeting to be called for that purpose. The commissioners from the county of Norfolk shall in like manner be nominated by the judge of the county court thereof. All vacancies in the board shall be filled in the same manner as the original appointments.

2. Be it further enacted, That the governor shall commission the said harbor commissioners, who shall hold their office for the term of four years, commencing on the first day of April, eighteen hundred and seventy-five, unless sooner removed by the governor, and the said commissioners shall be a board to be known as The Board of Harbor Commissioners of Norfolk and Portsmouth, and shall organize by electing one of their number president, with such other officers as they may deem proper, a majority of whom shall constitute a quorum for the transaction of business.

3. Be it further enacted, That the said board of harbor commissioners shall have full power to regulate and define the port wardens' lines along the water front of the cities of Norfolk and Portsmouth, and the Elizabeth river, and branches thereof, for five miles above and below the limits of said cities. They shall have power to fix the lines along said rivers within which the riparian owners may erect wharves, docks, and other proper erections and fixtures for commercial and manufacturing purposes. The said board, or a majority of them, shall have authority to cause the removal of any wharf, dock, wreck or other obstruction to navigation, or that may, in their opinion, be injurious to the harbor, at the expense of the owner or owners, or the parties causing the obstructions: provided, the rights of any owner or owners of wharves, whose lines have heretofore been fixed by authority of state legislation, are in nowise to be disturbed.

4. Be it further enacted, That for the purpose of enabling the said commissioners to carry out the purposes of this act, they are hereby authorized to employ the services of a competent engineer, who shall make, or cause to be made, under the direction of the commissioners, a survey of said harbor, Elizabeth river and branches thereof.

5. Be it further enacted, That hereafter, when any dredging or excavation shall be done in the harbor, the material excavated shall only be deposited at such places in the river as may be designated by the said harbor commissioners.

6. Be it further enacted, That the said board of harbor commissioners shall have power to make and enforce such rules and regulations for the preservation of the harbor as they may from time to time deem necessary.

7. Be it further enacted, That the board of harbor commissioners shall have power to appoint, annually, all harbor masters for the cities of Norfolk and Portsmouth, and assign their duties and fix their compensation, and may remove them at pleasure, and the powers of all harbor masters and port wardens, heretofore appointed and acting. shall cease and determine after the organization of the board.

8. Be it further enacted, That for the purpose of defraying

the necessary expenses incurred by the board of harbor commissioners in carrying out the provisions of this act, the county of Norfolk shall be assessed and shall pay two-sevenths of the estimated expenses thereof; the city of Portsmouth two-sevenths; and the city of Norfolk three-sevenths thereof: provided, that the said commissioners shall receive no compensation for their services, except it be allowed by their respective corporations, in which case the corporation making such allowance shall provide for the payment of said commissioners.

9. Be it further enacted, That no person shall build any wharf or other obstruction beyond the lines fixed by said commissioners, and any person doing this shall pay the sum of twenty dollars for every such offence, and shall moreover be fined in the sum of twenty dollars for every day such wharf or other obstruction shall remain; and no person shall hereafter build or extend any wharf or other obstruction in or upon the waters of the harbor of Norfolk or Portsmouth, Elizabeth river and branches thereof, without first obtaining, in writing, from said harbor commissioners, a permit for so doing, under a penalty of twenty dollars for every day such wharf or obstruction shall remain; and it shall be the duty of said board of commissioners to prosecute for the fines and penalties imposed by this act.

10. Be it further enacted, That it shall be the duty of the harbor commissioners, or a committee thereof, to examine from time to time, all the docks, public and private. in Norfolk and Portsmouth, and when it is the opinion of said commissioners, or a majority of them, that any such docks are not in a proper condition for the purposes for which they were designed and used, they shall cause a notice to be served upon the owner or occupier of said dock, to repair and deepen the same, and if such owner or occupier shall neglect or refuse to attend to such dock or wharf, after twenty days' notice, such person so offending shall forfeit and pay twenty dollars, and the further sum of five dollars for every day he, she or they, shall so neglect or refuse, and shall, moreover, pay all ·expenses incurred by reason of such neglect or refusal.

11. Be it further enacted, That the board of harbor commissioners shall publish an annual report of their proceedings, and furnish a printed copy of the same to the governor, auditor, judge of the Norfolk county court, and the mayor and corporations of Norfolk and Portsmouth.

12. Be it further enacted, That all acts and parts of acts so far as they conflict with the provisions of this act, are hereby repealed.

13. This act shall be in force from its passage.

CHAP. 205.—An ACT creating a Board of Harbor Commissioners of Norfolk and Portsmouth, and for the preservation of the harbor of Norfolk and Portsmouth.

Approved March 3, 1882.

1. Be it enacted by the general assembly of Virginia, That

Commission-
ers
for the purpose of preserving and improving the harbor of
Norfolk and Portsmouth, seven commissioners shall be appointed by the governor—three residents of the city of
Norfolk, two of the city of Portsmouth, and two of the county
of Norfolk. Any vacancy in said board—occasioned by death,
resignation, or otherwise—shall be filled in the same manner
as the original appointment.

Appointment
2. That said harbor commissioners shall be duly commissioned by the governor, who shall hold their office for the term
of four years, commencing from the date of their first appointment ; and the said commissioners shall be known as The
Board of Harbor Commissioners of Norfolk and Portsmouth
and Norfolk County, and shall organize by electing one of
their number president, with such other officers as they may
deem proper, a majority of whom shall constitute a quorum
for the transaction of business.

Powers, &c.
3. That the said board of harbor commissioners shall have
full power to regulate and define the port warden's line along
the water front of the cities of Norfolk, Portsmouth, and
Norfolk county, and the Elizabeth river and branches thereof
for five miles above and below the limits of said cities and
county. They shall have power to fix the lines along said
rivers, within which riparian owners may fix wharves, docks,
and other proper erections and fixtures for commercial and
manufacturing purposes. The said board, or a majority of
them, shall have authority to cause the removal of any wharf,
dock, wreck, or other obstruction to navigation, or that may,
in their opinion, be injurious to the harbor, at the expense of
the owner or owners or the parties causing the obstructions ;
provided, the rights of any owner or owners of wharves whose
lines have heretofore been fixed by authority of state legislation, are in no way to be disturbed.

Employ an
engineer
4. That for the purpose of enabling the said commissioners
to carry out the purposes of this act, they are hereby authorized to employ the services of a competent engineer, who shall
make or cause to be made, under the direction of the commissioners, a survey of said harbor, Elizabeth river, and branches
thereof.

Dredging
5. That hereafter, when any dredging or excavation shall
be done in the harbor, the material excavated shall only be
deposited at such places in the river as may be designated by
said harbor commissioners.

Regulations
6. That the said board of harbor commissioners shall have
power to make and enforce such rules and regulations for the
preservation of the harbor as they may, from time to time,
deem necessary.

Fees, &c.
7. That the governor shall, so soon thereafter as practicable, after the passage of this act, appoint two harbor masters
for the ciities of Norfolk, Portsmouth, and Norfolk county,
whose duties shall be assigned and compensation and fees
fixed by the board of harbor commissioners of Norfolk, Portsmouth, and Norfolk county, and who shall be under their
control and direction. One of said harbor masters shall be a

resident and citizen of the city of Norfolk, and the other a
resident and citizen of the city of Portsmouth or Norfolk
county.

8. That for the purpose of defraying the necessary expenses Expenses
incurred by the board of harbor commissioners in carrying
out the provisions of this act, the county of Norfolk shall be
assessed and shall pay two-sevenths of the estimated expenses
thereof, the city of Portsmouth two-sevenths, and the city of
Norfolk three-sevenths thereof; provided, that the said commissioners shall receive no compensation for their services,
except it be allowed by their respective corporations and board
of supervisors of Norfolk county; in which case the corporation or said board making such allowances shall provide for
the payment of said commissioners.

9. That no person shall build any wharf or other obstruc- Wharves, &c.
tion beyond the lines fixed by said commissioners, and any
person doing this shall pay the sum of twenty dollars for
every such offence, and shall moreover be fined in the sum of
twenty dollars for every day such wharf or other obstruction
shall remain; and no person shall hereafter build or extend
any wharf or other obstruction in or upon the waters of the
harbor of Norfolk or Portsmouth, Elizabeth river or branches
thereof, without first obtaining, in writing, from said board of
commissioners a permit for so doing, under a penalty of
twenty dollars for every day such wharf or obstruction shall
remain; and it shall be the duty of said harbor commissioners
to prosecute for the fines and penalties imposed by this act.

10. That it shall be the duty of the harbor commissioners, Duty of com-
or a committee thereof, to examine, from time to time, all the missioners.
docks, public and private, in Norfolk and Portsmouth and
Norfolk county, within the jurisdiction of said board, and
when it is the opinion of said commissioners, or a majority of
them, that any such docks are not in a proper condition for
the purposes for which they were designated and used, they
shall cause a notice to be served upon the owner or occupier
of said dock, and they shall repair and deepen the same; and
if such owner or occupier shall neglect or refuse to attend to
such dock or wharf after twenty days' notice, such person so
offending shall forfeit and pay twenty dollars, and the further
sum of five dollars for every day he, she, or they shall neglect
or refuse, and shall moreover pay all expenses incurred by
reason of such neglect or refusal.

11. That the board of harbor commissioners shall publish Annual report
an annual report of their proceedings, and furnish a printed
copy of the same to the governor, auditor, judge of Norfolk
county court, and to the judges of the corporation courts of
the cities of Norfolk and Portsmouth.

12. That all acts and parts of acts, so far as they conflict
with the provisions of this act, are hereby repealed.

13. This act shall be in force from its passage.　　　　Commencem't

Acts of Assembly, 1883–'84.

CHAP. 148.—An ACT to amend and re-enact sections 1, 2, 7, and 11 of an act creating a board of Harbor Commissioners of Norfolk and Portsmouth, and for the preservation of the harbor of Norfolk and Portsmouth, approved March 3, 1882.

In force February 23, 1884.

1. Be it enacted by the general assembly of Virginia, That sections one two, seven, and eleven of an act creating a board of harbor commissioners of Norfolk and Portsmouth, and for the preservation of the harbor of Norfolk and Portsmouth, be amended and re-enacted as follows:

Harbor commissioners to be appointed

§ 1. That for the purpose of preserving and improving the harbors of Norfolk and Portsmouth, there shall be appointed as soon as may be, after the passage of this act, a board of harbor commissioners, to consist of seven persons, three of whom shall be appointed by the councils of the city of Norfolk, upon the nomination of the chamber of commerce of Norfolk, and in the event that there be no chamber of commerce, then by the cotton exchange, two by the council of the city of Portsmouth, and two by the board of supervisors of the county of Norfolk.

Term of service

§ 2. The said commissioners shall hold their office for a term of four years, beginning on the first day of January, eighteen hundred and eighty-four, unless sooner removed from office, and until their successors shall have been elected and qualified, and a majority of them shall constitute a quorum for the transaction of business. The said commissioners shall be a board to be known as the board of harbor commissioners of Norfolk and Portsmouth, and shall organize by electing one of their number president, and such other officers as may be necessary for the proper dispatch of such business as may come before them. All vacancies which may occur in the board, shall be filled in the same manner as the original appointments.

Organization

Duties

§ 7. That the board of harbor commissioners shall have power to appoint, annually, all harbor masters for the cities of Norfolk and Portsmouth, and assign their duties and fix their compensation, and may remove them at pleasure; provided, however, that there shall not be less than two harbor masters for said port, one of whom may be a resident of the city of Norfolk. The powers of all harbor masters and port wardens heretofore appointed and acting shall cease and determine after the organization of the board.

Report to be made

§ 11. That the board of harbor commissioners shall publish an annual report of their proceedings, and furnish a printed copy of the same to the governor, auditor, councils of the city of Norfolk, council of the city of Portsmouth, and board of supervisors of Norfolk county; and in the discharge of the duties of their office shall be governed, in the matter of the expenditure of money, by the concurrent resolution adopted by the councils of the city of Norfolk, the council of the city of Portsmouth, and the board of supervisors of

Norfolk county; and before entering upon the discharge of their duties, the members of said board shall qualify by taking the oath of office required by the laws of this commonwealth.

2. All acts and parts of acts, so far as they conflict with the provisions of this act, are hereby repealed.

3. This act shall be in force from its passage. Commencem't

Regulations Adopted by the Harbor Commissioners.

HARBOR MASTERS—THEIR GENERAL DUTIES.

Their jurisdiction is concurrent over the harbor of Norfolk and Portsmouth.

They are vested with authority to designate the anchorage grounds of all vessels, and are required to keep the channel-way and track of steamers clear.

It is their duty to berth vessels at appropriate wharves and docks; and when called upon by the proprietor or occupant of any wharf or dock to change the berth of any vessel lying at such occupant's premises, it is made their duty to move such vessel to some other wharf, or to a safe anchorage in the stream.

They are charged with the execution of the police regulations which have been or may hereafter be adopted for the better government of the harbor, and will report all delinquents, and offenders to the committee on harbor police.

The practice of boarding vessels below, or on their arrival in the harbor, is deemed no longer necessary, and the harbor masters are henceforth relieved of this duty, but they are required to see that the regulations forbidding vessels from anchoring in the channel-way, or in the track of steamers is strictly observed.

They shall be entitled to receive, as compensation, fees, as follows, viz:

Three dollars ($3) per month from each steamer (except those trading through the canals, ferry boats, and tugs) that runs regularly to the port; and from all transient vessels arriving from or destined to any foreign port, as follows:

Schooners and Brigs - - - -	$3 00
Barks - - - - - -	4 00
Ships - - - - - -	5 00
Steamships - - - - -	5 00

They shall also be entitled to receive from all vessels in the coasting trade arriving here, whose length over all is 75 feet and upwards, a fee of $3, to be paid only once in a twelve month. The harbor masters are required to keep a register of all such coasting vessels for reference and for examination by the commissioners.

They are required to see that the regulations of the United States government requiring fog horns to be blown, or ships' bells rung, by all vessels anchored within the harbor during the prevalence of a fog, are strictly conformed to, and will report all delinquents to the committee on harbor police.

REGULATIONS REQUIRED TO BE OBSERVED IN THE

HARBOR.

1. No vessel having gunpowder on board shall approach any wharf nearer than 200 yards. Such vessel shall anchor out of the way of passing steamers, and shall keep a red flag flying while receiving or discharging powder.

The handling of powder to and from vessels in the harbor must be under the supervision of a harbor master, whose duty it is to see that every precaution against danger of ignition and explosion is adopted and rigidly observed.

2. All vessels at the end of wharves, or in docks, shall, when required, haul either way to accommodate vessels going in or coming out from such wharves or docks. They shall not occupy regular steamers' or sailing packets' berths, without permission from the recognized occupants of such wharves and docks. And they are required to rig in all fore and aft spars, have boats hoisted up under the bow, and davits turned up, as the harbor master may direct.

3. Vessels when not engaged in loading or discharging cargo shall give place to such vessels as are ready to receive or deliver freights. And if the captain or person in charge of any vessel refuses to move said vessel when notified by the occupant of the wharf at which she is lying, the harbor master shall order him to haul to some other berth, or in the stream; and should the captain or person in charge refuse to obey the orders of the harbor master, then the harbor master shall himself move the vessel at the owner's expense, by use of steam-tug if necessary, and shall be entitled to a fee of $5, to be recovered from the owners of the offending vessel.

4. Vessels dropping out from wharves or docks preparatory to departure for sea, must anchor under the direction of a harbor master, so as not to obstruct passing vessels in the channel-way.

5. All vessels, boats and lighters over ten tons burden shall have at all times a ship keeper on board, and all such are required to move whenever ordered to do so by a harbor master; and no vessel, boat or lighter shall anchor at or make fast to any wharf so as in any way to obstruct the passage of any regular ferry boat.

6. Whenever the services of a harbor master are required to move a vessel from the stream to any wharf, after being once berthed at her wharf, to land or receive cargo, or from any wharf to the stream, or from one wharf to another, the harbor master, when so employed, shall be entitled to receive from the master or agent of such vessel, for his services, a fee not less than $2 nor more than $5, according to the size of the vessel, viz:

For a medium size schooner - -	$2 00
For brigs and large schooners - -	3 00
For ships and barks - - - -	5 00

It is not intended to invest the harbor masters with any

right or privilege to superintend in person the shifting of vessels from berth to berth. This section is designed only to provide for cases when harbor masters are actually employed by masters or consignees, or when the authority of a harbor master is invoked to move a vessel from berth to berth against the will of the master.

7. It shall not be lawful for any boat or vessel propelled in whole or in part by steam to enter the harbor at or above the Naval Hospital Light, or to depart from said harbor or any part of it at a greater speed than four miles per hour. And the master or commander of any such boat or vessel who shall enter or depart from said harbor, within the above limits, at a greater sped than here prescribed shall forfeit and pay the sum of $50 for each and every offence, to be recovered before any justice of the peace of the city of Norfolk, city of Portsmouth, or county of Norfolk. One-half the fine to go to the informer and the remaining half to go to the commissioner's fund for defraying expenses. And in addition such master or commander shall be liable for any damage done to any vessel or wharf by his steamer going at a greater rate of speed than is here prescribed. This order, so far as relates to the speed of steamers, is not intended to apply to regular ferry steamers. Whilst this restriction as to the speed of steamers does not apply to ferry boats, it is understood, and is so ordered, that the said ferry boats' owners or managers shall be required so to sheathe the spiles in their docks as to prevent the waves from damaging contiguous wharf property.

The harbor masters will see that due notice of this section is served on the masters of all steamers.

8. The harbor masters have full authority, and they are hereby required so to regulate the manner in which a vessel shall lie at any of the public wharves, that the facilities for discharging and receiving cargoes may be afforded as generally as may be practicable, and as will best promote the public interest Any person having charge of any vessel, who shall refuse or neglect to obey the harbor master in carrying out this section shall forfeit and pay a fine of $5 for each and every offence.

9. No person in charge of any ship or vessel shall permit any fire to be kept on the deck thereof while lying at any wharf or dock within the harbor, between the hours of 10 o'clock at night and 5 o'clock in the morning, from the 1st of April to the 1st of October; and between the hours of 9 o'clock at night and 6 o'clock in the morning from 1st October to 1st April. Any one offending against this section shall forfeit and pay a fine of $20 for each and every offence.

10. Stone, coal, ballast, sand, manure, oyster shells, ashes or dirt of any kind whatsover shall not be taken on board any vessel lying at a public or private wharf, under a penalty of $20, unless the master of such vessel first obtain the written permission of a harbor master. And the harbor masters are required, before granting permission as aforesaid, to see that the master of such vessel has taken all necessary precautions

to prevent injury to the navigation of the harbor by any such articles falling therein.

11. If any person shall cast or throw any ballast, dirt, oyster shells, filth, or trash into the water in any part of the harbor of Norfolk and Portsmouth, or on the shores of said harbor below high water mark, unless for the purpose of making a wharf, after permission obtained for the purpose, and which wharf shall be sufficiently inclosed and secured so as to prevent injury to navigation, such person so offending shall forfeit and pay for every offence, not less than $20 nor more than $50 ; one-half to the informer and the remaining half to the commissioners' fund.

[The term " Harbor of Norfolk and Portsmouth " in this section, as well as in all other sections where it occurs, is meant to include the jurisdiction of the commissioners, viz:-- five miles above and five miles below the limits of the two cities.]

12. If any vessel shall be lying in any dock in Norfolk or Portsmouth, or at the entrances thereof, so as to obstruct any vessel that shall be coming into the same, or moving from one place to another therein, or going out of the same, the vessel so obstructing, unless actually engaged in loading or unloading, and then if deemed expedient by the harbor master, shall be removed to such place as shall be necessary to give room to the passing vessel, under a penalty at the rate of $5 per hour for the delay which shall be occasioned to the passing vessel, unless in cases where some unavoidable casualty or accident may make it impracticable to remove such obstructing vessel.

13. It shall be the duty of the captain or other person having in charge any vessel lying at any of the public wharves or docks, to top the yards, rig in the jib booms, and place the anchor or anchors on the deck of such vessel whenever required so to do by the harbor master, or the occupant of any wharf, or his agent; and any person having charge of any vessel who shall neglect or refuse to obey the directions aforesaid shall forfeit and pay a fine of $5 for each and every offence.

14. No ballast of any kind, or coal, shall be landed on any wharf or dock in the harbor, except by permission and under the supervision of the harbor masters, who are directed to see that every precaution is observed to prevent its falling into the water. And for such supervision the supervising harbor master shall be entitled to receive. from all such vessels. $1 per day for each day or part of a day they are engaged in landing ballast. Any one offending against this section shall forfeit and pay a fine not less than $5 nor more than $20. No fee shall be charged for supervising the landing of coal, but offenders shall be liable to the fine.

15. No pitch or tar, or other inflammable matter, shall be heated on board any vessel lying at any wharf or dock in the harbor. But the same may be done on a floating stage or lighter. Penalty $5 for every offence.

16. Vessels coming to anchor at any point above Hospital

Light must anchor on or near the flats as possible, so that the channel-way will not be obstructed; and if to remain over forty-eight (48) hours, they must be moored with both anchors, so as not to swing within one hundred yards of any wharf.

17. All vessels coming to anchor below the naval anchorage buoy abreast the Hospital Light, shall anchor in a direct line with said buoy, and shall be moored so as to keep the channel-way to the southward well open for vessels bound in or out.

18. Vessels whose draft of water will admit of loading on the flats out of the way of passing steamers will be permitted so to load, but no vessel whose draft of water when loaded is over eight feet will be allowed to load in the stream, except in cases of emergency, and then only by special permission from the harbor commissioners.

19. Shooting from the deck of any vessel or boat within the harbor is positively prohibited. Any violation of this order will subject the party so offending to a fine of $5.

20. Steamers of all classes are expected to use coal as fuel for their engines; but should any steamer plying in this harbor use wood as fuel, "spark catchers" or some other effectual spark extinguisher must be attached to the smoke stacks of all such steamers, so as to prevent the escape of burning flakes. A non-observance of this section will subject the offending steamer and owners to a fine of $20 for each and every offence; and to full damages for any loss that may be sustained by fire traceable to any such steamer using wood for fuel.

21. The dumping of ashes from steamers into the waters of the harbor is strictly forbidden, under a penalty of not less than $20 nor more than $50 for each and every offence. One-half to go to the informer and the remaining half to the commissioners' fund.

22. Whenever it becomes necessary to use a conveyance or to incur any expense in visiting localities with a view to defining lines for the construction of wharves or other improvements, such expense shall be borne by the parties making application for permits, for whose benefit the lines are to be defined.

23. Piles, *painted red*, have been driven along certain sections of the unimproved water front of the harbor to mark the established port warden lines. Similarly painted piles will be driven in all the unimproved sections so soon as port warden and limiting lines are decided upon for those sections. Masters of all classes of craft, and all other persons are forbidden from making fast to these piles, or to disturb them in any way, under a penalty of $5 for every offence.

It is ordered, that in all cases where a penalty is not affixed for a violation of any section of the harbor regulations, the penalty in each case shall not be less than $5 nor more than $20. One-half to go to the informer and the remaining half to the commissioners' fund, to be recovered as in all other cases, before any justice of the peace of the city of Norfolk, city of Portsmouth, or county of Norfolk.

In case application is made for any change in the limiting lines, it is ordered, that no resolution granting the privilege of extending any wharf or pier into the harbor beyond the prescribed limits shall be considered until four (4) weeks' notice of the application shall have been given in at least one of the newspapers published in Norfolk and Portsmouth, by advertisement inserted at least twice a week therein, for four (4) consecutive weeks. Nor shall any such application be considered or acted upon until a definite statement of the extension proposed is presented and filed with the secretary of the board of harbor commissioners; unless the exigencies of a case shall require immediate action, which exigency shall be determined by two-thirds of the members present. (Amendment adopted at meeting held 12th April, 1880.)

No wharf shall be run out, made, altered, enlarged or extended beyond the prescribed limits. And no person shall make, alter or extend any wharf without laying before the board of harbor commissioners a *plan* in duplicate of said wharf, and obtaining the written approval of the president of the board to the same. One copy of the plan, when approved, shall be filed with the secretary of the board, and the other returned to the person presenting it.

Any one offending against this section shall forfeit and pay a fine of not less than one hundred (100) dollars nor more than five hundred (500) dollars.

The following orders were adopted October 31st, 1881:

The attention of parties interested is called to the following orders of the board of harbor commissioners in relation to dumping of excavations:

. A dumping ground for the deposit of all excavations within the harbor and its approaches having been established at Craney Island flats, within defined limits, it is ordered, that all such excavations be dumped thereon, and nowhere else, under a penalty for each and every offence of not less than $50 nor more than $100, to be recovered according to law, of the master or owner of the offending tug.

It is also ordered, that no tug or other steamer with loaded dumpers in tow shall leave the dredge or dredges later than two hours before sunset, so that the dumping ground may be reached at or before sunset.

Any tug or other steamer offending against this order shall be fined not less than $50 nor more than $100, to be recovered as provided in the preceeding section.

One-half the penalty in either case to go to the informer, and the remaining half to the commissioners' fund.

PILOT LAWS.

OHAP. 62.—An ACT to repeal chapter 91 of the Code of 1873, and
all acts and parts of acts, in relation to pilots and piloting of vessels, and to enact a law to govern and regulate pilots and piloting
of vessels in the waters of the State of Virginia.

Approved April 21, 1882.

1. Be it enacted by the general assembly, That chapter Pilot laws
ninety-one of the Code of Virginia of eighteen hundred and amended.
seventy three, and all acts and parts of acts heretofore passed,
in relation to pilots and the piloting of vessels, be and the
same are hereby repealed, and that the following provisions
be and the same are hereby substituted therefor, so as to read
as follows :

2. The court of Elizabeth county shall appoint three per- Board of com-
sons, only one of whom shall be a branch pilot, and the cor- missioners
poration court of Norfolk city, four persons, only two of whom
shall be branch pilots, to constitute a board of commissioners
to examine persons applying for branches as pilots. The
board of commissioners shall hold its meetings in the city of
Norfolk, and four members thereof shall constitute a quorum.
And said commissioners shall have full authority to make such
rules as they may think necessary for the proper government
and regulation of pilots licensed by them.

3. The court by which any commissioner is appointed, may Court may re-
remove him for incapacity, neglect of duty or misconduct, and move commis-
may fill a vacancy happening in the office of commissioner sioners
from any cause.

4. Every person applying to the said board to be examined, Applicants to
shall produce a certificate of the court of the county or cor- be examined
poration in which he resides, that he is of honest demeanor, to give bond
and a citizen of the state, and furnish proof of his having
served as an apprentice to some pilot of the state for five years.
If the board of examiners find him qualified to act as a pilot,
they shall take from him a bond, in the penalty of five hundred dollars, and grant him a branch on his paying to said
board five dollars; and they shall return said bond to the
clerk of the corporation court. Every pilot holding a branch
shall renew the same every twelve months; for which renewal
he shall pay one dollar, and all pilots who have heretofore
held branches under the pilot laws of this state, shall renew
said branches within sixty days after the organization of the
commission herein provided for.

5. All pilots shall be arranged into three classes, and every Pilots arrang-
branch shall designate whether the pilot thereby commissioned ed in classes
belongs to the first, second, or third class.

6. Pilots of the first class may pilot and conduct vessels of Duties
every burthen and description; those of the second class shall
be confined to vessels whose draft of water does not exceed
fifteen feet, and those of the third class to vessels whose draft
of water does not exceed twelve feet.

7. Every pilot, or the company to which he belongs, shall Pilot-boat
keep one sufficient boat of at least thirty feet keel, which he

shall be attached to and cruise in, and any one acting as a
pilot without having such a boat, shall forfeit one hundred
and fifty dollars to any person who may sue for the same.

**Penalty for
failure to have
name display-
ed, &c: ex-
ception**
8. If any pilot boat shall not have her name, and the port
to which she belongs, marked ten feet below the head of her
foresail on each side, in letters at least nine inches long, the
owners thereof shall have no fees of pilotage, except in case of
steam pilot boats, which shall have her name on each bow
instead of on her foresail.

**Duty of com-
missioners in
regard to ap-
prentices**
9. If any apprentice of a pilot, being examined by the board
of commissioners which appointed his master, shall be judged
by them qualified, they may endorse on a copy of his master's
branch the name of the pilot boat, her port, and the class to
which said master belongs, and thereupon such apprentice
may conduct and pilot vessels, as his master might do, and
subject to the same regulations.

**Unauthorized
pilots; how
punished**
10. If any person, not authorized by law, or any pilot, after
removing from the state, shall undertake to conduct or pilot a
vessel to or from the sea; or to or from any port or place in
Virginia, or if any master or person on board any steamboat
or towboat, shall tow a vessel to or from sea, or to or from any
port or place in Virginia, except as authorized by this act,
without having a pilot on board of such vessel, if one shall
offer his service, he shall be deemed guilty of a misdemeanor,
and, upon conviction thereof, shall be imprisoned in the county
or city jail, for not more than three months, or fined any sum
not exceeding two hundred dollars, at the discretion of the
court; and any master employing any person not authorized
by law, or any pilot who has removed from the state, to act as
pilot of his vessel, shall forfeit and pay one hundred dollars
to any regular branch pilot who shall sue for the same; and
warrants for such offenders may be issued upon the oath of any
party complaining, by any justice of the peace of any county,
or mayor or justice of the peace of any city in this state, in
which such offender may be at the time; and, upon proof of
probable cause, the offender shall be bound, with security in
due form of law, to appear at the next term of the circuit,
county, or hustings court of said county or city, for trial of
such misdemeanor, and the circuit, county, or corporation court
of said county or city, shall have jurisdiction for the trial
thereof, as in other cases of misdemeanor.

**Exception in
favor of Mary-
land**
11. The preceeding section shall not prevent any pilot of
this state or Maryland, or any other person, from assisting a
vessel in distress, that he may fall in with, having Cape Henry
in view (and no authorized branch pilot appearing), nor from
conducting said vessel into Hampton roads, or any other harbor. Any such pilot, or other person aforesaid, shall be
entitled to full pilotage; but if he is not a pilot, he shall
deliver up the said vessel to any authorized pilot of this state,
who may offer his services to take charge of her, and then
shall receive from such pilot half the pilotage.

12. The master of every vessel (other than a coasting vessel
having a pilot license), inward bound from sea, shall take the

first Virginia pilot that offers his services, Cape Henry bear- ing west of south to Smith's point, Yorktown, Newport News or Norfolk, or any intermediate point; and any such vessel, outward bound, shall take the first pilot that offers his services at Smith's point, Yorktown, Newport News, or Norfolk, or any intermediate point, to sea; and any master refusing to do so, shall immediately pay to the said pilot full pilotage from the sea to Newport News, Smith's point, Yorktown, or Norfolk, from said ports to sea, as the case may be; but no master of a vessel coming from sea shall be compelled to take a pilot after arriving within the line at which Cape Henry bears west of south; provided further, that any registered vessel arriving within the line of Cape Henry, bearing west of south, without having taken a pilot, bound for Norfolk, Newport News, or Richmond, shall not be liable for pilotage; but the master may pilot his own vessel to Hampton roads, and there employ any steamboat or towboat to tow his vessel to her port of destination; but in no instance will any master be allowed to employ any steamboat or towboat below Hampton roads without paying full pilotage to the first regular pilot that offers his services to said vessel, and any master so employing a steamboat or towboat below Hampton roads without a pilot on board of such vessel, when one shall have offered his services, shall be liable to the penalty prescribed in section ten of this act. This provision applies only to inward bound vessels.

13. No master shall be required to have a pilot to conduct his vessel or steamboat above Newport News, Yorktown, Mobjack bay, Urbanna, or Smith's point, but he may, by himself, or by any person regularly employed on board, pilot his own vessel, or he may employ the services of any towboat to tow his vessel to her port of destination above any of the above-named points.

14. Pilots shall appoint agents—one for Norfolk city and one for Richmond—who shall grant licenses to coasting vessels trading in all the rivers of this state, for which license such agents shall receive ten per centum per ton for one year, and coasting vessels having such licenses shall be free to sail without pilots to or from sea; but all vessels sailing under a coasting license of the burden of seventy tons or more, coming from or going to sea, not having obtained a license from such agent, shall be subject to the same regulations and pilotage as registered vessels belonging to citizens of the United States.

15. The master of any coasting vessel wanting a pilot to any port in this state, shall signify it by a signal at his foremast or foretopmast head; whereupon a pilot shall repair to and pilot said vessel.

16. Pilots shall have pilotage at the following rates: For every vessel owned by citizens of the United States, and for every vessel owned by a citizen or subject of any foreign state, whose vessels are by treaty placed on the same footing as vessels of the United States, if the vessel be spoken or boarded

to the eastward of Cape Henry, there shall be paid for each foot the vessel draws, as follows: From sea to Smith's Point, West Point, Newport News, Norfolk, or any place between Smith's Point, West Point, Newport News, or Norfolk, vessels drawing ten feet and under, two dollars and fifty cents; vessels drawing thirteen feet and over ten feet, three dollars; vessels drawing fourteen feet and over thirteen feet, three dollars and fifty cents; vessels drawing sixteen feet and over fourteen feet, four dollars; vessels drawing over sixteen feet, four dollars and fifty cents. If the vessel shall be boarded or spoken twenty miles or more eastward of Cape Henry, twenty-five cents per foot shall be added to the foregoing rates. There shall be paid the same pilotage from Smith's Point, West Point, Newport News, or Norfolk, or any intermediate point to sea, as from sea to those places; and from Newport News to Jamestown, or any place between Newport News and Jamestown, one dollar and thirty-five cents per foot; from Newport News to Richmond, or any place between James-town and Richmond, two dollars and fifty cents per foot; and the same rates of pilotage shall be paid from said places respectively down. Vessels coming from sea to Hampton roads and thence to any port in Maryland, shall be subject to the same rate of pilotage as vessels bound from Newport News to sea. All vessels coming to Hampton roads, seeking, in ballast, shall only pay one-half pilotage in and one-half out; provided, however, that if such vessel coming to Hampton roads, seeking, is afterwards chartered to load in any port or place in this state, she shall pay the usual pilotage in and out as though she had come to a direct port. All steamers calling in any port or place in this state for the sole purpose of coal-ing, shall only pay one-half pilotage in, and one-half, pilotage out. All vessels that go from Norfolk to Newport News to load or to finish loading, and all vessels that go from Newport News to Norfolk to load or finish loading, shall, if they take a pilot, which shall be optional with the master, pay a fee of ten dollars to the pilot for transporting any such vessel to or from either place.

Concealing name of vessel; penalty

17. If the master of any vessel shall conceal or obscure the name thereof, or refuse to disclose the same when spoken by a pilot, he shall forfeit to the said pilot fifty dollars.

Detention of pilot

18. If any pilot notified to attend a vessel shall be detained, he shall have three dollars for each day's detention.

Pilot's pay

19. Any pilot who shall attend any vessel with his boat, at the request of the master or owner, shall have fifty dollars per day; any master carrying any pilot to sea, shall pay him wages at the rate of seventy-five dollars per month.

Following vessels having pilot

20. If any vessel having no pilot on board follow another that has a pilot, such pilot shall have pilotage for the vessel so following.

Detention of pilot

21. Any pilot being detained on board any sea-going vessel, shall be entitled to three dollars for each day he may be so detained, to be paid by the master, owner or consignee of such vessel. If any such pilot be carried beyond the limits of his

state against his will, he shall be entitled to recover the sum of three hundred dollars from the master or owner of the vessel upon which he may have been carried away. All vessels having a branch pilot, and arriving at the pilot station, shall remain there fifteen hours, if required, to give such pilot an opportunity to be taken off, under a penalty of fifty dollars.

22. Hereafter all vessels transported from the naval anchorage to the navy-yard by any pilot, shall pay the sum of twenty dollars. *Naval anchorage*

23. The first pilot who meets a vessel coming, in which his branch entitles him to conduct, shall have the right to take charge of and conduct her into York river, Hampton roads, Newport News, Norfolk, Mobjack bay, Urbanna, or Smith's point aforesaid, and to receive the pilotage allowed by law; but any pilot that boards a vessel off any vessel other than his boat, shall give the same to the first authorized pilot that offers his services from a lawful Virginia pilot-boat anywhere below the Thimble light; and the master of any such vessel employing a pilot from any other than a lawful Virginia pilot-boat, shall be liable to the first regularly licensed pilot that offers his services from a lawful pilot-boat of this state anywhere below Thimble light. *First pilot offering, to be employed*

24. Every pilot cruising or standing out to sea shall offer his services to the vessel of his class nearest to land or in most distress. *Duty of pilots*

25. The master and owner of every vessel shall each be liable to the pilot for his pilotage and other allowances, and also the consignee or supercargo of any vessel not owned by a citizen of the state; and if the said consignee or supercargo refuse to become responsible to the pilot for his fee, then the master or owner of said vessel shall deposit the amount of pilotage fees due in the hands of some responsible person before leaving her port of departure, subject to the order of the pilot. *Liability for pilotage*

26. Pilots may state their accounts, verified by affidavits, and lodge them with their agents in Norfolk, Richmond, Newport News, or Yorktown, or wherever they may think it necessary to appoint such agent for collection; and if any person liable on any such account, shall fail to pay the amount thereof to the agent or the pilot himself within three days' after demand made, he shall pay five dollars (in addition to said amount) to said pilot. *Pilot's accounts*

27. The board of commissioners may decide any controversy between pilots to whom it has granted branches, or between any such pilot and the master, owner, or consignee of any vessel, which may arise under any law concerning pilots. Its decision shall be final. If such decision requires the payment of money, the board shall enter a judgment therefor on the record of its proceedings; and on a copy thereof being put into the hands of any sheriff, constable, or sergeant, he shall enforce payment thereof as if it were an execution against the property of the debtor, and have the same fee. *Commissioners to decide controversies*

28. But no judgment shall be entered unless due notice be

Notice of judgment to be given before entering

given of the time and place of trial, and of the claim or charges to be preferred, and where the charge is against the pilot for neglect of duty or violation of law, such judgment shall in no case be for a longer suspension of the branch of the accused than twelve months, nor less than one month, at the discretion of the commissioners, unless where a longer time is expressly prescribed.

Exception

29. Nothing herein shall authorize such board to decide upon the liability of a pilot or his apprentice to any party injured by his negligence or misconduct, or to prevent such party from recovering for all damages occasioned thereby.

Clerk to board

30. The board shall appoint a clerk, who shall keep a record of all its proceedings, and the said commissioners, or any one of them, may administer an oath and issue a summons.

Examination of pilots

31. Each person who shall appear before the board to be examined as a pilot, shall pay to each commissioner present, and also to the clerk, one dollar. When the board makes a decision in a matter of controversy, the person against whom the decision is, shall pay to each commissioner one dollar, and to the clerk fifty cents.

Unlawful fees punishment for demanding

32. If any pilot shall, for any service, demand or receive less than the lawful fee, he shall forfeit the amount of said lawful fee, which may be recovered by any person who will claim the same, by warrant or by motion, one-half of which recovery shall be paid to the board of commissioners. Such pilot may, moreover, be suspended by said board, not exceed- ing six months. And if any pilot shall demand and receive greater fees than are allowed by law, he shall forfeit to master or owner double the amount of fees paid to him in any such case, to be recovered in the same manner.

Refusal of pilot

33. If any pilot or apprentice, without sufficient excuse, shall refuse, when requested by the master, to go on board any vessel and pilot her, or shall be intoxicated, or guilty of any other misbehavior or neglect of duty while in charge of a vessel, he shall be suspended not less than three nor more than six months.

Suspension of pilot

34. Whenever a pilot or apprentice shall be suspended, the fact shall be published in some newspaper printed in Norfolk, the cost of which shall be paid by such pilot; and if any pilot so suspended, shall be found on board of any vessel as a pilot. or shall offer to conduct any such vessel as such, he may be dismissed from such vessel by any pilot authorized to pilot her, to whom all the fees of pilotage shall be paid, and the board which gave him his branch, shall issue a warrant, directed to any sheriff or other such officer, requiring him to apprehend such suspended pilot or apprentice, and detain him in custody until bond shall be given, in penalty of not less than one hundred dollars, with condition for his good behavior dur- ing his suspension. which said bond shall be taken by the officer, and returned by him to the corporation court, and may be enforced by action, scire facias. or motion. Should such bond not be given, the officer shall confine him in the most convenient jail until it is given.

35. Any pilot first meeting a vessel coming from sea shall inquire into the health of her crew and the place from which she last came, and if she has a dangerous or infectious disease on board, or comes from any place from which vessels are required to perform quarantine in this state, or any port thereof, he shall direct said vessel to follow his boat, and carefully conduct her to the nearest place appointed for vessels to quarantine, and shall, as soon as possible, give notice thereof to the health officer of the port nearest thereto, for which service said pilot shall be entitled to an extra fee of seven dollars beyond the regular fees of pilotage, to be paid by the master or owner of said vessel; and if any pilot shall be permitted to go on board a vessel without being informed of contagious diseases being on board, and be obliged to remain on board, or perform quarantine in consequence thereof, he shall have three dollars for every day's detention, to be paid as aforesaid. *Duty of pilot on meeting incoming vessel*

36. Each pilot shall, if required, produce his branch at the time of demanding his fees before he shall be entitled to receive the same. *Certificate to be produced if required*

37. Nothing in this act shall be deemed to apply to vessels bound for any point on the Potomac, and no vessel bound to or from any point on the Potomac, shall be required to pay pilotage. But if she does take a pilot, she shall pay the regular rate to Smith's Point. *Exception*

38. This act shall be in force from its passage. *Commencement*

Quarantine.

CHAP. 114.—An ACT to constitute one quarantine district of the Elizabeth river and its branches, and to create a Board of Quarantine Commissioners and a Quarantine Medical Officer for said District.

Approved February 26, 1877.

1. Be it enacted by the general assembly of Virginia, That for the better protection of the cities of Norfolk and Portsmouth, and Norfolk county, against the introduction of infectious and contagious diseases by vessels arriving in the common harbor of said cities, or into any part of the Elizabeth river, and to secure uniformity in the administration of the laws and regulations concerning quarantine, appertaining to shipping in said river, the Elizabeth river and its branches shall constitute one quarantine district. *Quarantine district defined*

2. That a board of commissioners is hereby created, to be known as the board of quarantine commissioners for the district of Elizabeth river: the said board to consist of seven commissioners, three of whom shall be appointed by the councils of the city of Norfolk; three by the council of the city of Portsmouth; and one by the judge of the county court of Norfolk county. Each of said representations of three commissioners on said board shall embrace at least one practicing physician, if practicable. The said commissioners shall hold their office for the term of four years, commencing *Board of Quarantine commissioners created. One member to be a practising physician. Term of office*

25

on the first day of April, eighteen hundred and seventy-seven,

How vacancies filled unless sooner removed by the authority appointing them. All vacancies in the board shall be filled in the same manner as

How board organized the original appointments. The said board shall organize by electing one of their number president, with such other officers as they may deem necessary; and a majority of the

Quorum board shall constitute a quorum for the transaction of business.

Powers vested in board 3. That the said board of quarantine commissioners shall be invested with all the powers now granted by law to the councils of the cities of Norfolk and Portsmouth, and to Norfolk county. or by the general law on the subject, in regard to the establishment and regulation of matters of quarantine; and they shall prescribe such rules and regulations, conformably to existing law, as they may deem necessary, and have exclusive control of the quarantine appertaining to shipping for the Elizabeth river and its branches, and the cities, towns and villages, situated thereon. They shall meet

When to meet monthly, upon any day agreed upon by themselves; but the president of the board may, upon his own motion, and shall, at the request of any two members of the board, by written notice to each member, convene the board at any time, when circumstances may render prompt action necessary. The said

Business to be transacted at first meeting board shall, at their first meeting, or as soon thereafter as practicable, select a suitable quarantine anchorage, and shall adopt and publish, for the information and government of all concerned, rules and regulations for the management and enforcement of an efficient system of quarantine for said

Pilots to conform to regulations of board district. All pilots licensed by the laws of this state are hereby required to conform to the rules and regulations thus adopted, under the penalty of a fine of not less than twenty nor more than one hundred dollars. The said board shall

Quarantine officers to enforce regulations require the quarantine medical officer, hereinafter created, to faithfully carry out these rules and regulations; and they shall

Supervisory control of board have power to review the official action of said officer, and to revoke or reverse his decision in regard to any particular vessel; but in such case they shall record their reasons for so doing in the minutes of their transactions. The said board of quarantine commissioners shall not, as a board, nor shall any

Prohibition governing board of the members thereof, in their official characters, make any recommendation for the appointment of the quarantine medical officer, herein provided for.

Lazaretto to be provided and how 4. That the said board of quarantine commissioners shall have power, whenever in their opinion circumstances may demand it, by and with the consent of the councils of the cities of Norfolk and Portsmouth, to acquire by condemnation, as provided for by existing laws, or by purchase, a suitable site for a lazaretto, at any eligible point on Elizabeth river, and to erect thereupon one or more buildings, to be con-

Hospitals to be erected structed of wood, for the temporary accommodation and treatment of sick seamen and passengers arriving at the quarantine

Limit as to cost anchorage upon infected vessels; provided, the cost of such a site and the erection of the buildings thereon shall not exceed

the sum of five thousand dollars; and provided, further, that
the cost of the maintenance and treatment of the persons so *Who to pay for care of patients*
removed to the lazaretto buildings from infected vessels, shall
be paid by the masters or owners of said vessels, upon which
the costs thus incurred shall constitute a lien.

5. That the said board may, by and with the consent of the *Floating hospital in lieu of lazaretto permitted*
councils of the cities aforesaid, in lieu of the purchase of a
site and the erection of lazaretto buildings, provide and fit out
a floating hospital for the accommodation and treatment of
the same class of infected persons as is described in section
four of this act; provided the expense so incurred shall not *Proviso*
exceed the amount specified in said section; such floating
hospital to be moored, when having on board infected persons
at such point in the lower river, or Hampton roads, sufficiently *Where to be moored*
removed from the channel, so as not to endanger the health of
persons on board of passing vessels.

6. That the said board of quarantine commissioners shall *Compensation of quarantine officer*
pay the annual salary of five hundred dollars, in quarterly
instalments of one hundred and twenty-five dollars each, to
the quarantine medical officer created by this act; and in case *Proceedings to be had concerning selection of lazaretto or floating hospital*
they shall see fit to purchase the site and erect the lazaretto
buildings, or instead thereof, to provide and fit out the floating
hospital hereinbefore provided for, they shall make a report of
their proceedings, accompanied by a verified statement of all
the expenditures thereby incurred, to the councils of the
cities of Norfolk and Portsmouth, and to the county court of
Norfolk county.

7. That the governor shall appoint and commission a quar- *Quarantine officer to be appointed by governor*
antine medical officer for said district, who shall be a resident
of the city of Norfolk, or of the city of Portsmouth, or Norfolk *Residence prescribed*
county, and whose term of office shall be for two years from
the first day of April, eighteen hundred and seventy-seven, *Term of office*
unless sooner removed by the governor, and who shall be the
inspecting officer for all vessels arriving in Elizabeth river or *To be inspector*
any of its branches, subject to such inspection as shall be
required by and in accordance with the rules and regulations
of the board of quarantine commissioners created by this act;
provided that no one shall receive such appointment, who is *Proviso*
not a doctor of medicine of good standing, and who has not
had at least five years' experience in the practice of his profession.

8. That the quarantine medical officer shall board with *Duties*
promptness all vessels liable to his inspection, and no vessel
shall be detained in quarantine without his stated decision.
No vessel thus detained by him shall change her assigned
position without his written permission. He shall superin- *Quarantine regulations*
tend the thorough cleansing, by the most approved methods,
of any infected vessel, at the proper cost of such vessel. He
shall not allow pratique to any vessel once detained by him,
by reason of said vessel's having, at the time of his inspection,
infectious disease on board, or of her having had such disease
on board at any time during her voyage, without the express
sanction of the board of quarantine commissioners. He shall

have general superintendence and control of any lazaretto or floating hospital that may be established under the provisions of this act, and the care and treatment of any sick therein. He shall administer oaths and take affidavits in examinations as to the sanitary condition of vessels, and in relation to any alleged violation of the quarantine regulations; such oaths to have the same validity and effect as if administered by a justice of the peace. He shall have authority to direct, in writing, any constable or police officer to pursue, within the limits of his district, and arrest any person, who shall violate any quarantine regulation or obstruct him in the performance of his **Penalty for evasion or obstruction** duty; and any person violating the quarantine laws or regulations, or obstructing the quarantine medical officer in the discharge of his duty, shall be deemed guilty of a misdemeanor, punishable by fine of not less than twenty nor more than five hundred dollars, or by imprisonment of not less than one nor more than six months; and warrants for any offenders under this act, may be issued upon the oath of any party complaining, by any justice of the peace of any city or county, or the mayor of any city in this state in which such offender may be at the time; and upon proof of probable cause. the offender shall be bound, with security in due form of law, to appear at the next term of the corporation or county court of said city or county, for trial of such misdemeanor; and the corporation or county court of such city or county shall have jurisdiction for the trial thereof, as in other cases of misdemeanor. All fines recovered under the provisions of this act **How fines and penalties to be applied** shall be turned over to the said board of quarantine commissioners, to be used by them in carrying out the objects of this act.

Fees to be paid by masters of vessels 9. The quarantine medical officer shall exact of the master, owner, or consignee of each vessel visited by him in the performances of his official duties, a fee of seven dollars, for each necessary visit of inspection, and also the cost of cleansing, fumigation, or disinfection, whenever necessary; recoverable **Cost of cleansing vessel, &c** before the mayor or any justice of the peace of either of the said cities or said county. He shall defray all expenses attending upon his inspection of vessels out of the fees thus received, and he shall keep a true record of his receipts and expenditures, and report annually to the board of quarantine **Annual report** commissioners the items of the same. He shall also report to the said board, annually, on or before the twentieth day of December, the names and class of all vessels visited by him during the year, the disposition made of such vessels, and such other information concerning the quarantine service as he may deem expedient.

Where quarantine officer may be required to reside 10. The quarantine medical officer shall, when required by the board of quarantine commissioners, reside at or near the quarantine grounds or anchorage. He may, with the consent **may appoint a deputy** of the said board, appoint a deputy, who shall possess like qualifications, and be invested with the same powers as himself; but the said quarantine medical officer shall be held responsible for the conduct and compensation of such deputy.

11. That for the purpose of defraying the necessary ^{How expenses} expenses to be incurred by the board of quarantine com-^{apportioned} missioners in carrying out the provisions of this act, the city of Norfolk shall be assessed with, and shall pay three-sevenths thereof, and the city of Portsmouth shall be assessed with, and shall pay three-sevenths thereof, and the county of Norfolk shall be assessed with, and shall pay one-seventh thereof; provided that the said board of quarantine commissioners shall receive no compensation for their services.

12. That all acts and parts of acts inconsistent with the ^{Inconsistent} provisions of this act, are hereby repealed. ^{laws repealed}

13. This act shall be in force from its passage. ^{Commence-
ment}

[AMENDMENT.]

CHAP. 44.—An ACT to amend and re-enact the 3rd section of an act to constitute one quarantine district of the Elizabeth river and its branches, and to create a board of quarantine commissioners and a quarantine medical officer for said district, approved February 26th, 1877.

Approved January 29, 1878,

1. Be it enacted by the general assembly, That the third § 3, ch. 144. section of chapter one hundred and forty-four, acts of assem- ^{Acts of Assem-
bly 1876-7, con-} bly, eighteen hundred and seventy-six-seven, entitled an act ^{stituting one} to constitute one quarantine district of the Elizabeth river ^{quarantine
district of} and its branches, and to create a board of quarantine commis- ^{Elizabeth} sioners and a quarantine medical officer for said district, ^{river, &c.,} approved February twenty-sixth, eighteen hundred and ^{amended} seventy-seven, be amended and re-enacted so as to read as follows:

§ 3. That the said board of quarantine commissioners shall ^{Powers of} be invested with all the powers now granted by law to the ^{board of quar-
antine com-} councils of the cities of Norfolk and Portsmouth and to ^{missioners} Norfolk county, or by the general law on the subject, in regard to the establishment and regulation of matters of quarantine, and they shall prescribe such rules and regulations, conformably to existing law, as they may deem necessary, and have the exclusive control of the quarantine appertaining to shipping for the Elizabeth river and its branches, and the cities, towns and villages situated thereon. They shall meet ^{Times of
meeting} semi-annually, upon any day agreed upon by themselves, but the president of the said board may, upon his own motion, and shall, at the request of any two members of the board, by written notice to each member, convene the board at any time when circumstances may render prompt action necessary. The said board shall, at their first meeting, or as soon thereafter as practicable, select a suitable quarantine anchorage, and shall ^{Quarantine} adopt and publish, for the information and government of all ^{anchorage} concerned, rules and regulations for the management and enforcement of an efficient system of quarantine for said ^{Duties of} district. All pilots licensed by the laws of this state are ^{pilots} hereby required to conform to the rules and regulations thus adopted, under the penalty of a fine of not less than twenty nor more than one hundred dollars. The said board shall

Quarantine
medical officer

require the quarantine medical officer, hereinafter created, to faithfully carry out these rules and regulations; and they shall have power to review the official action of said officer, and to revoke or reverse his decision in regard to any particular vessel; but in such case they shall record their reasons for so doing in the minutes of their transactions. The said board of quarantine commissioners shall not as a board, nor shall any of the members, in their official characters, make any recommendation for the appointment of the quarantine medical officer hereinafter provided for.

Commencement

2. This act shall be in force from its passage.

Quarantine Regulations.

QUARANTINE DISTRICT OF ELIZABETH RIVER—Quarantine Regulations —Adopted April 30, 1877, by resolution of the Board of Quarantine Commissioners.

(As authorized by Act of Assembly, approved February 26th, 1877.)

No. 1. The following classes of vessels shall be subjected to the inspection of the quarantine medical officer, to wit:

(a) Such as have on board any case of infectious or contagious disease at the time of arrival.

(b) Such as have had any infectious or contagious disease on board at any time during the voyage, though there is no case on board at the time of arrival.

(c) Such as have sailed from any port at which any infectious or contagious disease prevailed at any time during the stay of the vessel at such port, or within sixty days previous to her arrival at such port.

(d) Such as shall arrive from any American port to the southward of the latitude of Cape Lookout between the 1st day of May and the 1st day of the ensuing November in each year.

(e) Such as shall arrive from any foreign port.

(f) Such as shall arrive from any other home port, which, for due reasons may have been interdicted by the board of quarantine commissioners, of which due notice shall be given to all concerned.

(g) Such as shall arrive from any American port between the 1st day of May and the 1st day of the ensuing November, if she shall have been in any port [foreign or domestic] south of Cape Lookout during any portion of sixty days previous to her arrival.

No. 2. The quarantine ground or anchorage for the inspection of vessels arriving within the limits of this quarantine district, via Hampton roads, shall be in the bight of Craney Island, and for those arriving from the southward, via the canals, at any point in the southern branch, not less than one and a half miles above the navy yard.

No. 3. All vessels liable to inspection shall come to, at said anchorages, until visited by the medical officer, and any master, pilot or other person having charge of any such vessel who shall bring her nearer the ports of this district than the aforesaid anchorages, without the sanction of the medical officer, shall be subject to a fine of not less than twenty dollars nor more than one hundred dollars.

No. 4. Any person [other than a licensed pilot] who shall board a vessel liable to inspection, either before or during the continuance of the quarantine term imposed upon her, without the permission of the medical officer, shall be subject to a fine of twenty dollars, and, in addition, to a forced residence upon said vessel, under the same restrictions as are imposed upon the crew, during her quarantine term.

No. 5. Any person landing from, or leaving a vessel while she is under quarantine restrictions, or procuring the landing of any part of her cargo, ship furniture, clothing, or chattels of passengers or crew, without the written permission of the medical officer, shall be subject to a fine of not less than twenty nor more than five hundred dollars, and be prosecuted for a misdemeanor.

No. 6. Any vessel having on board a damaged or infected cargo, shall be subjected to disinfection under the direction of the medical officer, before being allowed to come into port, and the concealment of the fact of damaged or infected cargo, furniture or clothing, shall be punished by a fine of not less than twenty dollars nor more than five hundred dollars, and a prosecution for misdemeanor.

No 7. Any vessel may be sent back to perform a quarantine term, and disinfection, under the orders of the medical officer, after arrival in port, upon the discovery of damaged cargo, [or such as may affect the health of either port,] during the discharge thereof: and a failure to give information to the medical officer of such discovery of damaged cargo shall be punished by a fine of not less than twenty nor more than five hundred dollars.

No. 8. Every vessel subject to inspection shall display the usual yellow flag upon her arrival at the quarantine anchorage and keep the same at her mast head until allowed pratique by the medical officer.

Ends of Streets.

CHAP. 163.—An ACT conferring Authority upon the Councils of the City of Norfolk in relation to the streets of said City.

Passed January 29, 1866.

1. Be it enacted by the general assembly, That the councils of the city of Norfolk shall be and they are hereby empowered to make such use of the ends of the streets of said city running to tide water, as they may deem necessary for the public interests. *(Authority of councils over ends of the streets)*

2. This act shall be in force from its passage. *(Commencement)*

Charter of the Norfolk City Railroad Company.

CHAP. 202.—An ACT to incorporate the Norfolk City Railroad Company.

Passed January 4, 1866.

Norfolk city railroad company

1. Be it enacted by the general assembly, That Thomas J. Corprew, John B. Whitehead, W. W. Wing, Edmund C. Robinson, Cicero Burruss and William H. C. Ellis, together with their associates, successors and assigns, are hereby created a body politic and corporate, under the name and style of The Norfolk City Railroad Company; and as such shall be subject to all the provisions of the Code of Virginia applicable to corporations, except as hereinafter provided.

Liabilities

Rights and powers

2. That it shall be lawful for said company to lay out, construct and equip, maintain and operate, with horse or mule power, a single or double track railroad in the city of Norfolk, throughout the entire length of Main street, down Market square to the Ferry wharf; up Church street to the Fair grounds in Norfolk county; and also through such other streets or parts of streets in said city as the directors may determine; and also to such other points in Norfolk county, not exceeding six miles, as said directors may determine upon: provided, that before such work shall be commenced, the consent of the council of said city shall be obtained thereto.

Duties of the company with regard to its tracks

3. The said company shall keep that portion of the street occupied by its track or tracks, embracing the space between said tracks and a distance of at least two feet beyond the outer rails thereof, well paved and in good repair, without expense to the corporation of the city of Norfolk: and the rails used for said tracks shall be of the most improved pattern for such purposes; and shall be laid at the distance of five feet five inches between the outer ridges or flanges thereof, and upon an even surface with the adjoining pavement, so as to form as little obstruction as practicable to the passage of carriages or other vehicles along or over said tracks.

Transportation and fare

4. That it shall be lawful for said company to transport passengers, light freights and baggage over said road or roads, hereby authorized to be constructed, and to collect fare and tolls for the same, not exceeding the sum of ten cents for passage to and from any point within the limits of the city, and the like sum for packages and bundles occupying the space of a passenger, within the said limits; and the sum of fifteen cents for the same passage and freight to and from any point within the said city, to and from any point beyond the limits thereof. The number of directors in said company shall not exceed nine, the president included.

Packages, &c

Directors

Capital

5. That it shall be lawful for said company to create and issue its capital stock to an amount not exceeding one hundred thousand dollars, in shares of fifty dollars each, and also to borrow money upon its bonds, secured by mortgage or deed of trust upon its property and franchises, to an amount not exceeding the amount of its capital stock, subscribed, paid in and

May borrow money

expended in the construction and equipment of its road, and for other purposes legitimately appertaining thereto.

6. That said company shall have at all times free and undisturbed use of their railway and other property; and if any person or persons shall wilfully or unnecessarily obstruct or impede the passage of cars on or over any portion of said road, or shall injure or destroy the cars, depots, or any other property belonging to said company, the person or persons so offending shall forfeit and pay to said company, for every such offence, the sum of five dollars; and shall remain liable, in addition to said penalty, for any loss or damage occasioned by his, her or their act as aforesaid. *Punishment for obstructing cars, &c*

7. That it shall be lawful for said company, for the purpose of constructing and equipping and operating said railway, to sell their bonds, with coupons attached, at a rate of interest not exceeding eight per centum per annum, to be paid semi-annually, to the amount of fifty thousand dollars, and also to borrow, upon their promissory notes duly executed under the authority of the board of directors, to an amount not exceeding fifty thousand dollars, and to lease their road to any person or persons, or domestic or foreign corporation: any of which corporations shall have power to subscribe to the stock of said company. *Authorized to sell coupon bonds* *Amount*

8. This act shall be in force from its passage, and shall be subject to amendment, modification or repeal, at the pleasure of the general assembly. *Commencement* *Control over*

Water Works.

CHAP. 104.—An ACT to Amend and Re-enact the first Section of an Act approved March 25th, 1871, entitled an Act to Amend and Re-enact the 1st and 4th Sections of an Act entitled an Act to Authorize the City of Norfolk to Construct Water Works for the use of the People of said City, passed January 14th, 1867.

Approved February 26, 1873.

1. Be it enacted by the general assembly, that the first section of the act approved March twenty-second, eighteen hundred and seventy-one, entitled an act to amend and re-enact the first and fourth sections of an act entitled an act to authorize the city of Norfolk to construct water works for the use of the people of said city, passed January fourteenth, eighteen hundred and sixty-seven, be amended and re-enacted so as to read as follows: *Charter of Norfolk city relative to water works amended 1870-71, c. 172, p. 254, 5, 1866-7, c. 61, p. 528*

§ 1. It shall be lawful for the city of Norfolk to construct suitable works to convey a supply of water from such place or places as the said city may select, into the said city; and the said city may acquire and hold for that purpose, slips of land not exceeding one hundred feet in width, and other lands at the termini and stations of their works in the city and county of Norfolk, and in any other county or counties in this commonwealth, not exceeding one thousand acres; and shall have the same rights and powers in respect to obtaining rights of *Power to city of Norfolk to construct water works* *Power to hold lands* *How to condemn them* *See Code of 1860, c. 56, p. 323, 324, 325*

way and lands for their pipes, acqueducts, reservoirs and other suitable structures and fixtures for securing and conveying water, and in respect to taking materials for construction, as are conferred upon railroad and other internal improvement companies by the code of Virginia; and may hold, use and employ such machinery, boats, apparatus and other appliances as she may deem proper for supplying the said city with water and for the transaction of the attendant business; provided, if in any case a part only of the land of any person is proposed to be taken by the said city, the commissioners in assessing the damages may, at their discretion, with the consent of the said city, reserve to the owner of said land such easements or rights of way in or over such part as they may deem proper; and in case of any such reservation the said city shall take and hold such part, in fee, subject to such easements or rights of way.

How works may be paid for

Power to issue bonds

§ 4. In order to provide for payment for the said works, the said city may issue bonds bearing interest not exceeding eight per centum per annum, which bonds shall be known as "the Norfolk city water bonds," the proceeds of which shall not be applied or used for other purposes, and all the net revenues or income derived from the said works and for the use of the water shall be applied exclusively to the payment of the interest and principal of the said bonds; and the councils of the said city are authorized to levy a special tax, to be knows as

Special tax to pay interest and principal of loans

the "water tax," upon all property in the said city, real and personal, and on such other subjects as may be assessed with state taxes, against persons residing in the said city; the said levy to be made in the mode prescribed by law and the constitution of this state for the levy of other taxes by the said city.

Commencement

2 This act shall be in force from its passage.

Old Fair Grounds.

CHAP. 164.—An ACT to Authorize the Councils of Norfolk City to use, hold, sell, lease and dispose of a Certain Tract or Parcel of Land, in Norfolk County, belonging to said City.

Approved April 9, 1874.

Whereas, under an act of the general assembly, entitled an act to authorize the city of Norfolk to purchase land for the purposes of an agricultural fair, passed January thirty-first, eighteen hundred and fifty-four, the said city of Norfolk has purchased, and now holds a piece or parcel of land, lying in Norfolk county, for the purposes therein mentioned, commonly known as the Old Fair Grounds; and whereas, the said parcel of land is no longer used for such purposes, and the councils of said city desire to sell, lease, hold, use and dispose of the same, for such other purposes as they may deem expedient for the interests of the city; now, therefore,

1. Be it enacted by the general assembly, that the select and common councils of the city of Norfolk be and they are hereby autorized and empowered to use, hold, sell, lease

and dispose of the said parcel of land for the purposes of an agricultural college, or for such other purposes as the said councils may deem proper.

2. This act shall be in force from its passage.

Salary of the Judge of Corporation Court.

CHAP. 50.—An ACT to amend and re-enact the fourteenth section of chapter thirteen of the Code, edition of eighteen hundred and seventy-three, in reference to the Pay of Judges of Circuit, Chancery, and Hustings Courts of Richmond, and Hustings Courts of Norfolk and Petersburg, so as to authorize the Council of the City of Portsmouth to increase the Salary and compensation of the Judge of the Hustings Court of said City.

Approved February 10, 1876.

1. Be it enacted by the general assembly of Virginia, That the fourteenth section of chapter thirteen of the Code of eighteen hundred and seventy-three, be amended and re-enacted so as to read as follows: §14, ch. 13, Code of 1873, amended

§ 14. The council of the city of Richmond are hereby authorized and empowered to add to and increase the salaries and compensation of the judges of the circuit court, of the chancery court, and of the hustings court of the said city; and the council of the city of Petersburg, and the council of the city of Norfolk, and the council of the city of Portsmouth, are hereby authorized and empowered to add to and increase the salary and compensation of the judges of the hustings court of said cities: provided, that the said addition and increase shall be a charge upon, and be paid out of the treasuries of said cities respectively: and provided further, that said increase shall not exceed one thousand dollars per annum, for any one of the judges of the courts of said cities; and that the city councils of said cities shall have the power to reduce the amount of addition whenever they may think proper; provided, that such reduction shall not take effect until after the expiration of the term of the judge then in office. §14

2. This act shall be in force from its passage.

Prohibiting City Officers from Contracting with the City.

CHAP. 314.—An ACT to prohibit and prevent the officers and agents of corporations from becoming contractors with the said corporations.

Approved April 2, 1877.

1. Be it enacted, That it shall not be lawful for any member of the council or board of aldermen, or any other officer or agent, including commissioners appointed for the opening of streets, of any city or other incorporated town, to be a contractor with the said corporation for any work or labor ordered to be done, or goods, wares or merchandize or supplies of any kind ordered by the said corporation to be purchased, or in any manner directly or indirectly, interested in the profits of any Who prohibited from becoming contractors

such contract; and every contract made in violation of this act shall be utterly void, and the officer or agent making it shall forfeit and pay to the state the full amount of money stipulated for by said contract, to be recovered by motion in the circuit court having jurisdiction over the said corporation; provided that this act shall not apply to towns of under two thousand inhabitants.

2. This act shall be in force from its passage.

[AMENDMENT].

CHAP. 209.—An ACT to amend and re-enact an act approved April 2, 1877, entitled an act to prohibit and prevent the officers and agents of corporations from becoming contractors with the said corporation.

Approved March 12, 1878.

Act approved 2 April 1877, amended — 1. Be it enacted by the general assembly, That the act approved on the second day of April, eighteen hundred and seventy-seven, entitled an act to prohibit and prevent the officers and agents of corporations from becoming contractors with the said corporations, be amended and re-enacted so as to read as follows:

No councilman or city official to contract for city work or supplies — § 1. Be it enacted by the general assembly, That it shall not be lawful for any member of the council or board of aldermen, or any other officer or agent, including commissioners appointed for the opening of streets, and including also all members of committees constituted or appointed for the management, regulation, or control of corporate property, of any city or other incorporated town, to be a contractor with the said corporation, or its agents or committee appointed or constituted to manage, regulate, or control its corporate property, for any work or labor ordered to be done, or goods, wares, or merchandise or supplies of any kind ordered by the said corporation, or such committee, as aforesaid, to be purchased, or in any manner, directly or indirectly, interested in the profits in any such contract; and every contract made in violation of this

Such contract to be void — act shall be utterly void, and the officer or agent or member of such committee aforesaid making it, shall forfeit and pay to **Penalty on officer** the state the full amount of money stipulated for by said contract, to be recovered by motion in the circuit court having jurisdiction over the said corporation: provided that this act **Proviso** shall not apply to towns of under two thousand inhabitants.

Commencem't — 2. This act shall be in force from its passage.

Assessment of Real Estate for Taxation.

CHAP. 241.—An ACT to provide a basis of municipal taxation on the real property in cities and towns.

Approved March 29, 1877.

Cities and towns not to exceed state's assessment of real property — 1. Be it enacted by the general assembly, That in cities and towns of this commonwealth, the assessment of real property for taxation, shall in no case exceed the value at which such property is assessed for the purpose of state taxation, and such cities and towns shall, in all cases, for purposes of taxation, adopt the state assessment.

2. That all acts or parts of acts in conflict with the foregoing section, whether contained in the charter of any city or town, or in the general law, are hereby repealed; provided, that nothing in this act shall in any wise affect any assessment of taxes made prior to the passage of this act, or any taxes payable during the year eighteen hundred and seventy-seven. *Conflicting acts repealed*

Proviso

3. This act shall be in force from its passage. *Commencem't*

Weights and Measures.

CHAP. 167.—An ACT to amend and re-enact section 8 of chapter 88 of the Code of 1873, as amended by an act approved February 13, 1877, in relation to weights and measures.

Approved March 20, 1877.

1. Be it enacted by the general assembly, That section eight of chapter eighty-eight of the Code of Virginia, edition of eighteen hundred and seventy-three, as amended by an act approved February thirteenth, eighteen hundred and seventy-seven, be amended and re-enacted so as to read as follows: *Act of Feb. 13, 1877, amended*

§ 8. A cord contains one hundred and twenty-eight cubic feet, being eight feet long, four feet high and four feet wide, or the equivalent thereof; and in all measurements, of wood, tan-bark or other things subject to such measurements, the foregoing shall be the true and legal standard, any usage, by-law, or ordinance of any corporation, railroad, or other company to the contrary notwithstanding. And in all sales by weight of the agricultural products hereinafter named, the number of pounds per bushel, as stated in the following schedule, shall be the true and legal standard: Barley, forty-eight pounds; beans (white), sixty pounds; blue-grass seed, fourteen pounds; buckwheat, fifty-two pounds; chestnuts, fifty-seven pounds; clover seed, sixty pounds; corn (shelled), fifty-six pounds; corn (in the ear), seventy pounds; corn-meal, fifty pounds; dried apples, twenty-eight pounds; dried peaches (peeled), forty pounds; dried peaches (unpeeled), thirty-two pounds; flax seed, fifty-six pounds; hemp seed, forty-four pounds; herds' grass (or red-top) seed, twelve pounds; Hungarian grass seed, forty-eight pounds; lime (un-slacked), eighty pounds; malt, thirty-eight pounds; millet seed, fifty pounds; oats, thirty-two pounds; onions, fifty-seven pounds; onions (top-sets), twenty-eight pounds; orchard grass seed, fourteen pounds; osage orange seed, thirty-four pounds; peanuts, twenty-two pounds; peas (black-eyed) sixty pounds; potatoes (Irish), sixty pounds; potatoes (sweet), fifty-six pounds; plastering hair, eight pounds; rye, fifty-six pounds; salt, fifty pounds; stone coal, eighty pounds; timothy seed, forty-five pounds; turnips, fifty-five pounds; wheat, sixty pounds. *Measurement of wood, &c*

Standard of bushel of grain, &c

2. This act shall be in force from its passage. *Commencem't*

Charter of the Cotton Exchange.

CHAP. 93.—An ACT to incorporate the Norfolk and Portsmouth Cotton Exchange.

Approved February 17, 1877.

The Norfolk and Portsmouth cotton exchange incorporated

1. Be it enacted by the general assembly, That the members of the association known as the Norfolk and Portsmouth cotton exchange, and all other persons who may hereafter become associated with them under the provisions of this act, are hereby created a body corporate by the name of The Norfolk and Portsmouth Cotton Exchange, with perpetual succession and power to use a common seal, and to alter the same at pleasure; to sue and be sued; to take and hold, by grant, purchase, and devise, subject to the provisions of law, relating to devises and bequests by last will and testament, real and personal property, to an amount not exceeding one hundred thousand dollars, for the purposes of such association; and to sell, convey, lease, and mortgage the same or any part thereof; to borrow money and issue bonds, and to do all and singular such acts as may be necessary to carry on the business and further the objects of said association.

General powers

Board of directors to be elected annually

2. The property, affairs, business, and concerns of the corporation hereby created, shall be managed by a president, vice-president, and treasurer, and five directors; who together shall constitute a board of directors, to be elected annually, at such time and place as may be provided by the by-laws; and the present officers and managers of said association, as now constituted, shall be the officers and managers of said corporation until their present term of office shall expire, and until others under the provisions of this act shall be elected in their place. All vacancies which may occur in said board, by death, resignation or otherwise, shall be filled by the said board. A majority of the members of said board shall constitute a quorum for the transaction of business.

Term of present officers

How vacancies to be filled

Quorum

Purposes of the corporation defined

3. The purposes of said corporation shall be to provide, regulate, and maintain a suitable building, room or rooms, for a cotton exchange in the city of Norfolk; to adjust controversies between its members; to establish just and equitable principles in trade; to maintain uniformity in its rules, regulations, and usages; to acquire, preserve, and disseminate useful information connected with the cotton interests throughout all markets; to decrease the local risks attendant upon the business; and generally to promote the cotton trade of the cities of Norfolk and Portsmouth; increase the amount, and augment the facilities with which it may be conducted. The said corporation shall have power to adopt a constitution for its government, and to make all proper and needful by-laws not contrary to the laws and constitution of the state of Virginia or of the United States.

Power over members

4. The said corporation shall have power to admit new members and expel any member in such manner as may be provided by the by-laws

5. The capital stock of the said corporation shall not exceed Capital stock
one hundred thousand dollars, divided into one thousand
shares of one hundred dollars each, which shall be paid in
cash or in instalments as may be required by the board of
directors. In case payment should be called for in instalments, any subscriber to the capital stock who shall fail to pay
such instalment within thirty days after the date fixed for such
payments, shall forfeit all instalments previously paid. All
certificates of stock shall be signed by the president and
countersigned by the treasurer.

6. Every member of the association who has already paid Regulations concerning stock
the regular initiation fee, shall be entitled to receive one share
of the capital stock in return therefor.

7. Every member of the association shall be required to be
the holder of at least one share of the capital stock of said
association in his own name.

8. No stockholder shall ever be held liable or responsible
for the contracts or faults of the association beyond the
amount of his stock therein.

9. Said association shall have power to appoint and license May appoint and license its own weights
its own weighers of cotton, who shall be known as the cotton
weighers for the cities of Norfolk and Portsmouth, who upon
being appointed, shall subscribe to the oath prescribed by the Oath of office
by-laws, and shall pay such annual assessment as the by-laws
may impose.

10. The following named stockholders shall constitute the First board of directors
board of directors, and shall hold their seats until their successors shall have been elected and qualified in accordance
with the constitution: William W. Gwathmey, president;
Kader Biggs, vice-president; H. C. Williams, treasurer; W.
D. Reynolds, George L. Arps, James R. Ricks, Washington
Reed, John N. Vaughan.

11. This act shall be in force from its passage. Commencem't

City Bonds.

Page 11, CHAP. 15.—An ACT to authorize the Council of the City of
Norfolk, to issue bonds for the purpose of redeeming certain outstanding bonds of said City.

Approved January 14th, 1878.

1. Be it enacted by the general assembly, That the councils
of the city of Norfolk be and they are hereby authorized to
issue and sell either registered or coupon bonds of said city, to
an amount not exceeding five hundred and forty thousand dollars, payable at such time, not to exceed thirty years, and at
such a rate of interest not to exceed six per centum per annum,
as the councils may deem best; provided, however, that the
money arising from the sale of said bonds shall be used and
applied by the said council for the payment and redemption of
the registered or coupon bonds of the city of Norfolk which

fall due in the years eighteen hundred and seventy-nine, eighteen hundred and eighty, and eighteen hundred and eighty-one, and for no other purpose whatever.

2. This act shall be in force from its passage.

Slaughter Houses.

CHAP. 127.—An ACT to prevent the erection of Slaughter Houses within half a mile of the City of Norfolk.

Approved March 1st, 1878.

1. Be it enacted by the general assembly of Virginia, that hereafter, except on tide-water, no slaughter house or slaughter pen shall be erected, established, and maintained, within half a mile of the limits of the city of Norfolk. Any violation of this act shall be deemed a misdemeanor, and shall be punished by fine and imprisonment; the fine not to exceed one hundred dollars, and the imprisonment not to exceed six months.

2. This act shall be in force from its passage.

Schools.

CHAP. 233.—An ACT to amend and re-enact the 20th Section, 19th Chapter, Code of 1873, in regard to duties of City Councils to make appropriations for School purposes.

Approved March 12, 1878.

1. Be it enacted by the general assembly of Virginia, That the twentieth section of chapter seventy-nine, of the Code of Virginia, edition eighteen hundred and seventy-three, shall be amended and re-enacted so as to read as follows:

§ 20. It shall be the duty of the city or town councils, and of every incorporated town of over five hundred inhabitants, which has been erected into a separate school district, to provide, in due time, and it shall have no power to withhold the sum or sums reported by the city or town school boards, and declared to be necessary for the proper maintenance and growth of the public schools of the city or town, except the city of Richmond the council of which said city shall have the discretion of the board of county supervisors in similar cases; provided, that the council shall not be required to appropriate a sum greater than double the amount received from school funds of the state during the same scholastic year; but the council may, in its discretion, appropriate a larger sum, but it shall not have power to impose a tax on property for school purposes exceeding three mills on a dollar in any one year.

City Bonds.

CHAP. 10.—An ACT authorizing the City of Nofork to issue its bonds for the purpose of retiring and refunding certain bonds now outstanding.

Approved March 28, 1879.

1. Be it enacted by the general assembly, That the city of Norfolk be authorized to issue its bonds to the amount of

three hundred thousand dollars, to bear interest at the rate of not more than six per centum per annum, and not to run more than thirty years, and that the money received from the sale of said bonds shall not be used for any other purpose than for retiring or refunding certain bonds of said city to the amount of three hundred thousand dollars, issued by virtue of an ordinance passed by the common council, on the fifth day of August, eighteen hundred and seventy, and by the select council, on the fifteenth day of August, eighteen hundred and seventy, bearing interest at the rate of eight per centum per annum, and redeemable after ten years from the date thereof.

2. This act shall be in force from and after its passage.

Work House.

CHAP. 95.—An ACT for the establishment of a work house of correction in the City of Norfolk.

Approved April 2, 1879.

1. Be it enacted by the general assembly, That the common and select councils of the city of Norfolk, with the approval of the mayor and judge of the hustings court, of said city, are authorized in their discretion, to establish a work house of correction for the punishment of boys and girls, under the age of fifteen years.

2. All persons under the age of fifteen years. who may be convicted of misdemeanor in any of the courts of said city, or before a justice of said city, may be punished in the discretion of the said courts or justices, by confinement in the said house of correction for a period not exceeding four months, in lieu of the punishment prescribed by existing laws for like offences.

3. All prisoners sent to the work house of correction, established under this act, shall be in the keeping of the present officer of the court having charge of prisoners, and shall receive like compensation for their keeping, and so forth.

4. This act shall be in force from its passage.

Chain Gang.

CHAP. 118.—An ACT to provide for the punishment of persons convicted of petit larceny, in the City of Norfolk.

Approved April 2, 1879.

1. Be it enacted by the general assembly of Virginia, That persons convicted under chapter three, section thirteen of the criminal code of the state, being chapter three hundred and eleven of the acts of assembly, eighteen hundred and seventy-seven, seventy-eight, and chapter three, section thirteen of the same, of petit larceny, in the city of Norfolk, may be punished with stripes, or, at the discretion of the court, may be sen-

tenced to hard labor in a chain gang in said city; provided, that the city of Norfolk shall pay all the expenses of said chain gang, and of guarding, finding, and clothing of such persons, and of properly providing for and taking care of the same.

2. This act shall take effect from its passage.

[The foregoing modified by act of 1881-82. Chap. 66.]

§ 5. And be it further enacted, That section twenty-nine, chapter ten, and section twelve, chapter twenty-five, of the criminal code of eighteen hundred and seventy-eight, and all other acts and parts of acts, so far as they relate to punishment by stripes, be and the same are hereby repealed.

Repeal of certain sections of criminal code

[From the Criminal Code. Acts of 1877-78.

How chain-gangs in cities, towns, and counties may be organized as a punishment for crime.

24. The common council of all cities and towns in this state containing a population of over five thousand inhabitants, and the trustees or other proper authorities of other incorporated towns of less than five thousand inhabitants, and the board of supervisors of each county, or if they shall not act, the judge of the county or corporation court of such county or corporation, are hereby authorized and empowered to establish chain-gangs, to be composed of persons hereinafter described, in their respective cities, counties, and towns, for the purpose and object of working on the streets, roads, and public property of such cities, counties, and towns; and all male persons above the age of sixteen years, who may be convicted of misdemeanor, or of any offence deemed infamous in law, and sentenced to confinement in jail as a punishment, or part punishment for such offence, or who may be imprisoned for failure to pay any fine or penalty which may have been imposed upon or assessed against such person upon such conviction, or upon conviction for any violation of any ordinance of any city or town which by said ordinance may be punished by confinement in jail or fine, may be required to work in such chain-gang: provided that any county which has not established a chain-gang of its own, may, by its supervisors or judge, contract to hire such convicted persons as are liable to work in a chain-gang, to the authorities of any county, city or town which has a chain-gang; such persons are subject to the rules and regulations established for the government of the chain-gang in which they shall be employed.

Chain-gangs authorized in towns

In counties

Purpose

Who shall compose chain gangs

Proviso

Rules and regulations for their government; how imposed.

25. Such common councils, trustees, or other proper authority, and boards of supervisors or judge, shall establish rules and regulations for the care, safe-keeping, and government of such persons while so employed, and shall provide for the payment of the expenses of said chain-gangs, and shall furnish the clothing necessary for such persons, to be paid out of their city, town, and county treasuries.

Proper authorities to establish rules for maintenance &c. of chain gangs, and provide for expenses out of city, &c., treasury

Order of judge; what to direct; may exempt for age or infirmity.

26. The judge shall order such persons as may be confined *Persons liable to work in chain gang to be delivered to contractor by order of the judge* or committed to the jail of his county or corporation, and liable to work in chain-gangs under the provisions of this chapter, to be delivered by the jailor to the person authorized to take charge of and work the chain-gang in his county, city, or town; which order shall specify the length of time each person *Order to specify the time* is required to work in such chain-gang. He may direct, if the *the offender is to work in chain gang* judge shall think proper so to do, that they be confined in the jail when not engaged at work. The jailor shall take a receipt *May be confined in jail during term* for every prisoner delivered by him under such order, which *Jailor to take receipt, which shall be his discharge* shall discharge him from all liability for the escape of such persons so long as they may not be in his custody.

27. If it shall be manifest that, from old age, bodily infirmity, *discharge from liability* or any other cause, any person otherwise liable to labor in the *Who are, and how, exempted from provisions of this act* chain-gang should be exempted therefrom, it shall be the duty of the judge to make an order to that effect, stating in the order the reason therefor.

Prisoners may be compelled to work out fine and costs.

28. All persons held to labor under the provisions of this *When fine and costs to be worked out* chapter for the non-payment of any fine imposed upon or assessed against them, shall be required to work out the full amount of all such fines or assessments, including the legal costs, at the rate of twenty-five cents per day for each day so *Rate per diem* held, Sundays excepted: provided that all persons held to labor *Proviso* under the provisions of this chapter, shall be entitled to a credit of twenty-five cents for each day of their confinement, *Statement of amount of fine and costs and days of labor to be made out, &c* whether they labor or not, as a credit upon any fine which may be assessed against them. A statement of the amount of the fine or assessment, together with the costs and the number of days labor required to discharge the same, shall be made out under the direction of the judge, and delivered to the person in charge of the chain-gang at the time he receives the delinquent: provided that no person shall be held to labor in any *Proviso* chain-gang for the non-payment of any fine imposed upon or assessed against him, for a greater period than six months.

Coroners' and Constables' Fees.

13. A coroner shall have, for taking an inquest on a dead *Fees of coroner when a physician* body, three dollars, except where the coroner is a physician and actually makes an examination of the dead body, in which case his fee shall be five dollars; and a sheriff, or constable for *Fees of sheriff or constable* summoning a coroner's jury and the witnesses, one and a half dollars.

Powder Officer.

CHAP. 154.—An ACT for appointment of Powder Offcer for the harbor of Norfolk and Portsmouth.

Approved March 3, 1880.

Appointment of powder officer authorized
Term of office
Compensation

1. Be it enacted by the general assembly of Virginia, That for the purpose of better security of life and property in the harbor of Norfolk and Portsmouth, one powder officer shall be appointed by the governor for the term of four years. The said officer shall superintend the handling of all powder to and from vessels of every and all kinds in the harbor, whose duty shall be to see that every prevention against danger of ignition and explosion is adopted and rigidly observed; for which services he shall receive from the consignee of the powder for transfer three cents per keg, and the said officer may be required to enter into a bond, in the penalty of five thousand dollars, for the faithful performance of his office before any officer authorized to take official bonds.

[AMENDMENT.]

CHAP. 290.—An ACT to amend an act passed February 27, 1880, entitled an act for appointment of powder officer for the harbor of Norfolk and Portsmouth.

Approved March 9, 1880.

Act 27th February, 1880, amended
Amendment
Commencem't

1. Be it enacted by the general assembly, That the act passed February twenty-seventh, eighteen hundred and eighty, entitled an act for the appointment of powder officer for the harbor of Norfolk and Portsmouth be amended by the addition of the following section:

§ 2. This act shall be in force from its passage.

ˉ2. This act shall be in force from its passage.

Misuse of Public Funds.

CHAP. 307.—An ACT to prevent and punish the misuse or misappropriation of public funds by public officers.

Approved March 9, 1880.

Offence
Penalty

1. Be it enacted by the general assembly, That if any state, city, county or town officer, agent or employee having custody of public funds, shall knowingly misuse or misappropriate the same, or knowingly dispose thereof otherwise than in accordance with the law, he shall be deemed guilty of a felony, and on conviction thereof, shall be confined in the penitentiary for a term of not less than one nor more than ten years, in the discretion of the jury; and any default of any such officer, agent or employee in paying over said funds to the proper authorities when required to do so by law, shall be deemed prima facie proof of his guilt.

Act to be given in charge to grand jury

2. The judges of the commonwealth shall give this act in charge to every grand jury empanelled in their courts.

3. This act shall be in force from its passage.

City Bonds.

CHAP. 28.—An ACT authorizing the city of Norfolk to issue its bonds for the purpose of retiring and refunding certain bonds now outstanding.

Approved January 19, 1882.

1. Be it enacted by the general assembly, That the councils of the city of Norfolk be and they are hereby authorized to issue and sell either registered or coupon bonds of the said city, to an amount not exceeding four hundred and thirty-four thousand dollars, payable at such time, not exceeding thirty years, and at such rate of interest, not to exceed five per centum, as the councils of said city may deem best: provided, however, that the money arising from the sale of such bonds shall be used and applied by the said councils for the payment and redemption of the registered bonds of the city of Norfolk, which will fall due in the years eighteen hundred and eighty-two, eighteen hundred and eighty-three, eighteen hundred and eighty-four, eighteen hundred and eighty-five; and the said money arising from the sale of said bonds shall be used for no other purpose whatever.

2. This act shall be in full force from its passage.

For issue of bonds for the purpose of retiring and refunding certain bonds now outstanding

Commencem't

Vaccination.

CHAP. 166.—An ACT to amend and re-enact section nineteen, chapter eighty-four of the Code of 1873, in relation to public health.

Approved February 21, 1882.

1. Be it enacted by the general assembly, That section nineteen of chapter eighty-four of the Code of eighteen hundred and seventy-three be amended and re-enacted to read as follows:

§ 19. The common council of any city, or town, and the board of supervisors of any county, when, in their judgment, occasion requires, may cause persons, residing within their limits, to be vaccinated with genuine vaccine matter; and the council of any city or town may enforce obedience to its ordinance by affixing fines and penalties for the violation of said ordinance. Should any person or persons, including children, who attend the public schools, be unable to pay for vaccination, such person or persons shall be vaccinated with genuine vaccine matter at the cost and expense of the city, town, or county, and provision shall be made therefor by the council of the city or town, or by the board of supervisors of the county.

2. This act shall be in force from its passage.

Act

May cause persons to be vaccinated

Commencem't

Penalty for Non-payment of Taxes.

CHAP. 220.—An ACT to prescribe the penalty for non-payment of taxes in cities and towns.

Approved March 6, 1882.

1. Be it enacted by the general assembly, That it shall not

Non-payment of city taxes be lawful for the authorities of any city or town in this state, to impose or receive, in any case, a higher rate of penalty for the non-payment of taxes, than is prescribed by the laws of the state in the cases of persons delinquent in the payment of state taxes.

2. All acts and parts of acts, and all provisions of the charters or ordinances of any city or town in this state, in conflict with this act, are hereby repealed and declared null and void.

Commencem't 3 This act shall be in force from its passage.

Proving City Ordinances.

CHAP. 9.—An ACT to prescribe the method of proving the ordinances and joint resolutions of municipal corporations.

Approved January 18, 1884.

Ordinances of corporations; how proven 1. Be it enacted by the general assembly of Virginia, That all ordinances and joint resolutions of any municipal corporation in the commonwealth shall be sufficiently proved in any court or cause by producing a copy of the same, certified by the clerk of the corporation, or a printed copy of the same; provided such printed copy purports to have been printed by the authority of the corporation; but in the latter case, without prejudice to the right of any party in interest to prove, by competent evidence, any error in the printed copy as compared with the ordinance or joint resolution as passed.

Commencem't 2. This act shall be in force from its passage.

Charter of City Gas Light Company.

CHAP. 20.—An ACT to extend, renew and amend the charter of the City Gas Light Company of Norfolk.

Approved January 18, 1884.

Extension of charter 1. Be it enacted by the general assembly of Virginia, That the charter of the city gas light company of Norfolk, granted by the act entitled an act to incorporate the city gas light company of Norfolk, passed January eleven, eighteen hundred and fifty, be and the same is hereby revised, renewed, amended and extended for a period of thirty years from and after the date of the passage of this present act.

2. That sections one, two and four of the act first above recited, be amended and re-enacted so as to read as follows:

Names and powers of corporators § 1. Be it enacted by the general assembly of Virginia, That Tazewell Taylor, Frederick W. Southgate, A. T. M. Cooke, Thomas Newton, Walter H. Taylor, Charles S. Almand, C. W. Newton, Richard Dickson, G. R. Drummond, William Selden, Thomas Bottimore, and W. C. Dickson, and such other persons as may now and hereafter be associated with them, shall be and they are hereby incorporated and made a body politic and corporate, under the name and style of the city gas light company of Norfolk, with full power to construct or purchase suitable works and machinery, either in Norfolk city, or Norfolk county, or both, for the manufacture, distribution and sale of gas, electricity or other material, from bituminous or other substances, for the purposes of public and private heating and illumination, and for power, both within the corporate limits of Norfolk city and without the same in Norfolk county, adjacent to said city; and for the purpose of carrying into full effect the works herein provided for, the said company shall have power to purchase and hold such real estate, not exceeding twenty acres, located either in the city or county of Norfolk, or both, as may be necessary for their works and the proper carrying on of their business; and they are hereby invested with all the powers conferred, and subjected to all the provisions prescribed by chapters fifty-six and fifty-seven of the code of Virginia, edition of eighteen hundred and seventy-three, except in so far as may be otherwise provided in this act.

§ 2. Be it further enacted, That the capital stock of the city *Capital stock how to be raised* gas light company of Norfolk, shall not be less than twenty thousand dollars, nor more than five hundred thousand dollars, to be divided into shares of one hundred dollars each, to be raised by subscription; for which purpose, if the stock be not otherwise subscribed, books may be opened under the superintendence of Charles S. Allmand, O. W. Newton, Richard Dickson, William Selden, G. R. Drummond, Thomas Bottimore, and W. C. Dickson, and such other persons as may be associated with them, or any two of them in conformity with the law in such case made and provided.

§4. Be it further enacted, That the said company shall be *Rights of company in carrying on business* authorized to open the streets, avenues, highways, and public parks and squares of the said city and county, for laying pipes, planting poles or placing and working such apparatus as shall be necessary to carry on the business of the said company; provided, that when the same shall be repaired by the said company, at its own cost and expense, subject to the approval of the inspector or engineer of said city, or the councils thereof; and provided also, that no poles shall be planted in the streets of the city by the said company, until the consent of the council thereto, shall have been first had and obtained.

3. This act shall be in force from its passage.   *Commencem't*

Prohibiting United States Officers from Holding State or City Offices.

CHAP. 145.—An ACT to amend and re-enact section 2 of chapter 11 of the Code of 1873, relating to the qualifications to hold office.

Approved February 22, 1884.

1. Be it enacted by the general assembly of Virginia, That section two of chapter eleven, code of Virginia, edition of eighteen hundred and seventy-three, be amended and re-enacted so as to read as follows:

§ 2 No person shall be capable of holding any such post, *Certain persons ineligible to office* who holds any post of profit, trust or emolument, civil or military, legislative, executive or judicial, under the government of the United States, or who receives in any way from United States, any emolument whatever, and the acceptance of any such post of profit, trust, or emolument, under the government of the United States, or who is in the employment of the United States government in any capacity, shall ipso facto, vacate any post of profit, trust or emolument, under the government of this commonwealth, or any town, city, or county thereof, and it shall be the duty of the constituted authorities of this commonwealth, to take such action as may be necessary to fill any vacancy so created, either by appointment or by causing an election or elections to be held, as may be provided by law, whenever the fact of such acceptance shall be brought to their attention.

2. All acts and parts of acts inconsistent with this act, are hereby repealed.

Commencem't   3. This act shall be in force from its passage.

To Prevent Obstructions of Streets by Railroads, and Hindering Trains.

CHAP. 391.—An ACT to prevent obstructions of streets, turnpikes and county roads or the crossings on railways.

Approved March 12, 1884.

1. Be it enacted by the general assembly of Virginia, That it shall not be lawful to obstruct free passage on any street, turnpike or county road, by standing cars or trains across said public highways, but a passway shall be kept open, except a passenger train while receiving or discharging passengers; nor shall it be lawful to stand any wagon, or other vehicle, on the track of any railway which will hinder or endanger a moving train.

2. If any person in charge of railway cars, or a train of cars, or a wagon or other vehicle, shall violate the provisions of the preceeding section, he shall be liable to arrest and a fine of five dollars before a justice of the peace.

Salary of Circuit Judge.

CHAP. 558.—An ACT to authorize the Councils of the city of Norfolk to add to and increase the salary of the Judge of the Circuit Court of the city, and to pay such increase from the City Treasury.

Approved March 19, 1884.

Whereas the great increase in the business and commercial prosperity of the city of Norfolk has greatly added to the duties and labors of the judge of the circuit court of that city, in the examination and granting of charters of incorporation, and other duties which are required to be done in chambers: therefore,

1. Be it enacted by the general assembly of Virginia, That the councils of the said city of Norfolk be and they are hereby

authorized and empowered to add to and increase the salary of
the judge of the circuit court of said city; provided that the
increase or pay allowed to the judge of said court shall not
exceed the sum of one thousand dollars per annum, and that
the same shall be paid out of the treasury of the said city.

Notice of Redemption of Bonds.

CHAP. 479.—An ACT providing how counties, cities and towns may
give notice to its holders of coupon bonds proposed to be redeemed.

Approved March 17, 1884.

1. Be it enacted by the general assembly of Virginia, That.
when any county, city or town wishes to redeem any of its outstanding redeemable coupon bonds, it may through its proper
officer give notice of its readiness to do so to the holder in
person or by a notice inserted once a week for two weeks in a
newspaper published in or near said county, city or town. It
shall be sufficient in said notice to give the number and
amount of such bond, and to fix a day for its presentation for
payment, which shall not be less than ten days from the date
of said personal notice, or the completion of said notice of
publication, as the case may be. If the bond shall not be
presented on the day fixed for its redemption, interest shall
cease thereon, and the holder shall be entitled to no interest
from that date.

2. This act shall be in force from and after its passage.

License Taxes on Corporations.

Approved March 15, 1884.

§ 108. It shall not be lawful for any incorporated company
doing business in this state, to exact or receive of persons
dealing with it, or charge to the account of such persons with
the company, the sum required by the state, county, city, or
town to be paid for the license or business of such company,
or any portion thereof, or any amount on account thereof.
Any company violating this provision, shall for every such
violation, be liable to a fine of one hundred dollars, one-half
of which shall go to the informer.

City Bonds.

CHAP. 29.—AN ACT to amend chapter 28 of the acts of assembly
1881-2, entitled an act authorizing the city of Norfolk to issue its
Bonds for the purpose of retiring and refunding certain bonds now
outstanding.

Approved August 27, 1884.

1. Be it enacted by the general assembly of Virginia, That
the act entitled an act authorizing the city of Norfolk to issue
its bonds for the purpose of retiring and refunding certain
bonds now outstanding, approved January nintcenth, eighteen

hundred and eighty-two, be and the same is hereby amended and re-enacted so as to read as follows:

Council to issue and sell bonds and for what purpose § 1. That the councils of the city of Norfolk be and they are hereby authorized to issue and sell either registered or coupon bonds of the said city, to an amount not exceeding three hundred and thirty-three thousand dollars, payable at such time not exceeding thirty years, and at such rate of interest not to exceed six per centum as the said councils of said city may deem best; provided however, that the money arising from the sale of such bonds shall be used and applied by the said councils for the payment and redemption of the registered bonds of the city of Norfolk, which shall fall due in the years eighteen hundred and eighty-four and eighteen hundred and eighty-five; and the said money arising from the sale of said bonds, shall not be used for any other purpose whatever.

Commencem't 2. This act shall be in force from its passage.

Schools.   Non Resident Tax-Payers Rights in.

CHAP. 132.—An ACT to amend and re-enact an act entitled an act to amend and re-enact an act entitled an act to secure to tax-payers in cities and towns the right of public school education for their children, approved March 17, 1884.

Approved November 27, 1884.

Repeal and amendment of previous act 1. Be it enacted by the general assembly of Virginia, That an act to amend and re-enact an act entitled an act to secure to the tax-payers in cities and towns the right of public school education for their children, approved March seventeenth, eighteen hundred and eighty-four, be amended and re-enacted so as to read as follows:

How resident tax-payers to have benefit of scools 2. That it shall be lawful for any person who is a tax-payer and citizen of Virginia, in any town, county, or school district of the commonwealth, and who is not a resident of said town, county or school district, to send his children to any public free school in said town, county or school district, subject to the laws regulating public free schools in said town, county or school district, as though said tax-payer resided in said town, county or school district. And any guardian who is a tax-payer for his ward or wards as aforesaid, shall be entitled to the privileges above named for his ward or wards, if citizens of Virginia: provided that children whose parents or guardian do not reside in any city of the commonwealth shall be received into the public schools of such city, only upon such terms and conditions as may be prescribed by the school board of such city.

3. This act shall go into effect on the first day of July,
Commencem't eighteen hundred and eighty-five.

Service of Process on Corporations.

CHAP. 164.—An ACT to amend an act entitled an act to amend and re-enact section 7 of chapter 166 of Code of 1873, in relation to service of process against or notice to a corporation.

Approved November 29, 1884.

1. Be it enacted by the general assembly of Virginia, That section seven, chapter one hundred and sixty-six of Code of eighteen hundred and seventy-three, as amended by an act approved March eighteenth, eighteen hundred and eighty-four, entitled an act to amend an re-enact section seven, chapter 166 of code of eighteen hundred and seventy-three, in relation to service of process against or notice to a corporation, be amended and re-enacted so as to read as follows:

§ 7. It shall be sufficient to serve any process against, or notice to a corporation on its mayor, rector, president or other chief officer, or in his absence from the county or corporation in which he resides, or in which is the principal office of the corporation against or to which the process or notice is, if it be a city or town, or the president of the council, or board of trustees, or in his absence, or the recorder or any alderman or trustee, and if it be not a city or town, on the cashier or treasurer, and if there be none such, or he be absent, on a member of the board of directors, trustees, or visitors. If the case be against a bank of circulation and be in a county or corporation wherein the bank has a branch, service on the president or cashier of such branch bank shall be sufficient; and if the case be against some other corporation, whether incorporated by the laws of this state or any other state or country, transacting business in this state, or on any agent thereof, or any person declared by the laws of this state to be an agent of such corporation; and if there be no such agent in the county or corporation, publication of a copy of the process or notice as an order is published under the eleventh section of this chapter, shall be sufficient. Service on any person under this section shall be in the county or corporation in which he resides, or in which the principal office of the company is located; and the return shall show this, and state on whom, and when the service was, otherwise the service shall not be valid.

What shall be sufficient process on and notice to corporations.

2. This act shall be in force from its passage.

Commencem't

Extracts from the Constitution of the Commonwealth.

ARTICLE V.

Sec. 15. No law shall embrace more than one object, which shall be expressed in its title; nor shall any law be revived or amended with reference to its title, but the act revived or the section amended, shall be re-enacted and published at length.

Sec. 23. The legislature shall have power to provide for the

government of cities and towns, and to establish such courts
therein as may be necessary for the administration of justice

ARTICLE VI.

Government of Cities and Towns.

Sec. 14. For each city or town in the state, containing a
population of five thousand, there shall be elected on the joint
vote of the two houses of the general assembly, one city judge,
who shall hold a corporation or hustings court of said city or
town, as often, and as many days in each month, as may be
prescribed by law, with similar jurisdiction which may be
given by law, to the circuit courts of this state, and who shall
hold his office for a term of six years: provided, that in cities
or towns containing thirty thousand inhabitants, there may be
elected an additional judge to hold courts of probate and
record, separate and apart from the corporation or hustings
courts, and perform such other duties as shall be prescribed
by law.

Sec. 15. Also the following enumerated officers, who shall
be elected by the qualified voters of the said cities or towns:
One clerk of the corporation or hustings court, who shall also
be the clerk of the circuit court, except in cities or towns containing a population of thirty thousand or more; in which
city or town there may be a separate clerk for the circuit
court, who shall hold his office for a term of six years.

Sec. 16. One commonwealth's attorney, who shall be the
commonwealth's attorney for the circuit court, and shall hold
his office for a term of two years.

Sec. 17. One city sergeant, who shall hold his office for a
term of two years.

Sec. 18. One city or town treasurer, whose duties shall be
similar to those of county treasurer, and shall hold his office
for a term of three years.

Sec. 19. One commissioner of the revenue.

Sec. 20. There shall be chosen by the electors of every city,
a mayor, who shall be the chief executive officer thereof, and
who shall see that the duties of the various city officers are
faithfully performed. He shall have power to investigate
their acts, have access to all books and documents in their
offices, and may examine them and their subordinates on oath.
The evidence given by persons so examined, shall not be used
against them in any criminal proceedings. He shall also have
power to suspend or remove such officers, whether they be
elected or appointed, for misconduct in office or neglect of
duty, to be specified in the order of suspension or removal;
but no such removal shall be made without reasonable notice
to the officer complained of, and an opportunity afforded him
to be heard in his defence. All city, town and village officers,
whose election or appointment is not provided for by this constitution, shall be elected by the electors of such cities, towns
and villages, or of some division thereof, or appointed by such

authorities thereof as the general assembly shall designate. All other officers whose election or appointment is not provided for by this constitution, and all officers whose offices may be hereafter created by law, shall be elected by the people, or appointed, as the general assembly may direct. Members of common councils shall hold no other office in cities, and no city officer shall hold a seat in the general assembly. The general assembly, at its first session after the adoption of this constitution, shall pass such laws as may be necesary to give effect to the provisions of this article. General laws shall be passed for the organization and government of cities, and no special act shall be passed, except in cases where, in the judgment of the general assembly, the object of such act cannot be attained by general laws. Nothing in this article shall affect the power of the general assembly over quarantine, or in regard to the port of Norfolk, or the interest of the state in the lands under water and within the jurisdiction or boundaries of any city, or to regulate the wharves, piers or slips in any city. All laws or city ordinances in conflict with the provisions of the preceeding sections, shall be void from and after the adoption of this constitution.

SEC. 21. All regular elections for city or town officers, under this article, shall be held on the fourth Thursday in May, and the officers elect shall enter upon their duties on the first day of July succeeding.

ARTICLE VIII.

Education.

SEC. 11. Each city and county shall be held accountable for the destruction of school property that may take place within its limits by incendiaries or open violence.

ARTICLE X.

Taxation and Finance.

SEC. 1. Taxation, except as hereinafter provided, whether imposed by the state, county, or corporate bodies, shall be equal and uniform, and all property, both real and personal, shall be taxed in proportion to its value, to be ascertained as prescribed by law. No one species of property, from which a tax may be collected, shall be taxed higher than any other species of property of equal value.

SEC. 2. No tax shall be imposed on any of the citizens of this state for the privilege of taking or catching oysters from their natural beds with tongs, in the waters thereof; but the amount of sales of oysters so taken by any citizen, in any one year, may be taxed at a rate not exceeding the rate of taxation imposed upon any other species of property.

SEC. 3. The legislature may exempt all property used exclusively for state, county, municipal, benevolent, charitable, educational and religious purposes.

SEC. 4. The general assembly may levy a tax on incomes in excess of six hundred dollars per annum, and upon the following licenses, viz: the sale of ardent spirits, theatrical and circus companies, menageries, jugglers, itinerent pedlars, and all other shows and exhibitions for which an entrance fee is required; commission merchants, persons selling by sample, brokers and pawn-brokers, and all other business which cannot be reached by the *ad volorem* system. The capital invested in all business operations shall be assessed and taxed as other property. Assessments upon all stock shall be according to the market value thereof.

SEC. 5. The general assembly may levy a tax, not exceeding one dollar per annum, on every male citizen who has attained the age of twenty-one years, which shall be applied exclusively in aid of public free schools; and counties and corporations shall have power to impose a capitation tax, not exceeding fifty cents per annum, for all purposes.

SEC. 6. The general assembly shall provide for a re-assessment of the real estate of this state in the year 1869, or as soon thereafter as practicable, and every fifth year thereafter; provided, in making such assessment, no land shall be assessed above or below its value.

SEC. 16. Every law which imposes, continues or revives a tax, shall distinctly state the tax, and the object to which it is to be applied, and it shall not be sufficient to refer to any other law to fix such tax or object.

Election of State Officers for the City.

The clerk of the courts in 1888, for six years.

The commonwealth's attorney in 1886, for two years.

The city sergeant in 1886, for two years.

The city treasurer in 1888, for three years.

The commissioner of the revenue in 1886, for two years.

APPENDIX.

Town Point Lots and Ends of Streets.

Opinion of JUDGE D. TUCKER BROOKE,

In the Corporation Court.

APRIL TERM, 1885.

IN THE MATTER OF	Unlawful Trespass.
J. W. LEE,	
vs.	Upon an appeal from a
WM. O'CONNOR.	Justice of the Peace.

This is an action of unlawful trespass instituted before a justice of the peace, and comes here upon an appeal from his decision. The act complained of as a trespass consisted of the defendant passing with a truck over a certain portion of Jackson street, in the city of Norfolk, of which the plaintiff claimed to have exclusive right of possession under a lease from the city of Norfolk, conveying to him the "end of Jackson street" with other property belonging to the city. The right of the city to make the lease referred to is based upon an act of the general assembly of Virginia, passed January 29, 1866 (acts 1865-6, p. 277), authorizing the city councils of the city of Norfolk "to make such use of the ends of streets of said city running to tidewater as they may deem necessary for the public interest." The defendant was at the time of the alleged trespass, an employe of the tenant of the owner of property abutting on Jackson street.

The questions presented are:

1. Did the city of Norfolk have the right to give exclusive use and possession of the end of Jackson street to the plaintiff?

2. If the city had the right was the locus of the alleged trespass within that portion of Jackson street falling within the words "end of Jackson street?"

The first question at once resolves itself into two branches.

a. The right of the city of Norfolk prior to the act of 1865-6.

b. The right of the city of Norfolk after the passage of that act.

(a) In the year 1705, in the 4th year of Queen Anne, while yet Virginia was a colony and the beds of her rivers, creeks and bays were in the crown (2 Min. Ins. 557) the Virginia

general assembly with the consent of the crown passed an act
establishing certain towns as ports. Among these was Norfolk,
on the Elizabeth river (3 Hen. St. at L. 415). By one of the
sections of that act (ibid p. 412) it is provided as follows:
"And if any person having a lott in town upon the water side,
will build out into the water before his own lott, for the better
conveniency of landing and shipping off goods, such persons
shall have the whole benefit of such building, and the land
so built upon shall be reckoned as part of his own lott, and it
shall entirely be his as the lott itself," etc.

It will be observed that this provision was an innovation
upon the law of riparian rights, under which the owner of
property bordering upon tidewater acquired at that time a fee
simple title only down to high water. But it was an innovation made by a duly authorized power, applicable only to the
ports, or towns established by that act, and for the express
purpose of facilitating commerce.

In this condition of affairs, in the first year of George III.
1761, an act was passed enlarging the limits of the port of
Norfolk, which had by previous acts been made a borough, and
giving to owners of lots in the annexed territory the same
privileges, etc., theretofore bestowed upon lot owners of the
original town. The 4th section of this act, reciting that a certain lot of public land, called the Fort Land, in the borough of
Norfolk, was daily washing away by the washing of the river,
and that neither the county nor the borough of Norfolk were
in condition, financially, to correct the evil, established what
we may call the Fort Land company, vesting the fee simple
title of said land in trustees for the benefit of the said company. The 5th section of this act, however, gave to the county
and to the borough of Norfolk if the county should refuse, the
right to acquire the said Fort Land from the company by purchase for the benefit of the inhabitants of the county or
borough as the case might be. (7 Hen. St. at L. 435, 510, 511,
512). The Fort Land company, however, refused to accept
the benefits of that act, unless the borough of Norfolk, to the
exclusion of the county, should have the authority to buy the
said land, and accordingly the act of 1 George III, 1761, was
amended to suit the views of the company by the act of 2
George III., 1762. (7 Hen. St. at L. 511.) And by act of 7
George III, 1766, the trustees of said company were given a
perpetual succession. (8 Hen. St. at L. 269-70.) We find
then in 1766, the Fort Land, owned in fee simple by a private
corporation, with the right in such corporation under the then
statute law, to build out into the water in front of their land,
and upon so doing to acquire the title to the land built upon,—
the only limitation to this right of acquisition being the
obstruction of navigation, and this limitation being deduced
by the principle of *exclusion*, from the fact that the purpose of the grant was to facilitate commerce. And this was the
condition of affairs when by revolution, Virginia acquired her in-
dependence of England and became a sovereign state. By virtue
of her revolution and consequent acquisition of an independent

sovereignty, she became as sovereign the owner of the beds of rivers, creeks, etc., within her territorial limits, and though it may be admitted that she became such owner with full power, as a necessary incident of her sovereignty, to avoid any prior grant of the same or any part thereof by the predecessor sovereignty, the crown of England, which she should deem derogatory of her sovereignty or subversive of her interest, yet the question still remains whether in the exercise of this incident of sovereignty she ever did avoid the royal act by which the Fort Land company became entitled to acquire in fee, by building on it, the land under water fronting their property. That she has avoided the grant of a predecessor sovereign to her *own* citizens for the purpose of promoting the prosperity of one of her *own* ports, is not to be presumed in the absence of clear statutory provision. No such statute seems to have been passed prior to 1792, in August of which year the Fort Land company, or as it was then usually called the Town Point company, conveyed the Fort, or Town Point, land to the borough of Norfolk. There can seem no doubt, therefore, that the borough of Norfolk acquired by that conveyance the Fort, or Town Point, land with all the rights incident thereto, just as it had been held by the company, including the right to acquire title to the land covered by water in front of its property, by building upon it, etc. In the same year the borough of Norfolk caused this land to be laid off and platted into lots, streets, etc., running the streets on the plat to the extent of their rights of property, viz: to the *channel* of the river, which expression, considered in the light of the special legislation under which they held, must be construed to mean to the point to which they could go without impeding common navigation, and not, as contended by counsel, only to low water mark. There seems no room for doubt that the borough of Norfolk, at the time of such purchase, in 1792, had under the original grant to the Town Point company, it not having been avoided by the state of Virginia in the exercise of her sovereignty, the right to lay out and open these particular streets to the channel or line of common navigability, and to sell lots binding on them down to the same point ; and so far from its appearing that the state did ever avoid the right of the borough of Norfolk to exercise all the privileges bestowed by act of 4 Anne, 1705, upon lot owners in the port of Norfolk, owning lots on the water, she seems to have acknowledged and confirmed those rights, only confining them within the original intent that they should not be exercised so as to impede navigation.

In the year 1801 an act was passed providing for the appointment for the borough of Norfolk of three discreet persons as *wardens* of the port, a part of whose duty it was to give notice in writing to the *"owner"* of any dock or wharf, deemed by them a nuisance, to remove such nuisance either by deepening the place or filling it up. And by another section of the act, reciting that the *"owners"* of lots on rivers and creeks were constantly extending their wharves and breastworks beyond each other, whereby navigation is greatly obstructed, the wardens are directed to run a line on the water front of the borough, having due regard to the depth of the water from one end of the town to the other, so as not to obstruct the navigation of the river, beyond which line no person should extend any wharf or breastwork. This is the origin of the port warden's line in Norfolk, and from the language of the act it is the line of *navigability*.

This act is a clear acknowledgment on the part of the state of *ownership* by individuals of wharves and docks filled up and extended to the line of navigability, and was so construed by our court of appeals in Hardy vs. McCullough, 23 Gratt., and to construe it otherwise would be to divest the titles to nine tenths of the wharf property in the city of Norfolk, all of which is the result of filling or building and not of alluvion or gradual accretion. Nor can § 1, ch. 52 code of 1873, be fairly construed as adverse to this view. That section expressly recognizes the existence and validity of former grants of the beds of bays, rivers and creeks, and does not pretend to avoid them when made by special grant or compact according to law.

It follows then that the borough of Norfolk, as a private owner, in 1792 had the right, which was not afterwards taken from her, to lay off these streets to the channel of the river, or to the line of common navigability, (soon after definitely defined by the port wardens), and to sell lots binding upon these streets down to the same point or line. And accordingly in 1792 the borough did exercise this right and sold the lots by advertisement, with express reference to the plat showing the streets. One of these lots by successive conveyances has become the property of Tunis' estate, whose tenant employed the defendant to do the act complained of as a trespass. What, then, considering the borough of Norfolk as a private owner, merely, was the effect of this dedication of these streets and sale of lots binding upon them. In considering this question as bearing on the case at bar, the defendant is to be considered,

(a¹) Simply as an individual, one of the general public, claiming no right in the premises not common to other individuals of the community;

(a²) As an employe of the tenant of the owner of the adjoining property, claiming special rights under such owner. In more general terms, Mr. O'Connor in this case represents the rights of, first, the *public*, and, second, the owners of lands abutting on the streets.

"Where the owner of land in a city lays out a street through it and sells lots on each side of it, the rights of different parties concerned" are as follows:

The *public* have an easement of way, or right of passage.

The *corporation* (or city) has the right to make ordinances, and the state to make laws as to the way in which this right of way or public street shall be used.

The grantees of lots bordering on the street, in addition to this privilege common to them with other members of the public, have peculiar rights; they are purchasers by implied covenant from the grantors of the right to have that interval of ground left open for ever; and though the city or state were to close the street as a public highway so as to deprive the *general public* of its easements, they could not divest the lot owners of their right to have that space left open as a street, because that is a private right vested in them by purchase from the owner of the soil.

2 Smith's Leading Cases, 186 (Dovastin vs. Payne).

Seventeenth Street, 1 Wendell, 202.

Lewis Street, 2 Wendell, 472.

Livingston vs. Mayor New York, 8 Wendell, 85.

Alden vs. Murdock, 13 Mass., 256.

New Orleans vs. United States, 10 Peters, 666-720.

Parker vs. Framingham, 8 Mete, 260-266.

And this easement of the public extends throughout the entire length of the street.

Taylor vs. Commonwealth, 29 Gratt., 793.

Applying these principles to the case at bar, and considering the city of Norfolk merely as a private owner, we find that the general public, and the defendant O'Connor as a member of that public, had the right, after these streets were opened and until they should be closed as streets by the proper authorities, to have them kept open for the use of the public throughout their entire length as lawfully established (that is, as we have endeavored to show, to the port wardens' line), and that the owners of property abutting on these streets, have for themselves and their employes (the defendant O'Connor being one of their employes) the additional right to have that space of ground, identical and co-extensive with Jackson street to the port wardens' line, kept open for all the practical purposes of a street for the benefit of such lot owners.

(b) Are these rights, then, affected by the acts of 1866-7, which referred to the "ends of streets running to tidewater?" That act provides that the city councils of the city of Norfolk may make "such use of the ends of streets running to tidewater as they may deem necessary for the public interests." Now it will not be contended that by that act the state of Virginia intended, even if she had the right after the implied surrender of her title by the act of 1801, as above recited, to resume by virtue of her sovereignty, her title to the bed of the river in front of lots in the city of Norfolk, which had been by her predecessor sovereign, the crown of England, granted to the owners of lots on the water, and confirmed by her by the act of 1801. But unless such a construction prevails, Jackson street and all other streets on the Town Point land, are legally streets down to the port wardens' line; and being so, until it is formally closed as such by the proper authority, the general public (and Mr. O'Connor as one) have an easement over it throughout its entire length to the port wardens' line. Was this street closed as a street, or intended to be so, by the act of 1865-6 above recited? No one will contend for that construction of the act. But if that construction be admitted, the effect is only to deprive the public, and Mr. O'Connor in his

character as a member of it, of the easement; it cannot deprive
the owners of lots abutting on it and their employes (among
others the defendant O'Connor) of their right to have the
space kept open for all practical purposes of a street for their
benefit; because that is a private right acquired by purchase.

See cases cited above.

It follows, therefore, that under that act the city can give no
one possession of any part of Jackson street down to the port
wardens' line, to the exclusion of the general public without
closing it a street; and even then it can give no such possession to the exclusion of lot owners of property abutting on
this street.

In this view of the case the defendant was lawfully on the
street (wherever the exact point may have been, provided it was
within the port wardens' line) both in his capacity as a member of the general public, and, *a fortiori*, as an employe of a
tenant of the owner of property abutting on the street.

These views, it is thought, are not in conflict with the doc-
trines established by the authorities quoted by the counsel for
plaintiff, except possibly the case in 3 Hughes' Reports. The
court admits, in the views above expressed, the position that
the beds of rivers, creeks and bays, etc., where not previously
granted, belong to the state and that the rights of riparian
owners do not give them title; but the view of the court is
that these beds, etc., down to port wardens' line in the borough
of Norfolk, were previously granted by the crown of England,
and approved by legislative enactment in 1801, to the owners
of lots on the water in said borough.

The case in 3 Hughes may be at variance with the opinion
above expressed, but that case is not binding authority
upon this court, and a careful examination of it tends to
deprive it largely of that persuasive authority which the
rank and dignity of the court deciding it would otherwise give
it. There the court, starting out with the definition that a
"street is a way upon land, usually a paved way, lined or
intended to be lined on either side with houses,"—a definition, the necessary logical conclusion of which is to continue
a street running towards tidewater at least to *high water* mark
—finally fixes the termination of Randolph street at Nevill's
north line, a point as shown by the platt, several feet above
high water mark, and decides that the lot lying between
Nevill's north line and high water mark does not abutt on
Randolph street.

So far I have discussed this question upon the theory that
the city of Norfolk as the fee simple owner of the property in
question, had, under the circumstances above recited, *property
rights* in the soil to the port wardens' line, other than mere
riparian rights, which gave her as a private owner the right to
lay out these streets to that line. The case of the city of
Norfolk vs. Cooke, 27 Gratt, is however, a strong authority
for the position that on general principles the city of Norfolk
as a municipality, has a right to extend its streets to the port
wardens' line. The general principles referred to seem to be

these: The dedication of a street to tidewater, carries with it, for the purposes of the dedication the riparian rights of the original owner, so as to invest in the municipality the right to build out (extend its street out) in the water so as not to impede navigation, and the port wardens' line marking the limit to which such extension may be made without injury to navigation, the municipality may extend its streets to the port wardens' line.

These views render it unnecessary to discuss the 2nd point, whether the locus of the alleged trespass was within that portion of Jackson street falling within the words "the end of Jackson street."

I am, therefore, for reversing the decision of the magistrate.

OFFICERS OF THE CITY,

September 1st, 1885.

Mayor . . . . William Lamb.
Treasurer . . . . . . Wallace W. Hunter.
Auditor . . . . . . Benjamin F. Tebault.
Collector of City Taxes . . . . George W. Black.
Commissioner of the Revenue . . Charles B. Langley.
City Attorney . . . . . . A. B. Seldner.
City Engineer . . . . . William T. Brooke.
Health Officer . . . . . Dr. James D. Galt.
Clerk of the Market . . . . . J. W. Blick.
Keeper of the Almshouse . . . . George T. Keefe.
Superintendent of Cemeteries . . . Keley Harrison.
Keeper of Calvary Cemetery . . . A. B. Campbell.
Sealer of Weights and Measures . James N. Pebworth.
Weigher of Hay . . . . . . J. J. Burke.
Gauger and Inspector of Liquors . . John S. Fontane.
Inspector of Streets . . . . . A. A. Runaldue.
Janitor of the City Hall . . . . . D. C. Bell.
Weigher at the Market Scales . . . C. H. Battley.
Weigher at the Scales on Roanoke Square   Geo. W. Battley.
Custodian of Christ Church Clock . . Dixon Brown.

GRAIN INSPECTORS AND MEASURERS.

R. O. James,   C. A. Davis,
W. Roberts,   Josephus Scott,
B. S. Gray,   John C. Dalby,
R. K. Hudgins,   Humphrey Hudgins,
J. N. Wilkinson,   H. H. Woodhouse,
Edward Pearce,   A. E. Owen,
C. H. Batley,   Thomas B. Gresham,   John L. Smith.

THE COURTS.

Judge of the Circuit Court: Honorable George Blow.
Judge of the Corporation Court: Honorable D. Tucker Brooke.
Commonwealth's Attorney: Thomas R. Borland.
Sergeant: Frank Slade.
Clerk of the Courts: Samuel Kimberly.

JUSTICES OF THE PEACE.

First Ward: E. R. Johnson.
Second Ward: George R. Wilson.
Third Ward: W. Hunter Saunders, (Police Justice).
Fourth Ward: Charles H. Todd.
High Constable: A. W. Chapman.

POLICE DEPARTMENT.

Commissioners: William Lamb, Mayor, ex-officio.
Washington Taylor.   R. Y. Zachary.
Chief of Police: J. A. Roland.
Mayor's Clerk: Joseph A. Wright.

FIRE DEPARTMENT.

Commissioners: Walter A. Edwards, James B. Camp, Hugh
N. Page.
Chief Engineer: Thomas Kevill.
First Assistant Engineer: John A. Brimmer, Jr.
Second Assistant Engineer: Edward Church.
Fire Marshall: A. Gordon Milhado.

WATER DEPARTMENT.

Commissioners: George C. Reid, J. G. Womble, George W.
Dey, Treasurer.
Superintendent: Herbert L. Smith.
Registrar: John R. Todd.
Engineer at Pump House: William Wright.

STREET, SEWER AND DRAIN DEPARTMENT.

Commissioners: Elias E. Guy, President; Richard H. Wright,
Treasurer.
Inspector of Plumbing: W. A. Foster.

BOARD OF HEALTH.

Benj. P. Loyall, President;   Dr. W. T. Sutton,
Dr. M. Fitzgibbon, Dr. W. A. Thom, Jr., Kader W. Dozier.
Sanitary Inspector: J. Pettis.

SINKING FUND COMMISSIONERS.

Dr. William Selden,   Walter H. Taylor.

HARBOR COMMISSIONERS.

Charles Reid, President; Richard A. Dobie, Walter H. Doyle.
Norfolk City.

William H. Peters,   B. W. Baker.
Portsmouth.

T. J. Nottingham,   Henry Kirn.
Norfolk County.

QUARANTINE COMMISSIONERS.

William B. Rogers,   Dr. William J. Moore,   B. P. Loyall.
Norfolk City.

W. H. Peters,   Dr. James Parish,   J. T. Borum.
Portsmouth.

Dr. R. Halstead.
Norfolk County.

COMMON COUNCIL.

Barton Myers, President. C. W. Grandy, Vice-President.
First Ward: J. Adelsdorf, J. Arnold Dalby, R. F. Lawler, Jas.
R. Guy, C. O. Wrenn.

Second Ward: W. A. Graves, Jr., Geo. Tait, W. Y. Johnson,
M. T. Cooke.
Third Ward: C. A. Nash, D. Humphreys, W. R. Jarvis, Harry
Hodges.
Fourth Ward: J. E. Fuller, J. W. Grinnell, C. H. Robinson,
D. W. Jones.
Clerk: John A. Moore, Assistant to the Treasurer.

SELECT COUNCIL.

W. H. Holmes, President.   A. S. Martin, Vice President.

First Ward: W, F. Allen, W. A. Power, W. W. Webster.
Second Ward: George H. Newton, A. Deiches.
Third Ward: D. W. Jordan. C. L. Upshur.
Fourth Ward: Peter W. Wilson, W. E. Pettie.
Clerk: Boswell T. Camp, Messenger to the Councils.

The Mayors of Norfolk.

List of the mayors of Norfolk, from the date of the original
charter to the borough of 1885:

The first mayor was Samuel Boush, appointed by the charter
of the borough under date of September 15th, 1736, in the
tenth year of the reign of King George II. Mayor Boush
died in less than two months after his appointment to the
office. George Newton, 1736. John Hutchins, 1737. Robert
Tucker, 1738. John Taylor, 1739. Samuel Smith, 1740.
Josiah Smith, 1741. George Newton, 1742. John Hutching,
1743. John Taylor, 1744. John Phripp, 1774. Edward
Pugh, 1746. Thomas Newton, 1747. John Tucker, 1748.
Robert Tucker, 1749. Durham Hall, 1750. Wilson Newton,
1751. Christopher Perkins, 1752. Josiah Smith, 1753. Geo.
Abyvon, 1754. John Hutchings. 1755. Richard Kelsick,
1755. Josiah Smith, 1756. John Phripp, 1757. John Tucker,
1758. Robert Tucker, 1759. Wilson Newton, 1760. Christopher Perkins, 1761. Paul Loyall. 1762. Archibald Campbell, 1763. Lewis Hansford, 1764. Maximillian Calvert, 1765.
James Taylor, 1766. Geo. Abyvon, 1767. Cornelius Calvert,
1768. Maximilian Calvert, 1769. Charles Thomas, 1770.
George Abyvon, 1771. Paul Loyall, 1772. Charles Thomas,
1773. George Abyvon, 1774. Paul Loyall, 1775 ; the records
do not show how long he served. James Taylor. 1778, whose
term expired in June. Cornelius Calvert, 1778. George
Abyvon, 1779. Thomas Newton, Jr., 1780. Paul Loyall,
1781. James Taylor, 1782. George Kelly, 1783. Robert
Taylor, 1784. Cary H. Hansford, 1785. Thomas Newton,
Jr., 1786. Benjamin Pollard, 1787. George Kelly, 1788; (he
was the last mayor that presided over the common council ; on
the 9th of August, 1788, the common council was presided
over for the first time by its first president, Richard E. Lee, Esq.;
a court of aldermen was then established and the mayor presided over it, and was thereafter elected by the aldermen.)
Robert Taylor, 1789. James Taylor, 1790. John Boush, 1791.

Cary Hansford, 1791. Thomas Newton, Jr., 1792. Robert Taylor, 1793. Thomas Newton, Jr., 1794, served two months. James Ramsey, 1794. Seth Foster, 1795. Samuel Moseley, 1796. George Loyall, 1797. Baylor Hill, 1798. John K. Read, 1799. Seth Foster, 1800. John Cowper, 1801. Wm. Vaughan, 1802. Thomas H. Parker, 1803. Miles King, 1804. Luke Wheeler, 1805. Thomas H. Parker, 1806. Richard E. Lee, 1807. John E. Holt, 1808. Miles King, 1809. William B. Lamb, 1810. Miles King, Jr., 1811. William B. Lamb, 1812. Miles King, Jr., 1813. William B. Lamb. 1814. John E. Hoit, 1815. William B. Lamb, 1816. John E. Holt, 1817, served four months, less one day, and resigned. James Taylor, 1817, served one day and resigned. (The resignation of Mayor Holt one day before his term expired, made him eligible to the office for the succeeding term.) John E. Holt, 1817, served one year, less one day. John Tabb, 1818, served one day. John E. Holt, 1818, served one year, less one day. Wright Southgage, 1819, served one day. John E. Holt, 1819. Wright Southgate, 1820, served two days and resigned. John E. Holt, 1820. George W. Camp, 1821, served three days and resigned. John E. Holt, 1821. John Tabb, 1822, served four days. John E. Holt, 1822. William B. Lamb, 1823, served a few days and resigned. John E. Holt, 1823. William A. Armistead, 1824, served a few days and resigned. John E. Holt, 1824. John Tabb, 1825, served three days and resigned. John E. Holt, 1825. Isaac Talbot, 1826, served five days. John E. Holt, 1826. Daniel C. Barraud, 1826, served three days. John E. Holt, 1827. George T. Kennon, 1828, served four days. John E. Holt, 1828. Thomas Williamson, 1829, served two days. John E. Holt. 1829. Giles B. Cook, 1830, served ten days. John E. Holt, 1830. Wright Southgate, 1831, served ten days. John E. Holt, 1831. John E. Holt (nineteenth term); no record of any intervening election; he died in office October 12th, 1832. Miles King, 1832 till 1843. W. D. Delaney, 1843 till 1851. Simon S. Stubbs, 1851. Hunter Woodis, 1853. Simon S. Stubbs, 1854. Hunter Woodis, 1855; he died in office in the fall of same year, a victim of the yellow fever. Ezra T. Summers, 1855. Finley Ferguson, 1856. William W. Lamb, 1858, also in 1860 and 1862, and was serving as mayor when the United States military authorities entered Norfolk. William H. Brooks, 1863. James L. Belote, 1864. Thomas C. Tabb, 1865. Wm. W. Lamb, 1866. John R. Ludlow, 1866-68. Francis De-Cordy. 1868-70. John B. Whitehead. 1870-72. John R. Ludlow, 1872-74. John B. Whitehead, 1874-76. John S. Tucker, 1876-80. William Lamb, 1880-86.

INDEX.

Index to City Charter.

www.ingramcontent.com/pod-product-compliance
Lightning Source LLC
Chambersburg PA
CBHW030404270326
41926CB00009B/1260